Merry Christmas

To CAPT DONALD ARNOLD

FROM BLANCHE RUBENKING

1968

WHERE LIFE
MATURES

I CORINTHIANS

WHERE LIFE MATURES

by

ROY L. LAURIN

Bible Expositor, Pastor, Conference
and Radio Speaker, Author

DUNHAM PUBLISHING COMPANY
GRAND RAPIDS, MICHIGAN 49506

Printed in the United States of America

PREFACE

T HE FIRST Epistle to the Corinthians is a presentation of Christian truth which has a maturing and developing effect.

The book itself begins with a description of Christian people who are in the spiritual childhood of carnality. At its conclusion it presents a matured and fully grown Christian who says, "When I became a man, I put away childish things."

Life matures as one observes the laws of spiritual growth which are found in the First Epistle to the Corinthians. This is normal Christianity.

This is a revision of an earlier edition and is presented for the help it can offer any Christian or Christian worker in his life and service.

Roy L. Laurin

ACKNOWLEDGMENTS

PLATO ON BORROWING THOUGHTS

"Bees cull their several sweets from this flower and that blossom, here and there where they can find them, but themselves after make the honey which is purely their own. So he who borrows from others and blends together what shall be absolutely his own, he is not obliged to discover whence he had his materials, but only to produce what he has done with them."

FROM MONTAIGNE

CONTENTS

INTRODUCTION

TO INTRODUCE you to the book properly, we speak of three things. These three things constitute a sort of literary vestibule in which we stand before we enter the building proper. They are the writer, the reason and the outline.

The writer obviously was Paul. This Epistle is number four in the chronology of Paul's writings.

The reason becomes apparent from the nature of the writing. Examine the contents and you immediately discover the reason. It was not a casual religious writing sent to a distant church. It was directed specifically toward matters that were vital to the very fate of Christianity itself.

Here was a church in the midst of a heathen city. It was strategic to the cause of Christ. Yet, it was engaged in things which were contrary to the principles and practices of Christianity. Here were to be found serious quarrels among its members. There were numerous factions boasting about their particular religious heroes. Here was a member scandalously immoral, and the church completely indifferent to it.

Besides this, there were excesses and irregularities in public worship. The Lord's Supper, for one thing, was shamefully disgraced. Their services were disorderly. The members would shout out their testimonies and go into excesses of tongue speaking. They were entertaining mistaken views of the Resurrection. They were even compromising with the heathenism around them.

Paul, therefore, writes to rebuke, to correct, and to challenge; and what he writes becomes a document of great importance to all Christendom of all places and ages. It is a reminder to us of the human element that exists in the church and how seriously we may handicap the cause of Christ by letting

that predominate. Consequently, we have a document of
Christian literature which sets forth the fact of divine things
to counterbalance the existence of human things.

The outline puts the contents of the Epistle in three divisions.

1. The Divine Origin of Christianity. Chapters 1-3.

2. The Divine Order in the Church. Chapters 4-11.

3. The Divine Objectives of the Christian. Chapters 12-16.

Here the Divine Origin of Christianity is thrown into contrast against the human factionalism that tended to put it
on the basis of human parties. Paul rescues Christianity from
that abuse and shows its lofty origin.

Here, also, the Divine Order in the Church is thrown into
contrast against the irregularities and abuses of the Corinthian congregation. There was a supreme authority for decency, order and purity. It did not come from a Corinthian
hierarchy nor did it rest in the independent responsibility of
each member. It was nothing less than the authority of
Jesus Christ, the great Head of the Church.

Here, likewise, the Divine Objectives of the Christian are
thrown into contrast against the petty party-seeking interests
and the personal irregularities of the Corinthians.

Thus, in setting forth these three great things: the Divine
Origin, the Divine Order, and the Divine Objectives of Christianity, the Church and Christian, Paul sets the tempo of a
new order of life and a new level of thinking as well as a
new manner of living not only for Corinth and its Christians
but for all Christendom, even to this twentieth century.

The book of First Corinthians is not a literary accident. It
is not placed at this point in the canon of Scripture because
of the whimsical choice of compliers. It is here because of
the Holy Spirit's wise and orderly arrangement of truth, and
it is related to preceding and succeeding books in the truth
of the Christian's common identity of being "in Christ."

We have therefore—

Romans.......................in Christ justified
Corinthians..................in Christ sanctified
Galatians....................in Christ crucified
Ephesians....................in Christ seated
Philippians..................in Christ satisfied
Colossians...................in Christ completed
Thessalonians................in Christ glorified

The matter which is before us in the First Epistle to the Corinthians narrows down to this consideration: is Christianity something to be contemplated or something to be practiced? Is it just religious ethics or is it a demonstrable life? Does it belong inside the walls of a building called a church or should it be taken into homes and market places? Is it a human invention or a divine revelation? If it is the former of these things, then let us abandon it, except as a venerable relic of religion. If the latter is true, then let us get down to business as Christians and do something about it.

The Christian church stands today at the crossroads. It must decide whether it is going to institutionalize Christianity or whether it is going to personalize it. "Institutional Christianity represents a gigantic business enterprise. There are 212 communions in the United States, with 232,000 churches— each one with a separate business organization. These churches have a membership of 45,000,000 people and spend each year for their current budgets the sum of $817,000,000. Church properties are valued at $3,800,000,000 and this does not include such items as parsonages, hospitals, schools, and endowment investments." Its place as an institution cannot be questioned but it will be a fatal day when the institution takes the place of the individual.

First century Christianity was personal. The institution was secondary. The heart of it was the disciple. The disciple did his own praying. Now we pay for prayers to be said. The disciple did his own studying because the various New

Testament books were written to the disciples and not to the apostles. The disciple did his own witnessing and evangelizing. Now we have delegated that to professionals. The disciple had a church in his home. Now we have isolated Christianity to buildings called churches and institutionalized them to such a degree that they have become vast factories of religion which fabricate prayers and music and philosophies. It is all so exceedingly convenient and easy. We no longer need to pray or study or meditate or minister. But with all this we have lost the vision and virility of the early Christian and we have lost to ourselves the personal benefits of the personal demonstration of our faith.

This day calls for a new advance in Christian living. Let us dare to set the standard and proclaim it, not merely by preaching it at people, but by living it before people.

SECTION ONE

THE DIVINE ORIGIN OF CHRISTIANITY

I CORINTHIANS 1-3

CHAPTER I
FACTS AND FACTIONS

CHAPTER II
INSPIRATION AND INTERPRETATION

CHAPTER III
SPIRITUALLY AND CARNALITY

CHAPTER I

FACTS AND FACTIONS

I Corinthians 1

WE SHOULD take note of the differences between the book of Romans and this book of Corinthians. Romans begins with our old nature. Corinthians begins with our new nature. Romans requires justification. Corinthians requires sanctification. Romans leads sinners to Christ. Corinthians leads Christians to Christlikeness. Romans presents the appeal of a new faith. Corinthians presents the appeal of faithfulness.

With this in mind, we find it easy to enter into an appreciative understanding of its teaching. Almost with its first words we find it searching us with its appeal for Christlike living and a faithful faith.

I. THE FACT OF CHRIST. Verses 1-9.

Christ is the great pivotal fact of the introduction to the book. He is mentioned no less than nine times and in the mention is revealed the importance of His relation to the new society of Christians which had been planted in pagan Corinth.

While the letter deals primarily with grievous sins and grave problems of conduct in the Christians of Corinth, Paul does not commence by upbraiding them for these things. He begins with the fact of Christ. He begins not with a criticism but with a constructive fact which, if remembered, will become the basis of a stronger faith, a sweeter fellowship and a surer faithfulness.

Let us begin with Christ in all our considerations and deliberations. If we begin here, we will come out at the right place. If we live here, we will proceed to an adventure of enduring reality. Our danger is that we may begin with de-

15

nominational distinctions or personal preferences or selfish desires. Of course, if we begin there, we shall end disastrously. Let us begin every consideration and every deliberation with the great fact of Christ.

Our attention is called to nine features of the great fact of Christ as found in verses 1-9.

1. Christ the Great Fact of Authority. Verse 1.

"Paul, called to be an apostle of Jesus Christ through the will of God, and Sosthenes our brother."

The authority with which Paul speaks is to be found in the fact that he is "an apostle of Jesus Christ." The origin of Paul's Christianity was not in the organization of some religious society. It was not in a choice but rather in a call. That call was the summons of God's will with the consequent effect that Paul could speak with authority. We need the voice of authority today. That voice of authority must be the voice of a man only as the human voice vocalizes the divine voice.

Bewildered human beings have cupped their hands over their ears to shut out the din of bombs and the babel of religious pleas in order that they might catch the sound of some authoritarian voice. Unless we hear soon the voice of authority, we are going to end in a chaotic confusion which will be disastrous to our whole civilization. In order that the sound and effect of this voice may quickly come to our beleaguered civilization, let us hasten to it with the Bible and be the effective sounding boards against which its voice may be heard.

Paul's apostleship is linked with Sosthenes' brotherhood. One speaks of authority and the other of association. One deals with origins and the other deals with effects. If there be need for authority, there is also a need for the linking of life and effort in the common things.

Too many of us deny ourselves the joy of service because we have no conspicuous places nor high titles. We would like to relegate and confine Christian service to the apostles. Here it is, placed in the hands of brothers, and we are made brothers in a common service.

Jesus taught us that ability was the measure of responsibility. It was not merely a matter of preferment or place. What you can do is what you ought to do.

Here is a father who is busy sprinkling his lawn. He is holding a hose with its sprinkling attachment and the water gushes forth in forceful plenty on the dry grass. His little girl, wishing to help, has found her little toy sprinkling can, and in her childish way is pouring little streams of water here and there. It mattered little to the grass whether the water came through the large sprinkler or the little can. The only thing that mattered was the water. So it matters little to the world how talented the receptacle may be that furnishes it with the water of life. What is of importance is that it gets the water. Do not be too concerned about how much you do—but be sure of what you do.

Let us get back to the great fact of the world's first and fundamental need of Christ and, whether we are eloquent or halting, educated or ignorant, apostle or brother, let us be the vehicles to fill that need.

2. Christ the Great Fact of Character. Verse 2.

"Unto the church of God which is at Corinth, to them that are sanctified in Christ Jesus, called to be saints. . . ."

The appeal of this letter was addressed to the members of a Christian church, whose Christian experience is assumed. From this point of beginning there was to be a continuance in Christ that is here technically called sanctification. In fact, two things are mentioned here. First, it speaks of their being sanctified; second, it speaks of their being saints. Sainthood is a state of character into which all believers are brought by the new birth. Sanctification is the process by which this sainthood is enhanced and beautified and made practical in daily living.

We have scant interest in that idea of sanctification which puts Christians into some sort of pious coma, folds their hands and places a halo of holiness over their heads. It is, on the contrary, the operation of the Spirit of God upon our sensibilities and faculties whereby they are purified and developed into the loveliness of Christ. This is true saintliness and real sanctification.

3. Christ the Great Fact of Unity. Verse 2.

" . . . with all that in every place call upon the name of Jesus Christ our Lord, both theirs and ours."

The provision of instruction and the intention of inspiration were not confined to a single church such as Corinth. The wide sweep of revelation encircled Christendom as far and as long as it existed. Be intent to hear and alert to act, for God speaks in a document of truth that will enrich your life and enhance your spiritual inheritance. Yes, it is "ours to walk with a large heart in a narrow path."

4. Christ the Great Fact of Satisfaction. Verse 3.

"Grace be unto you, and peace, from God our Father, and from the Lord Jesus Christ."

Here are two things which are to each other as cause and effect. Grace is the cause while peace is the effect. Having the grace of God we possess the peace of Christ.

Satisfaction, after all, is not something we find on the outside, after a long search. It is not something that comes after we have made a supreme effort to be good. It is something which comes from the inside. It is something which has its source and springs in the divine reality in the regenerated human personality.

We have committed the folly of trying to materialize satisfaction. Then when disaster has swept things out of our hands, we are bereft of hope. It is only what we hold in the heart that can give quality to the quantity of life.

None of us dare deny the reality of the pleasure which comes from material things, but that pleasure is only temporary and artificial unless it is made spiritual. Christ in the heart enhances all that is in the hand. So Paul's salutation does not wish them a material prosperity nor a physical sufficiency. He prays for grace and peace.

Faith thrives on facts. Christian faith is not built on mysteries and mysticisms. Therefore, the more apparent the facts, the more forceful and substantial the faith. The more knowledge we have of the facts, the more useful will be our faith.

Here in the opening portion of the Corinthian letter where the human element nearly brought disaster to the Church, we have it counteracted with the teaching of the divine origin of Christianity.

5. Christ the Great Fact of Sufficiency. Verses 4, 5.

"I thank my God always on your behalf, for the grace of God which is given you by Jesus Christ; That in everything ye are enriched by him, in all utterance, and in all knowledge."

Notice the generous commendation which Paul gives. He knew the worst about these people, yet he writes the best. He is not being dishonest for he is not substituting flattery for censure. The censure comes later, and it is given justly and properly. But, regardless of their shortcomings, there were things in them which were commendatory.

This is a fine thing for us to remember. We are so quick to speak with censure and so slow to speak with praise. A lawyer once said: "I never say anything harmful about another person unless I can prove my statement before a court of law and twelve impartial jurors; and even then I don't say it."

Even Paul's commendation had in it the elements of a condemnation. Their possession of the grace of God and their fullness of gifts should have prevented their disorders and their improper conduct. To them, much had been given and of them much was required. They were without excuse.

Their sufficiency should have meant their success. Yet it proved to be the opposite.

How is it with us? Are we any better than they? What have we done with the abundant advantages and opportunities we have received? How has our performance measured up to our privileges? Perhaps most of us would be disappointed with the comparison.

The enrichment of these Corinthians is represented in two things as found in verse 5.

(1) *"All utterance."*

Who was it that was enriched for utterance? Was it the apostles or the disciples? It was the disciples. They were to be voices of utterance for God. The authority and the sufficiency of their utterance was to be the grace of God. We have shut up the utterance of spiritual things into the voices of a few. We have made it ecclesiastical and surrounded it with canonical law and constitutional restrictions. But in Corinth, as in the other early churches, there was an utterance that belonged to the people. It was personal and not professional.

(2) *"All knowledge."*

The promotion and extension of Christianity were not left to the culture and erudition of Grecian civilization. It was something that belonged to the Christian church within its own assembly. In other words, the tools they used were not borrowed from the world. Their wisdom was not sharpened on worldly wits. It was a philosophy and an erudition distinctly Christian. It was spiritual as well as mental.

6. Christ the Great Fact of Witness. Verse 6.

"Even as the testimony of Christ was confirmed in you."

These people were witnesses. As such, their responsibility was to give "the testimony of Christ." In one sense, it means that they confirmed the testimony of Paul to Christ. But in an equally important sense they were to confirm their own testimony with both lip and life. For this they had at hand an adequate equipment. It was all utterance and all knowledge. Thus, they could plead neither ignorance nor inability. It was a part of their spiritual equipment. Whether it was used was another matter. That other matter is something which should give modern Christians grave reason to doubt their faithfulness to Christ.

7. Christ the Great Fact of Expectation. Verse 7.

"So that ye come behind in no gift; waiting for the coming of our Lord Jesus Christ."

We are dealing with the text of a scriptural document. It states something specific. Facing that statement, we have no right, even if we have the desire, to substitute our own opinions for the self-evident revelation of this utterance.

The statement speaks of "waiting for the coming of our Lord Jesus Christ." Here were people who were believers in and followers of Christ because He had come. Being such believers and followers there was before them the prospect of His coming again. We have no right to say that this does not mean what it says. It was evidently believed in by the church closest to the earthly ministry of Christ. It was, therefore, not a doctrinal invention. It was a fact of revelation.

The first coming was a fact of experience. The second coming is a fact of expectation. One was history; the other is prophecy.

That which was the hope of the early Church has become the lost hope of the latter day Church. It has almost disappeared from the list of modern church faith. To ignore it we must renounce the testimony of those closest to Christ and repudiate the self-evident meaning of the Scriptures.

8. Christ the Great Fact of Confirmation. Verse 8.

"Who shall also confirm you unto the end, that ye may be blameless in the day of our Lord Jesus Christ."

Here we discover that confirmation is not an act but an effect. It is not a rite performed by man but a result which proceeded from our faith in Christ. It was said of those who were waiting for the coming of Christ that Christ would confirm them unto the day of His Coming.

To confirm means to make sure. This establishment in the faith was a spiritual thing. It was not a human confirmation of something, but divine. It was not administered by rite but established by grace.

The specific effect of this confirming was their security. They were confirmed unto the end and were to be delivered blameless.

Arthur S. Way says, "He it is who shall keep you steadfast until that final consummation, so that none shall dare arraign you in the Great Day of our Lord Jesus the Messiah."

9. Christ the Great Fact of Fellowship. Verse 9.

"God is faithful, by whom ye were called unto the fellowship of his Son Jesus Christ our Lord."

Against the dark picture of the faithlessness of man we have the faithfulness of God. Here is our hope. If today one sees the return of Corinthian corruption, let us not allow our hopes to dwindle because man has failed. Instead, let our hopes be settled on one great fact—"God is faithful."

The practical benefits of this divine faithfulness are conditioned here upon our fellowship. We are united to Him through Christ by the union of fellowship. This fellowship is in reality a partnership. It is the vital union of life. It is the mystical union of faith. The benefits of this union arise out of our participating in this fellowship. It is through this fellowship that we shall prove His faithfulness.

It is too bad that with the substantial facts of our faith before us we must witness the disgraceful spectacle of factions arising among Christians. It points out to all of us that the facts of the faith are not enough. We not only need truth but grace. Knowledge must be accompanied by love.

It is often, yea too often, the case that where there is
the most knowledge of the facts of the faith you will find
the most factions. Here at Corinth, they were enriched "in
all utterance and in all knowledge." They lacked none of the
gifts. But knowledge without love and gifts without grace
will lead to disastrous factions which will disgracefully divide those disciples whom Jesus prayed might "be one."

Perhaps fundamentalists and all who espouse the conservative cause of Christ should use CORINTHIANS as a textbook of Christian ethics. Their contentious conduct makes
them eligible for the role of modern Corinthians. They need
the impact of this indictment which is delivered against dis-
paragement between faith and practice. Here is a flaming
philippic against conservative corruption.

II. The Factions Among Christians. Verses 10-17.

In spite of the fact of the union of fellowship into which
all believers are brought by their faith in Christ we face this
spectacle of factions.

As long as churches are made up of human beings, we
will have the deficiencies of humanity. This does not mean
that the ideals of Christianity are frustrated and limited and
made impossible just because of our humanity. It only means
that as long as Christians behave as humans and not as Christians, as long as they live in carnality instead of spirituality,
as long as they remain under the dominion of the flesh and
refuse the dominion of Christ, there will be the kind of factionalism that existed so conspicuously at Corinth.

1. The Plea for Unity. Verse 10.

"Now I beseech you, brethren, by the name of our Lord Jesus
Christ, that ye all speak the same thing, and that there be no
divisions among you; but that ye be perfectly joined together
in the same mind and in the same judgment."

Here was an impassioned plea that these Christians might
be unanimous in their faith. This was essential in any case,

for unless they were unanimous here, they would be divided elsewhere. Unity must begin in the mind and heart. It is not something which is created by constitutions and commandments.

There are instances in the religious world where unity is achieved at the expense of individuality. It is achieved because people surrender their minds and allow others to think for them. They surrender their wills and allow others to act for them. This, of course, is not the unity of the Spirit. Spiritual unity does not mean the destruction of our thinking but rather the moulding of our collective Christian thinking within the mind of Christ.

The secret of unity is not human dictation in every particle of thought and practice. This would be abject slavery. Unity comes when we recognize the common leadership of Christ and surrender to the influences of the Holy Spirit.

In 1887 the celebrated musician, Leopold Damrosch, organized a music festival in New York. For this festival he trained groups of singers in such separated places as New York, Brooklyn, Newark, Philadelphia, and Albany. All were drilled separately to concert perfection and when they came together for the festival, they sang in perfect harmony, all because they had been drilled by the same leader to the same pitch. Unity may be achieved out of diversity if Christians will allow Christ to direct their lives to the pitch of God's will. When this is done, we shall "be perfectly joined together in the same mind and the same judgment."

2. The Presence of Factionalism. Verse 11.

> "For it hath been declared unto me of you, my brethren, by them which are of the house of Chloe, that there are contentions among you."

This factionalism was not denominationalism. It was something far worse. It was infinitely more destructive to the unity and efficiency of the Christian community. One can see some purpose in a dignified denominationalism where the emphasis of one group balances the emphasis of another group. But here it was contentious strife and selfish wrangling. This sort of thing is a blight on Christianity and should be shunned as carefully as hypocrisy and apostasy.

Someone has observed that "the smallest man is often the biggest problem." Small-statured Christians are Christianity's biggest problem. It is not the giant critic from without but the little contender from within that constitutes the major peril to the common front assault the Church should make against the forces of unrighteousness.

3. The Perversion of Liberty. Verses 12, 13.

> "Now this I say, that every one of you saith, I am of Paul; and I of Apollos; and I of Cephas; and I of Christ. Is Christ divided? was Paul crucified for you? or were ye baptized in the name of Paul?"

The perversion of Christian liberty led the factionalists to split up into parties and cliques, each naming their own heroes. To one faction it was Paul. To another it was Apollos. To another Peter (Cephas). And to another party it was Christ. These latter were the most arrogant of all. They contended that they would submit to no human teachers and claimed direct dependence on Christ.

The evils of this factionalism might have arisen out of perfectly legitimate likes and dislikes. Some preferred the straightforward preaching of Paul, others the eloquence of the philosophic Alexandrian Apollos, still others the authoritarian utterances of Peter. But with these preferences, they forgot that, after all, the importance and excellence of the gospel lay not in the messengers but in the message. There is just as much peril in sermon-tasting as there is in heretical inquiries. One may lead to destructive factionalism from within, as the other may lead to destructive assaults from without.

The result at Corinth was as recorded; they adopted party cries. Instead of a witness to Christ in which their energies were united in unison, some were saying, "I am a partisan of Paul;" others, "I of Apollos;" others, "I of Peter." Paul asks the pertinent question, "Is Christ divided?"

There were two tests that Paul submitted to these partisans, the tests of crucifixion and baptism. In other words, he was asking them, Who died for you and to whose name do you pledge allegiance? In neither case was it any man but Christ. Therefore, let faith and allegiance be totally and wholly given to this Christ. Let no man's name be the insignia of our faith or our loyalty. Subscribe it all to Christ. If this were true of all of us today, it would revolutionize Christianty. Let Christ once more become the leader of the united party of Christians.

4. The Priority of Preaching. Verses 14-17.

"I thank God that I baptized none of you, but Crispus and Gaius; Lest any should say that I had baptized in mine own name. And I baptized also the household of Stephanas: besides, I know not whether I baptized any other. For Christ sent me not to baptize, but to preach the gospel: not with wisdom of words, lest the cross of Christ should be made of none effect."

Paul was not belittling baptism. He had, in fact conducted this rite in the case of some of the believers. But he refrained from engaging in it generally lest people would become attached to him rather than to Christ. He had not been sent to ceremonialize but to evangelize. His task was clear. It was to preach the gospel as far and wide as the providence of God would permit.

But what gospel would he preach? Remember, he describes himself as being sent. He was both under commission and command. Therefore, his message was of the nature of his mission. It was not his invention but God's revelation. It was not of philosophic eloquence but the facts of the Cross.

This was the gospel of Paul of the first century. It turned that world upside down. It defeated the calculations of world schemers. It conquered the strongholds of evil. It transformed myriads of sinners. It is the only hope of the twentieth century world. Let us give it a renewed proclamation and demonstration.

The emphasis of Paul's message to Grecian Corinth is as significant as the emphasis of his message to Roman Rome. To Rome with its vaunted power and might he strikes the theme of his message in these words, "I am not ashamed of the gospel of Christ; for it is the power of God unto salvation to everyone that believeth; to the Jew first, and also to the Greek" (Rom. 1:16). To Corinth with its boasted wisdom and culture he strikes the theme of his message in these words, "But we preach Christ crucified, unto the Jews a stumbling-block, and unto the Greeks foolishness; but unto them which are called, both Jews and Greeks, Christ the power of God, and the wisdom of God" (I Cor. 1:23, 24).

In the preliminary part of his message to cultured and philosophical Corinth he sets forth the gospel as being "the wisdom of God" just as in the preliminary part of his message to imperial Rome he sets forth the gospel as being "the power of God." Here is a difference; to Corinth it is set forth as being both the power and the wisdom of God.

III. The Factor of the Cross. Verses 18-31.

The Cross is set forth here as distinct from and as opposed to the wisdom of the world. There is a difference which is carefully made between the wisdom of God and the wisdom of the world. What the Scriptures differentiate, we should respect.

The Cross is set forth as God's way of salvation in distinction to the wisdom of man which is set for as the world's way of salvation. The agency of the one is preaching while the agency of the other is philosophy. Here we have the eternal controversy between preaching and philosophy. Between the two is a chasm as wide and as untraversable as the one between truth and error, light and darkness. There is no place at which they ever unite except at the cross, at which place wisdom must capitulate to God. This means that there is a perpetual difference between the message of the gospel and the wisdom of the world. The moment we compromise this difference, so far as the gospel is concerned, that moment we have robbed it of its power. This, of course, does not mean that the gospel has nothing in common with wisdom. Indeed it has. It has much in common with science and philosophy, but only as these things reveal and reflect the truth which is eternal in the gospel.

The great difference between the gospel and philosophy lies in the fact that the gospel is a revelation while philosophy is an invention.

In the seventeenth verse Paul declares his preaching to be "not with wisdom of words lest the cross of Christ should be made of none effect." Just what does he mean when he says "not with wisdom of words"? We remember, first of all, that Paul was being used by the Holy Spirit to create through inspiration the literature we know as the New Testament. He was, therefore, careful not to inject the wisdom of words.

For us today, interpretation is to follow the pattern of inspiration. The tools of inspiration were words just as the tools of interpretation are words. What Paul wrote by inspiration, we are to understand by interpretation. Both require the use of words. Paul was careful, however, not to use the wisdom of words. We must also be careful not to use the wisdom of words. Nevertheless, words are necessary and while it must not be the wisdom of words, it can be words of wisdom.

The gospel, the most priceless message in the world, deserves the best kind of presentation. It is a mistake to think that simplicity is simple-mindedness and shabbiness. It should be surrounded with an intellectual respectability that is both simple and profound. It should be presented with the best words in the best order, but never with words that strive to make it conform to human systems of philosophy and religion.

When Paul spoke of making the cross of Christ of "none effect," he referred to that patronizing presentation of the gospel in the mould of human words which reduced it to something that conformed to human wisdom. This would make it of none effect. Instead of being the way, it would be *a way*. Instead of being one gospel, it would just be another religion. Whereas the Scriptures are specific in declaring that the message of the cross is the only way. Therefore, preaching and philosophy can never be made one for they are diametrically opposed. They proceed from different sources and produce different results. The world of the twentieth century is dependent upon the message of the first century for its salvation.

There are many ways by which we make the cross of "none effect." We make the cross of none effect when we make it merely a symbol. It is that, to be sure, but it is much more. The cross is much more than a crucifix. A crucifix may only be an object of religious veneration whereas the cross is the power of regeneration.

We make the cross of none effect when we make it a ceremony. To ritualize the cross, so one can visualize it, may only serve to materialize it. It can become as material to us as any physical object we handle.

We make the cross of none effect when we make it a concept—just words. A religious or philosophical concept may be theologically exact. It may be as exact as the law of gravitation, but it is only when faith puts it to work that one will experience the saving effects of the cross in life.

The immediate importance of all this rests in one thing. Here we have divine facts and human factions. If the facts are kept in mind, the factions will never exist. The factions arose because the people failed to comprehend the significance of two great facts. First, they failed to comprehend the significance of the Christian message. Second, they failed to comprehend the significance of the Christian messengers. Here were people who were exalting the messengers above the message. They were dividing over men instead of uniting around a message. The message was divine. The messengers were human. All of the factionalism that has ever existed has been needless. Had we kept in mind the true significance of the message, we would have placed our emphasis there. As long as preachers are men, the message will be presented and represented in a faulty manner. But, in any case, it was wrong to say that one's allegiance belonged to Paul or Apollos or Peter, because there was but one gospel and that gospel came from God, not from men.

The message Paul presented here was not only intended for consumption at home, that is, among the Christians at Corinth; but it also was intended for the cultured and wise of that day who denied the claims of the gospel upon both intellect and conscience.

1. The Foolishness of Preaching. Verses 18-21.

> "For the preaching of the cross is to them that perish foolishness; but unto us which are saved it is the power of God. For it is written, I will destroy the wisdom of the wise, and will bring to nothing the understanding of the prudent. Where is the wise? where is the scribe? where is the disputer of the world? hath not God made foolish the wisdom of this world? For after that in the wisdom of God the world by wisdom knew not God, it pleased God by the foolishness of preaching to save them that believe."

You may observe that it does not say the preaching of foolishness. There is a great deal of such which is passed out under the label of Christian propaganda. That is not the kind of foolishness which is meant here. Here it means that the cross is unphilosophical. It does not fit ideas of the wise. It does not follow their arguments. They want something which is more acceptable and agreeable. They want something that parallels their own minds. They want something, further, which will not disturb their conscience nor require them to change their ways of life.

For these reasons, the preaching of the cross is to them

an absurdity. For these reasons the unadulterated message of the gospel will always be unacceptable to the intellectuals. It is only when we adulterate it with religious and philosophical forms and ideas that it finds acceptance. When we do this, the cross of Christ is "made of none effect." An emasculated gospel is worse than no gospel, for it is a fraud and a deception.

Let us be proud to stand without reservation and equivocation for the gospel of the cross as given by Christ and as declared by Paul. Apart from this, there can be neither intellectual respectability nor moral responsibility. It is not a question of what we think but of "thus saith the Lord." It is not a matter of human speculation but the solid and assured fact of divine revelation. Here we should stand, proud and happy, secured and assured to have the high honor of an ambassadorial portfolio from the King.

The time will come in the life of every one when he must make a choice. That choice has personal consequences. Upon it hinges the whole pattern of present life and the nature of our future life. That choice is between the wisdom of the word and the wisdom of the world. This is precisely the thing which is being discussed in the portion of the book in which we are presently interested. It deals with the foolishness of preaching as against the futility of philosophy.

(1) *The attitude of the lost.* Verse 18.

"The preaching of the cross is to them that perish foolishness."

We must be careful to notice that it is not the preaching which is considered foolishness but the content of what is preached. The word used for preaching here does not have its ordinary meaning of proclamation. It is the word "logos" which means word or discourse, and which, significantly enough, was used of the Lord Jesus Christ.

We have in contrast the word of the cross in verse eighteen and the wisdom of words in verse seventeen. The word of the cross is presented in a person while the wisdom of

words merely declares a philosophy. The scriptural way to
God is not the way of a philosophy but the way of that
Person who said, "I am the way, the truth, and the life;
no man cometh unto the Father but by me."

Notice what emphasis preaching places on Jesus. It is
the preaching of His cross. This is a preaching intellectuality
regards as foolishness. Oh, yes, they admire and extol the
idealism of Jesus. But they deny the realism of Jesus. They
admire the life of Jesus, but would pass over the death of
Jesus. They believe in the example of Jesus, but turn from
the redemption of Jesus. When the spectacle of a Saviour
hanging on a cross is presented as God's way to life, they
say it is absurd. They do not object to the cradle of Jesus,
but they are most vigorously opposed to the cross of Jesus.
And why? It lies in the very nature of the cross. The Cross
means death to human effort. It precludes any possibility of
self-salvation. It requires faith and abolishes works. It sets
forth a picture loathsome to the sensibilities of culture and
philosophy. Cicero said, "the cross speaks of what is so
shameful, so horrible, it should never be mentioned in polite
society."

The Cross not only speaks of the purity and heroism of
Jesus, but, by its very existence and necessity, shows the depravity and wickedness of human nature. For this reason,
the proud intellectualist says it is foolish and absurd. But
why does he say this? He says it because he has in his own
nature what the Cross came to reveal—the impotent and im-
poverished state of sinfulness.

"The preaching of the cross is to them that perish foolishness." It does not say that those who say the cross is foolishness and that those who reject the Saviour will perish. It
says something far worse. It declares that those who are
already lost and perishing are saying that the preaching of
the cross is foolishness. We are judged by the very words
of our mouths and the very words of our mouths indicate our
character.

No wonder Paul wrote in II Corinthians 4:3, "If our gospel be hid, it is hid to them that are lost." Not hid, mind you, to those who will be lost a long time from now, but who are lost right now. They are lost while they live. Their destiny is in their birth. Born once, they possess a nature of the destiny of death. Born twice, they possess a new nature of the destiny of life.

To the perishing the cross is foolishness because it demands the death of one in order to provide life for all. To the perishing the cross is foolishness because it requires the blood of one righteous Man in order to provide cleansing for all unrighteous men. To the perishing the cross is foolishness because it requires saving faith by all men in the redeeming work of one Man.

Why does it require the all to depend upon the One? Here God deals with a fundamental life fact. It is the fact of spiritual life. Man being spiritually dead must become spiritually alive. As, in the beginning, the physical life of all came out of One, so in this new beginning the spiritual life of all must come out of One. None of us created his own physical life. None of us can create his own spiritual life. Life was received as a gift of nature. Life eternal must be received as a gift of the new order. Therefore, all men are shut up to the one Man as the fountain-head of the new order of life.

For this reason, Scripture declares, "He that hath the Son hath life and he that hath not the Son of God hath not life." Being saved is far more than a question of religion. It is a matter of biology—of having life. It is a law of God in nature that life can come only from antecedent life. In other words, life from life.

These cultured and philosophical people who were perishing had espoused a religious theory of spontaneous generation through which they maintained that a person may become gradually better and better until in the course of the process of gradual betterment, he reached a satisfying state of perfection.

These were the people who were crying "foolishness" when confronted with the cross. The cross stands for a new creation; not spontaneous from within human nature but instantaneous from the divine nature; not from below but from above; not of flesh but of faith; not from man but from God.

The Cross of Christianity is opposed unalterably and eternally to the philosophical opinions of cultured intellectuals. And we defy them to prove themselves right. We defy them to prove by their own arguments, by their own opinions, that they are right. The very laws of life about them condemn them and reveal their inane folly. They are condemned by the very things they espouse.

On the other hand, we find the teachings of Jesus and the message of the cross which require a new birth to life to be justified on every hand. The law of biogenesis teaches us that as in the natural world there is no life except by the higher reaching down to the lower, so in the spiritual world there is no life save by God reaching down to man and transforming his nature through a process of birth. For, "except a man be born again he cannot see the kingdom of God."

But there is another attitude men take to the preaching of the cross.

(2) *The attitude of the saved.* Verse 18.

"But unto us which are saved it is the power of God."

Theirs is not simply an attitude of philosophical argument and explanation, but of personal experience. Christianity is much more than academic question to be settled by philosophers and scientists. It is a laboratory experience of life to be established by proof. Jesus declared that proof would come through experience. He said, "If any man will do his will, he shall know of the doctrine, whether it be of God, or whether I speak of myself." Therefore, to those who have already experienced this power, and who are now saved, the cross is not a proposition. It is a demonstration. It is not a promise. It is a power. Moreover, it is divine power because it is "the power of God."

Now we submit the inescapable consequence of this whole matter. It is its reduction to terms of personal responsibility and such responsibility as must make a choice for or against the message of the cross. This verse declares that there are but two attitudes and two classes. It is either the attitude that it is foolishness, or that it is the power of God. It is either that we belong to the class of those who are lost or the class of those who are saved.

The distinguishing difference here is not one of personal wickedness and vileness. It is just intellectual anarchy. It is philosophical unbelief. It is cultured atheism. We do well to remember that hell is not populated altogether by bad people but by a lot of good people who thought they were not bad enough to be saved.

The inevitable consequence of the course of the human intellect which considers the preaching of the cross to be foolishness is to defy God and deify man. It will seek to abandon a practical piety and establish man in a position of so-called splendid isolation from God. For all practical purposes this is nothing more than respectable atheism.

Within recent times a conference of outstanding American churchmen and scientists met to discuss the separation which exists between science and religion. Here were some of the world's foremost thinkers representing, as far as possible, the collective cultural and intellectual opinion of our day. Before this conference a paper was read from Albert Einstein in which he said, "In their struggle for the ethical good, teachers of religion must have the stature to give up the doctrine of a personal god." This remark is open to diverse interpretation. To some it is avowed atheism. But whatever Einstein personally meant and whatever he personally believes, it is at any rate an ethical and practical atheism. Einstein wants to get rid of "the doctrine of a personal God interfering with natural events." But who wants any other kind of a god? What good is any other kind of a god?

Einstein's brazen plea for the abandonment of a personal God who interferes with natural events is a modern example of an ancient folly. As far as the Scriptures are concerned, they do not teach us the fact of a personal God interfering with natural events. They do teach us, however, of a personal God intervening in natural events. Between interfering and intervening, there is a great difference.

God has intervened twice in human affairs; once in creation and once in redemption. Twice will become thrice when He shall intervene in national affairs and natural events at the return of Christ.

The crisis in our world can be met only by a faith in a personal God intervening in human affairs.

Lord Bacon quotes: "I had rather believe all the fables in the legend and the Talmud and the Koran, than that this universal frame is without mind; and, therefore, God never wrought miracles to convince atheism, because His ordinary works convict it. It is true that a little philosophy inclineth man's mind to atheism, but depth in philosophy bringeth men's minds about to religion; for while the mind of man looketh upon second causes scattered, it may sometimes rest in them and go no further; but when it beholdeth the chain of them confederate, and linked together, it must needs fly to Providence and Deity."

If the wise choose to speak of the foolishness of preaching, we dare to counter with remarks about the futility of philosophy.

Paul goes on, after stating the two attitudes that men have to the cross, to show the futility of philosophy and also the ultimate triumph of the preaching of the cross.

(3) *The futility of philosophy.* Verses 19, 20.

"For it is written, I will destroy the wisdom of the wise, and will bring to nothing the understanding of the prudent. Where

is the wise? where is the scribe? where is the disputer of this
world? hath not God made foolish the wisdom of this world?"

To cast one's lot with the philosophical thinking of God-
defying men is to put oneself on the losing side, for the wisdom of such will be destroyed and the understanding of such
will come to nothing.

After all, Paul is saying in verse twenty, it is the vaunted
wisdom of the wise which is absurd. If their wisdom was
the truth, then why did not God choose their wise men,
their scribes and their debaters to become His messengers?
But He did not. Where then is the wise? Where then is the
scribe? Where then is the disputer? Here are the three departments of philosophy. "The wise" is the thinker. "The
scribe" is the writer. "The disputer" is the speaker. All of
these God has ignored in His plans to save the world. Thus,
man's highest wisdom becomes the utmost folly, for if it does
not lead him to God it is the grossest foolishness, and we submit that this is a fact true of modern intellectuality.

(4) *The triumph of preaching.* Verse 21.

"For after that in the wisdom of God the world by wisdom
knew not God, it pleased God by the foolishness of preaching
to save them that believe."

If God has rejected the wisdom of the world, then we observe that He has employed the foolishness of preaching.

It is utterly impossible for man to know God through intellectual processes. It takes a life process, not a thought
process. The question of the book of Job is pertinent, to
the point: "Canst thou by searching find out God?" Men think
God is a thought to be reduced to a sentence. They think
He is a formula to be proved in a test tube. God would not
be God if He were such! Then "whence cometh wisdom? and
where is the place of understanding? . . . Behold, the fear
of the Lord, that is wisdom; and to depart from evil is understanding" Job 28:20, 28).

Salvation is not by thinking but by believing, for "it pleased God by the foolishness of preaching to save them that believe." Whom does God save? Make no mistake about this. Let no intellectual dishonesty creep in here. The text says—"them that believe." It does not say—them that are good. It does not say—them that think. It does not say—them that are moral. Nor does it even say—them that are religious. All of these will be true as an effect of salvation but never as the cause of salvation. Whoever is saved will be good, think right, be moral and religious; but these will be expressions of what they are instead of experiments in what they want to become. It will be the finality of a fact of life and not the futility of a hope of philosophy.

Another question appears here. By what does God save these who believe? The answer is very plain, "by the foolishness of preaching." Not by the act of preaching but by the content of preaching. Preaching does not save anyone but preaching the cross saves all who believe.

2. The Substance of Preaching. Verses 22-25.

The substance of preaching is the cross. There can be no variations and no substitutions.

Mahatma Gandhi asked some missionaries who visited him during a fast to sing a hymn for him. "What hymn?" they inquired. "The hymn that expresses all that is deepest in your faith," he replied. They sang—

> "When I survey the wondrous Cross,
>   On which the Prince of Glory died,
> My richest gain I count but loss
>   And pour contempt on all my pride.
> Were the whole realm of nature mine,
>   That were a present far too small,
> Love so amazing, so divine,
>   Demands my soul, my life, my all."

You are invited to notice three things about the substance of this preaching.

(1) *The reaction.* Verses 22, 23.

> "For the Jews require a sign, and the Greeks seek after wisdom: But we preach Christ crucified, unto the Jews a stumblingblock, and unto the Greeks foolishness."

There is a twofold reaction. To the Jew requiring a miraculous and spectacular religious sign as an evidence of the divine reality, the cross is a stumblingblock. They wanted Messianic wonders and the overturning of Rome's despotic powers. They could not reconcile a cross with a Messiah and, consequently, it became a stumblingblock. While to the Greek, filled with philosophical inquiry and seeking after wisdom, the cross was an absurdity.

The way to God, however, is neither religious pageantry nor mental culture. It is the way of a spiritual biology which requires birth into a new life. That life is inherent in the cross, for Christ's death released His life so that what was once His becomes ours. It is like the seed that must die in order to live, and out of that death comes the multiplication of life.

(2) *The result.* Verse 24.

> "But unto them which are called, both Jews and Greeks, Christ the power of God, and the wisdom of God."

To the unregenerate it may be either a stumblingblock or foolishness. But to the regenerate, whether Jew or Greek, it is Christ "the power of God," and "the wisdom of God." He is God's power for the empowering of human nature. He is God's wisdom for the enlightenment of the human mind.

Henry Rogers said: "It is adapted to human nature, as a bitter medicine may be to a patient. Those who have taken it, tried its efficacy, and recovered spiritual health, gladly proclaim its value. But to those who have not, and will not try it, it is an unpalatable potion still."

(3) *The reason.* Verse 25.

> "Because the foolishness of God is wiser than men; and the weakness of God is stronger than men."

Here is a gospel which seems foolish to men, yet it is wiser than their wisdom. It seems weakness to men, yet it is stronger than any power men possess. Here is a way of salvation regarded to be weak and foolish, yet it is a way that exhibits both divine wisdom and power. Thus, what men say is God's weakness turns out to be a profound wisdom for the culture of the human mind.

Here, indeed, is a respectable faith. Here is something to be proud of. Here is a cause worthy of our best. Herein is the ultimate triumph of all for which we believe and live. Let us take new hope and new courage and press on.

3. The Instruments of Preaching. Verses 26-31.

(1) *The instruments of God's choice.* Verse 26.

> "For ye see your calling, brethren, how that not many wise men after the flesh, not many mighty, not many noble, are called."

The genius of the gospel has been in its consecrated, Spirit-filled men. It did not advance its cause by political influence of wealthy patrons from the nobilities of society. It began in a cradle, was disciplined in a carpenter shop, tested on the highways and in homes, glorified through crucifixion, and sent world-wide through the lips and lives of common people. The instruments which have been employed by God have come from the humble walks of life. The early disciples were neither high born nor highly cultured. The original disciples were manifestly ill-suited as purveyors of so great a message as the gospel. They were low-born peasants. They were uneducated. They were Jews whom the world despised. They belonged to the smallest geographical section of the ancient world. Prior to the crucifixion, they were a dozen weak, vascillating, incompetent men. After the Resurrection and Pentecost they were bold, fearless, resolute, death-defying, intrepid revolutionists of a new life. The difference lay in the transforming of their natures and the indwelling of God in their lives.

It says that "not many wise men . . . mighty . . . noble, are called." It is careful that it does not say *not any*. There have been the wise, the mighty, and the noble like Count Zinzindorf and Madame Guyon. But it has only been such of these as have been willing to surrender to the dominion of Christ and serve under the sacrifice of the cross.

Lady Huntington was an English noblewoman of great distinction who had been converted under the street preaching of Roland Hill, a flaming evangelist. She remarked once that she owed her salvation to the letter "m." If it had been "not any wise . . . mighty . . . or noble" she could not have been saved.

The world has advanced its cause and based its prospects on power and prestige. It has pyramided power on worldly honor. In the ultimate end it will all fail. The final solution of world affairs will ultimately rest in the godly virtues of simple men and in the righteous lives of a nobility of honor which proceeds from Christ.

The glory of the Russian Czars, the Ottoman Sultans, the Moguls of India, the Mongols and Manchus of China, the Conquistadors of Spain, the Shoguns of Japan, the Hohenzollerns, Hapsburgs, Borgias, Caesars, Bourbons, Napoleon, Alexander, Bismarck, Charlemagne and all the rest have passed or will vanish from the earth, except in name and tradition. But "the meek shall inherit the earth."

And so we have the Scripture roster of "not many wise . . . mighty . . . noble." Does it say "not many wise . . . mighty . . . noble"? Yes, but of this minority of nobility we have our present and current examples. A columnist of a Dallas newspaper published an invitation which was both rare and beautiful. The invitation, written on panelled parchment printed in gold bore these words: "1890-1940, You are cordially in-

vited to rejoice with Miss M. Richardson honoring the golden
anniversary of her conversion at 10 o'clock Tuesday morning,
the third of September, 1940. How sweet the time has been!"
At the bottom of the panelled parchment were some scriptures which had endeared themselves to her heart through
fifty golden years of proof.

What a beautiful and fitting thing to do! A golden anniversary of a wedding day! Yes, it is very common. But it is
a golden anniversary of conversion, a betrothal to Christ.
How beautiful! Who was this one who sent out the panelled
parchment in gold that "cordially invited to rejoice?" Locally,
she is a beloved teacher of English in a college in Canyon,
Texas. Her brother is Admiral Richardson, Commander-in-
chief of the United States Navy. She is one of the "not many"
but she is one, thank God, and the beauty of her deed breathes
the nobility of her faith. Here is a faith that the years
have tested and proved. In the golden letters that sum up
her faith on her invitation to rejoice, there is found this confession, "For the Lord God is a sun and a shield; the Lord
will give grace and glory; no good thing will he withhold
from them that walk uprightly. O Lord of hosts, blessed is
the man that trusteth in thee."

Are you discouraged sometimes and do you consider that
you cannot matter because your position is low and your place
is obscure and your person is humble? You are challenged to
rise up in the dignity of a divine calling, to remember that
you can be an instrument for greatness since you possess its
qualification right now.

(2) *The purpose of their choosing.* Verses 27, 28.

"But God hath chosen the foolish things of the world to confound the wise; and God hath chosen the weak things of the
world to confound the things which are mighty; And base things
of the world, and things which are despised, hath God chosen,
yea, and things which are not, to bring to nought things that are."

Arthur S. Way's translation gives this passage added illumination—"Nay, God chose out the unwisdom of the world, that its success in regenerating humanity might put to shame the philosophies which had failed in the task; the strengthless ones of the world God chose out, that their success might put to shame the strong rulers who had failed. The lowly-born of the world, the things condemned, God chose them out—aye, and agencies whose very existence was unsuspected, that by their success He might show the futility of existing systems."

The philosophies of men have failed to make both better men and a better world. Look at the world any time. The philosophies and cultures of centuries are dragged through pools of innocent blood and covered with the ashes of incendiary bombs and buried under the debris of sacred buildings.

Into this bankrupt civilization of the first century, God put foolish things and weak things and base things and despised things to achieve what wisdom and nobility and might had failed to do. Thus, the gospel moves out upon the stage of human events, supplanting the failures of philosophy, and becomes the human agency of Almighty God for the remaking of the world. What a thrilling spectacle to behold!

The foolish found in Christ a saving knowledge and a spiritual wisdom which utterly puts to shame the wisdom of philosophy.

The weak found in Christ a spiritual life and a moral strength which routed every foe.

The base and the despised and the nonentities found in Christ a nobility of life and a distinction of character that made them saints and martyrs and heroes. They became a new nobility; a nobility that shall never end.

(3) *The principle of their choice.* Verse 29.

"That no flesh should glory in his presence."

How far we have gone from this nobility of grace is apparent in our modern churches. Listen to the boasting and bragging that goes on among Christians. Listen to the introductions given to preachers and teachers in which they are lauded, patronized and eulogized. There is a fitting courtesy to be extended anyone who labors in the Master's name, but the extremity to which this is carried is disgusting and nauseating to discerning and sensible Christians.

Factionalism had sprung up in Corinth around human personalities. Classes and cliques arose because of this factionalism. One would have thought that Christianity had arisen in these men. It was not so. It was of divine origin. The message was divine! the messengers were human. Any elevation of the messengers above the message would be fatal and tragic. Alas, it happened in Corinth and it has happened today. Let us rescue Christianity from the friends who have hugged it to their bosoms of self-satisfaction and have shut it up in their own little groups of sectarianism. Let us give it back to the world as a revelation from God that will save humanity.

(4) *The sufficiency of their calling.* Verses 30, 31.

> "But of him are ye in Christ Jesus, who of God is made unto us wisdom, and righteousness, and sanctification, and redemption: That, according as it is written, He that glorieth, let him glory in the Lord."

This is to say that we draw our life, our hope and our sufficiency not from men like Paul, Apollos, and Peter, but from God through Christ.

It is declared here that certain things are made available to us in Christ. The statement of the text as we have it indicates four things. The fact is that it is one thing, and out of that one thing there issue three things. Thus, Christ is made unto us "wisdom" and out of Him, as our wisdom, are three great facts of Christian character and experience including: "righteousness," "sanctification," and "redemption."

The leading fact is that Christ becomes the source of wisdom. This is given in contra-distinction to the philosophies of the wise. Theirs is a transient and changing wisdom but His is eternal. He is set forth in His incarnation as the *logos* or word which means science, discourse, or learning. It is wisdom personified in Christ and personalized in us. Thus, Christianity is not an abstract philosophy; it is a concrete way of life.

From Christ, our "wisdom," proceed three great facts of personal character and experience.

a. Righteousness.

This means our justification. In Christ we attain to a state of life impossible otherwise or elsewhere. It means pardon for sin and peace of heart.

b. Sanctification.

This is the quality of our life as the previous fact referred to the position of our life. Being separated from God by sin we now become separated unto God by salvation.

If our justification is "of Him" then it is equally true that our holiness is "of Him." Holiness merely means the quality of Christian character. It is not only something we do but something done in us. Whatever follows in the way of a noble life is the outworking of His inworking.

c. Redemption.

This is the ransom of life from the bondage of sin's power. It is a new freedom. It is not merely judicial freedom as is true of justification, nor character freedom as is true of sanctification. It is volitional freedom plus an equipment of power which enables us to rise up out of our defeat, failure and weakness, to outlive life disasters and live out Christ's life.

Yes, He is all of these to us. To the mind He is the Spirit of enlightenment. To the heart He is the Spirit of love. To the life He is the Spirit of power.

CHAPTER II

INSPIRATION AND INTERPRETATION
1 *Corinthians* 2

A S YOU read and consider the substance of this second chapter in the light of the content of the first chapter, you will, undoubtedly, face a question similar to this: If Christianity presents such an extraordinary message, how can people of ordinary intelligence understand it? Where does a divine revelation and its human interpretation meet? Or, you may think of it like this: What code must I use to decipher it? To what school must I go to learn it? What authorities must I consult to interpret it? These are pertinent and important questions. Their answers, while not categorically present in this chapter, are nevertheless found here.

To begin with, we notice to whom this message to Corinth was addressed—"Paul . . . unto the church of God which is at Corinth." It was not a sealed document to the clergy but a spiritual message to the laity. We can be sure then that what was addressed to them can be understood by them. It is for this reason that we have the correctly logical presentation of truth. In the first chapter we see the character of the revelation while in the second chapter we see its conception. First, who gave it. Second, how to receive it.

I. PROCLAMATION AND DEMONSTRATION. Verses 1-5.

1. The Proclamation. Verses 1, 2.

"And I, brethren, when I came to you, came not with excellency of speech or of wisdom, declaring unto you the testimony of God. For I determined not to know anything among you, save Jesus Christ, and him crucified."

46

Paul refers to a personal visit which he made to Corinth. He had gone there directly from Athens where he had delivered his notable address at the Areopagus on the subject of the Unknown God (Acts 17). There he had contended with the philosophers. He was, however, untouched by their influence. When he went to Corinth, he did not try to imitate the methods of the philosophers. He did not use their philosophical verbiage. It was not "with excellency of speech or of wisdom."

Just how much has a modern message the right to use attractive speech? Does not Paul deny that right? We can be quite sure that he does not. Paul used attractive speech himself. Read I Corinthians 13 for proof of that. Read any of his message, for that matter. What this does prohibit is the ostentatious display of human knowledge and personal talent. Let the message be as attractive as the instrument through which it comes can shape it, but let both its content and its messenger be subordinated to a crucified spirit. There is place for beauty and culture, but there is no place for personal display and demonstration.

We do not need to point out that at a dinner the manner, the atmosphere, and the service with which food is served have much to do with its enjoyment. The gospel, likewise, may be presented in a palatable way or it may be presented shiftlessly and slovenly. In no case must its substance be subordinated to its service. The message is always more important than the manner but the manner enhances the message.

Two things explained the great success of Paul as a gospel messenger. One was consecration and the other was concentration. It was consecration to the Master and concentration on His message. "For I determined not to know anything among you, save Jesus Christ, and him crucified."

Philosophy could extol Christ's life, but preaching must proclaim Christ crucified. The life of Christ set forth ethics but the death of Christ set forth redemption. He said, "And

I, if I be lifted up from the earth, will draw all men unto me."
This lifting up was on the cross. It is the high point of the
Christian message.

But why the cross?

(1) *It reveals what man is.*

He is biologically and spiritually sinful. The cross revealed
that, by its necessity, as it also did by its perpetration.

(2) *It reveals what God is.*

There is to be found divine love—"Father, forgive them;
for they know not what they do."

(3) *It reveals what sin is.*

There "He hath made him to be sin for us, who knew no sin."
The bitterest dregs of the cup He drank are found in the
words He uttered, "My God, my God, why hast thou forsaken
me?"

(4) *It reveals what salvation is.*

There the omnipotence of God is directed to the production
of new lives and new destinies. Men and women defeated
by the common foe find a new Champion, and they go forth
to a victorious life. Thus, the cross marks the defeat of sin as
the tomb marks the defeat of death, and both reveal the power
of the gospel's salvation.

No wonder Paul walked into Corinth with a cross and a
Christ to preach instead of poetry, philosophy, astronomy,
economics or a book review.

2. The Demonstration. Verses 3-5.

> "And I was with you in weakness, and in fear, and in much
> trembling. And my speech and my preaching was not with en-
> ticing words of man's wisdom, but in demonstration of the Spirit
> and of power: That your faith should not stand in the wisdom of
> men, but in the power of God."

The proclamation resulted in demonstration. It was the
manner of the proclamation that produced the demonstration.
It was not the eloquence or the elocution of the messenger

but the peculiar content of the message. Make the proclamation right and you will make the demonstration certain.

There came out of the circumstances surrounding the Civil
War the story of a man with a branded hand. Captain
Jonathan Walker was a kind-hearted sea captain who lived
during the slave-trading days; he was strongly opposed to
slavery and most sympathetic to the cause of the slave. Four
intelligent Negroes approached him on the subject of his
aiding them in their escape from Florida. It was Captain
Walker's answer to their request that was to change his
whole life.

Upon hearing their plea and seeing that they were of a high
type of Negro who would really achieve something by gaining their freedom, Captain Walker consented to do what he
could to help them escape. Being a good sailor, he decided
to attempt the 800 miles to the Bahama Islands in an open
boat with a small sail.

Finally the day came for the attempt. The men who were
to go were told to meet him that night with supplies for the
trip. They met as pre-arranged, and with his human cargo
the captain headed straight for the open sea.

Hope was high in the hearts of all the men. Their start
being made at night, they were sure to be well on their way
before morning came and the fact could be discovered that
they and Captain Walker were missing. The Florida Keys
were safely passed, and the captain, with his years of navigation experience behind him, felt sure of his objective. Had
he not considered everything? Could he not navigate correctly? Most certainly. Would not the supplies hold out? More
than enough for the trip. Were the fugitives afraid? No! Death
itself was preferred to the suffering they had endured. And
yet, when success seemed certain, the worst thing possible
happened.

The captain was no longer young and at midday the blister-
ing heat of the tropical sun in a small boat in the open sea
proved too much for him, and he fell unconscious from his

seat. Completely out of sight of land, panic seized the men, and though they were above the average in intelligence they knew nothing of the ways of the sea or navigation.

Thinking him to be dead, they placed Captain Walker in a sheltered portion of the boat and covered him with a piece of canvas. They drifted about without any sense of direction, until a few hours later they were picked up by the revenue boat sent out in pursuit. The slaves were returned to their master and Captain Walker was thrown into jail.

Because he could not furnish bail, the captain was held for a year before he could obtain a hearing. When finally tried, the verdict was a foregone conclusion. The captain was found guilty of aiding in the attempted escape of the slaves, and sentenced to be placed in the pillory on a public road where it would be the privilege of anyone who wished to pelt him with rotten eggs. From there he was to be returned to his cell, his right hand lashed to the bars, and the letters "SS" to be branded into his palm with a red-hot iron. On top of all this he was sentenced to one year in prison, fined $600 and all the costs of the trial.

Though it is hard to believe, this cruel sentence was carried out, and he was placed in the pillory and pelted with rotten eggs for an hour. Upon returning to the jail, great difficulty was encountered in finding a blacksmith who would make the branding iron. The first one approached said, "No, sir! I make irons to brand horses, mules and cattle; but to burn the flesh of a fellow man, I will not!" A smith was found eventually who would make the iron, but he refused to heat it. Finally the iron was heated, and in the right palm of this man was branded the symbol "SS," signifying—"slave stealer."

After his release Captain Walker spent a number of years traveling about the country, lecturing on the subject of slavery. About the year 1863 he settled down on a small fruit farm at Lake Harbor, Michigan, where for a number of years he was able to make a good living for himself and his family. In the year 1877 his health failed rapidly and he had to give up farming. He passed on peacefully at the age of 79, on April 30, 1878. His grave in Evergreen Cemetery, at Muskegon, Michigan, is marked by a tombstone upon which a branded hand is engraved.

Such was the experience of the man whose love and sympathy for slaves resulted in his being punished and put to shame because he espoused their cause.

But there is another record that surpasses this by far because we play an important part in it. The fact is, we were the slaves who had been sold to sin and that harsh master, Satan. We were serving him, for he held us captive at his will. Has this sad fact ever occurred to us before? Have we been aware of the terrible plight that we were in? Oh, that men would realize the danger, and be convinced that it is true!

Thank God for another Man, the Man Christ Jesus, whose love, sympathy, and grace abounded toward those who are slaves to sin. He has rescued them and set them free from the awful clutches of Satan and the consequences of sin! At what cost was this done! It was indeed the greatest price ever paid. Calvary! Calvary with all its unfathomable depths of anguish, pain, agony, suffering, which no human can fathom; and then—the blood—His blood—that precious blood which flowed from His blessed head, His hands, His feet, and His side; that was the price paid to set us free. No wonder Paul said, "For I determined not to know any thing among you, save Jesus Christ, and him crucified."

II. INSPIRATION AND REVELATION. Verses 6-10.

Paul has been speaking of the wisdom of the philosophies which he has just contacted at Athens. He respects it out of the spirit of tolerance, but he rejects it as an avenue by which he may find God and by which he may succeed in the ultimate good in life. He has just said that he wants the faith of these Corinthians to stand in the power and not in the wisdom of man. He knows that man's wisdom is unstable and insecure. What is true today is false tomorrow. What is science today is an exploded theory tomorrow.

Paul comes now with a new wisdom. It is something utterly foreign to Athens and entirely new to Corinth. Where did he get it? What is it like? How will it work?

1. The Higher Teaching. Verse 6.

> "Howbeit we speak wisdom among them that are perfect: yet not the wisdom of this world, nor of the princes of this world, that come to nought."

Arthur S. Way's translation helps out at this point. "And yet for an audience of ripe understanding. I have a higher teaching, a divine philosophy. But it is not a philosophy which this world will recognize as such; no, nor the rulers of this world, who are on the point of passing into nothingness."

There you have it—a new and higher philosophy. It is the teaching of the Christian gospel. Its agency of propagation is preaching. Its instrument of understanding is revelation. It embraces all the past of history and all the future in prophecy. It reveals God to man and man to himself. The crux of its revelation is the cross. Apart from that cross, this gospel has neither a message nor a meaning.

Paul begins a new line of reasoning. He does not reason back to the cross but from the cross. He does not try to think back to God in order to find Him but from a God he has already found. Paul found a new philosophy—the philosophy of faith.

This wisdom has its patrons and recipients. It has a vast company of those who have been inducted into a new life. They are called "perfect." It does not mean sinless, but rather matured and fully developed. These perfect ones are the same that are thought of as being "foolish," "weak," "base," and "despised." One is God's category and the other, man's category. How different!

2. The Untaught World. Verses 7, 8.

"But we speak of the wisdom of God in a mystery, even the hidden wisdom, which God ordained before the world unto our glory: Which none of the princes of this world knew: for had they known it, they would not have crucified the Lord of glory."

What is revealed to some is hidden to others. It remains a "mystery," something which is hidden.

When Paul says that he speaks the wisdom of God in a mystery, he does not refer to something impossible to the understanding. The Bible is not filled with symbols and parables that are beyond understanding. If so, it would be just a literary form of mysticism and idolatry. In fact, it would be bibliolatry. We would be no better than educated idolaters. Instead, it is a mystery with a meaning. It has a meaning both simple and profound. But take notice, it is a meaning which is not native to the natural intelligence of men. Men may be naturally religious but they are not naturally spiritual. The key that unlocks this mystery is not of the mind but the spirit.

The secret of its understanding lies in the nature of its beginning. Where did it begin? Last year? In the last century? In the first century? No! It is declared in verse seven to be that "which God ordained before the world."

Creation and redemption, natural law and spiritual law, all have a common origin both as to time and place. They began in God before the world. "The world we inhabit must have had an origin; that origin must have consisted in cause; that cause must have been intelligent; that intelligence must have been supreme. It is that supremeness we know as God." And the God of that physical creation is the God of our spiritual creation. The God of nature is the God of the Bible.

The most abysmal ignorance that exists in the world today is the ignorance of wise men about divine things. We know about the stars, the soil, the atmosphere, and our bodies. We are geniuses of invention. Knowing all this about God's works, however, we know little about God.

It was so in the first century—"which none of the princes
of this world knew: for had they known it, they would not
have crucified the Lord of glory." It was ignorance that caused
the crucifixion of Jesus. What kind of ignorance? Not the
ignorance of superstition. That world was not like ours, but
it had its measure of enlightenment. It was saturated with
philosophy but still it was ignorant of God. And if it was
ignorance that crucified Christ, it is ignorance that rejects
Him. Of course, we are a highly enlightened people. Yes, in
facts, but not in faith. Those who reject Christ are as far from
God as those who crucified Him.

We take our lack of spiritual knowledge in a stride of glib
contentment. Whatever we do not know, we reply by saying
God knows. But here is a means by which we may know.

Dr. Wm. Osler was making a visit to a very modern hospital
in London. The staff was proudly showing him every part
of the building. Dr. Osler picked up some patients' charts in
the course of his tour. He noticed a system of abbreviation.
S.F. for scarlet fever. T.B. for tuberculosis. D. for diptheria,
etc. Finally, he saw the initials GOK on numerous charts.
Turning to one of the doctors he said, "I observe that you
have a sweeping epidemic of GOK on your hands. I am un-
familiar with what it means. Just what is GOK?"

"Oh," said the doctor, "when we can't diagnose a disease
we say God only knows and so it becomes GOK."

Whether true or not, as far as those medicos were concerned,
we add up our ignorance of life's problems with the same
GOK. We indeed have a sweeping epidemic of GOK. It is
everywhere. But it need not be, for there is an avenue of understanding open to us. Let us follow it to our enlightenment
and we shall follow it into peace and blessing.

If this is to be so the Bible cannot be left in the church. It
is neither a one-building book any more than it is a one-day
book. Let us rescue it from the restrictions that religious
forms have put around it. Let us take it in our hands, treasure
it in our hearts and live it out in our homes.

"Religion," it is said, "is not a way of looking at certain things, but a certain way of looking at all things." We have got into the habit of thinking that it is a way of looking at certain things. We take our Sunday look at God (some only take an Easter look). We say this belongs to religion, this belongs to science and this belongs to economics. The consequence is that religion, so-called, is just a way of looking at certain things. We have become its masters. We tell it what it can and cannot do. We set its limits and boundaries. In the first place, Christianity is not a religion. It has no place in the category of human religions. It is vastly more, and in our consideration of it, we must understand it as "a certain way of looking at all things." Through it we look at life on Monday and Saturday as well as Sunday. Through it we look at life in the home, school and shop as well as in the church. Through it we look into the future as well as the past. Through it we plan for time as well as eternity. And through it the Bible is a book for common people in the common things of life as well as for the profound mysteries of spiritual revelation.

3. The Revealing Spirit. Verses 9, 10.

"But as it is written, Eye hath not seen, nor ear heard, neither have entered into the heart of man, the things which God hath prepared for them that love him. But God hath revealed them unto us by his Spirit: for the Spirit searcheth all things, yea, the deep things of God."

We usually mistake this to mean the things of a glorious hereafter. We understand it to mean the preparations of heaven which neither eye nor ear nor heart can now penetrate but which revelation sets forth. But this is not so. It has no reference to the unknown and unseen glories of heaven, but rather to the possible glories of our present life. It refers to the fruits of redemption to be experienced by men in the body. It refers to the spiritual experiences possible to believers who find them both promised and provided in the

Bible. It refers to the things discussed in the context. Thus, the Bible becomes a treasury of good things for today! There is provided with the treasury a key to unlock it. Make no mistake here. God never provides a divine treasury and a human key. Both are of the same nature. The author of the Bible is the teacher of the Bible. Thus we find that "God hath revealed them unto us by his Spirit: for the Spirit searcheth all things, yea, the deep things of God."

We have then two things: first, that which God "hath prepared" in verse nine; and that which God "hath revealed" in verse ten. Both are in the past tense and indicate something done.

We are creatures living in physical and spiritual poverty while all around us is a world of wonder. While, as we have already indicated, this statement has primary reference to the present spiritual blessings of the believer, there is also the anticipation of God's abundant provisions and preparations for the future.

We do know that the gospel holds the prospect of a vast physical change in all of nature. What is being accomplished today is but "the outskirts of His ways."

The wonder of radio is only in its infancy. The very soil at our feet, our clothing, our breath have possibilities of radio activity. Hills that shall sing and trees that shall clap their hands are not as impossible as we think.

God not only "hath prepared" but He "hath revealed." How? "By His Spirit." Where? In the Bible. Here is declared the new wisdom. Here is detailed the new way of life. Here are defied the old problems. Here are defeated the life-long enemies. Become acquainted with the Bible and you become acquainted with the prospects of a better life. This life is entered through the new birth. It is sustained and developed through the new wisdom of this Book. It is matured and perfected and finally delivered back to its Creator and Redeemer under the sponsorship of Jesus Christ. And all of these things which God hath prepared are prepared "for them that love Him." Thus, it is the affinity of God's love and man's love. Match your love for God with God's love for you and you have the magic meeting place of life's mystery.

The fact has been already set forth that we have in the Bible a revelation of God and from God. This fact is fundamental to the Christian faith. It is also important to understand what kind of revelation we have and how that revelation can be apprehended and comprehended by the common people to whom it was written.

III. INTERPRETATION AND ILLUMINATION. Verses 11-16.

As an introduction to the verses of this section, let us note a distinction between certain things that appear at this point.

1. Inspiration and Revelation.

Inspiration is how the Bible came while revelation is what the Bible is. Inspiration is the cause while revelation is the effect. Inspiration is the inflow while revelation is the outflow. Inspiration is the method God used while revelation is the result of what God said. Therefore, we say that the Bible is a divine revelation which came by divine inspiration.

2. Revelation and Interpretation.

Revelation is the sixty-six units of the Bible's message while interpretation is the method by which this message may be translated into human terms.

Suffice it to say that the Bible contains the solution of its own secrets. This solution is as old as the Bible. No modern discoveries have provided any new solutions. In other words, the interpretation is according to the revelation. Since the revelation was spiritual, the interpretation will be spiritual.

No human being and no human organization have a monopoly on the Bible. None have exclusive rights to its pages. None have prior authority for its interpretation. None have any mystical key to its understanding. The interpretation belongs to all to whom the revelation was sent.

3. Interpretation and Illumination.

If the revelation came by the inspiration of the Holy
Spirit, then that revelation will be interpreted and understood by the illumination of the Holy Spirit.

Inspiration came to a few men while illumination comes
to all men. Inspiration communicated the message while illumination communicates the meaning of the message. Inspiration was a guarantee of the purity of the truth while
illumination is a guarantee of the power, authority, and validity of the truth.

If inspiration produced what eye had not discerned and
ear had not heard and mind had not conceived, then illumination makes them plain and plausible. This is so because
"God hath revealed them unto us by his Spirit: for the
Spirit searcheth all things, yea, the deep things of God."

The Christian has two great personal agencies for the
enrichment of life. One is Jesus Christ and the other, the
Holy Spirit. The work of both mark the beginnings of Christianity. The first of these two beginnings was Calvary and
the second was Pentecost. Here were two great outpourings.
One was an outpouring of blood—the life of man. The other
was an outpouring of the Spirit—the life of God. Through
the one came redemption and through the other came illumination. The one had to do with the living Word and the other
with the written Word.

All of the foregoing adds up to one sum, namely, the conclusion that the message of the Bible is neither plausible nor
possible except on the terms of understanding laid down in
the Bible. Those terms are not ecclesiastical priority, not
intellectual ability but spiritual illumination. This, as you
see, is the only reasonable and fair thing, for it instantly takes
the Bible out of the hands of classes and cliques and makes
it available to all.

You are asked to observe three things in these verses:

(1) *The spirit of man and the Spirit of God.* Verse 11, 12.

"For what man knoweth the things of a man, save the spirit of man which is in him, even so the things of God knoweth no man, but the Spirit of God. Now we have received, not the spirit of the world, but the spirit which is of God; that we might know the things that are freely given to us of God."

In other words, since one must be on the human level to know the human mind, so one must be on the divine level to understand the divine mind. There are three levels in life. The physical or animal, the mental or "soulical," and the spiritual or divine. A man's dog has certain things in common with his master on the physical level. The dog can eat food, drink water, and sleep. But the dog cannot appreciate his master's music, art or literature. To understand these he must be lifted from his animal level to his master's human level. Now, in human affairs we are all on the human level and all capable by reason of a common equipment to understand the human mind. It is only by this spirit of man that we understand the things of man. By the same token it is only by the Spirit of God that we understand the things of God. Man must be lifted to the next level, which is the spiritual. On that level the Spirit of God communicates with the spirit of man through the intellect and he is enabled to understand the things of God.

You will be careful to notice that the basis of this communication is spiritual and then mental. The mind is the vehicle of both apprehension and expression, but it is such a mind as is sensitized and energized by the Spirit of God.

Since none but the human spirit can know what is in the human mind, so none but the divine spirit can know what are the thoughts, plans, and purposes of God. This makes the illumination of the Holy Spirit essential in understanding and living the Bible.

But someone asks, "How do we get the Holy Spirit?" That is a pertinent question. Have Christ, and you will have the

Spirit. To possess Christ by the new birth is to possess the Spirit for this new light. He is the source of our spiritual life and, being the source of our spiritual life, He will also be the secret of our spiritual illumination. It is declared of these very Corinthians, "Now we have received, not the spirit of the world, but the spirit which is of God; that we might know the things that are freely given to us of God."

Here are found a fact and a purpose. The fact is that being Christians they had received the Spirit of God. He was their possession and He is yours now, if you are Christ's. The purpose is to "know the things that are freely given to us of God."

The Bible is either a book of mystery or a book of meaning. To the mind full of the spirit of man it is mystery, but to the mind full of the Spirit of God it has meaning. Regeneration will result in illumination.

The Bible will be as different as a distant landscape viewed through the naked eye or through a telescope. If you have ever been at the Grand Canyon and stood in the observation room at Desert View, you will remember that difference. With the naked eye the distant multicolored cliffs are but masses of earth. But when the telescope is moved across their face you see trees and rocks in bold detail. Yet the glass added nothing to what was there when your eye looked unaided. It discovered nothing that was not already there. So it is with the Bible. Viewed as human literature by human minds, it presents a far-off spectacle of beauty. But, viewed under the illuminating lens of the Spirit of God, its truths stand out with bold beauty. Not a single truth has been added nor a single character inserted. The page is just magnified and illuminated to see what is unseen to the naked intelligence.

Furthermore, the Bible will be as different as if you looked at a pile of stones under common light or under ultra-violet light. Take a pile of stones into a dark room and turn a common electric light on them and they reveal nothing unusual. Shine ultra-violet rays on them and they become amazing objects of beauty. A host of new colors and shades replace the old drabness of the rocks, and they live in a new beauty. The light adds no new qualities to the stones but causes certain inner qualities of the stones to fluoresce. The ultra-violet light ray is the unseen part of the violet end of the spectral band of light and is a perfect illustration of both the position and action of the Holy Spirit in illuminating the pages of Scripture. The Bible is fluorescent to the illumination of the Holy Spirit. It contains truth that does not respond to the light of the human intelligence, but the instant it is placed under the uncommon and unseen light of the Spirit, it fluoresces with a new and remarkable beauty.

In that case, let us not view the Bible as mere literature but as revelation requiring illumination. Let us read it reverently. Let us open its pages and scan its contents with the Spirit's eye. And when we do, it will live with living men and women and its truths will walk up and down in our hearts.

The mission of the Christian minister is not to deal directly with the problems of the state but rather to produce a condition of mind in those to whom he ministers so that they are enabled to deal with their own problems. This, in turn, will react to the benefit of both the community and the commonwealth.

In days of grave international chaos and confusion and national crisis, the greatest service we can perform is to produce this state of mind by teaching the Bible in such terms of spirituality and simplicity that its hearing will result in great personal and national blessing.

(2) *The teaching of man and the teaching of the Spirit.* Verse 13.

> "Which things also we speak, not in the words which man's wisdom teacheth, but which the Holy Ghost teacheth; comparing spiritual things with spiritual."

In this verse lie the two great facts of inspiration and interpretation.

a. Inspiration.

It is declared in the words "which things also we speak, not in the words which man's wisdom teacheth but which the Holy Ghost teacheth." This is inspiration. It is the inspiration of words and is what we technically call verbal inspiration. If the Bible is inspired at all, it is inspired in its words. The inspiration of thoughts is not enough. Thoughts are made of words. Inspired thoughts mean inspired words. You cannot have correct sums without accurate figures. You cannot have good music without correct notes. In the Bible we have inspired thoughts through inspired words.

The apostle is saying that he did not take divine truths and express them in human words. Of course, the words were human in the sense that they were in common usage, but they became filled with a divine content. They were not empty philosophic platitudes. They were not aristocratic ethical expressions. They were pregnant with divine power. Hence, we have a Bible whose words are inspired.

b. Interpretation.

This is declared in the words "comparing spiritual things with spiritual." This refers to the human interpretation of the words of divine inspiration. What is divinely inspired must be humanly interpreted. But how? By "comparing spiritual things with spiritual." That is, using spiritual methods. The communication of spiritual things must be by spiritual methods. This requires spiritual men. Thus, spiritual men and spiritual methods will bring to light the wonder of spiritual words.

What are the spiritual methods? We do not disparage learning when we say that in any interpretation of Scripture human wisdom must be subordinate to spirituality. Intellectuality alone will never unlock the spiritual secrets of spiritually inspired words. It takes a mind filled with the Holy Spirit. It takes a life which is born again. It takes prayer and acquaintance with God. Through these spiritual methods will come a communication of spiritual things that will enrich the world.

(3) *The natural man and the Spiritual Man.* Verses 14-16.

a. The natural man. Verse 14.

"But the natural man receiveth the things of the Spirit of God: for they are foolishness unto him; neither can he know them, because they are spiritually discerned."

This natural man is an unspiritual man. He has not been born again. He has a soul life but not a spirit life. He is spiritually dead. As such, his perceptions are limited to body and mind (or soul) whereas the Scriptures belong to the realm of the spirit. Consequently, without a spiritual capacity he cannot receive spiritual things. They are foolishness to him because he has only a natural capacity while they are of spiritual origin.

b. The spiritual man. Verses 15, 16.

"But he that is spiritual judgeth all things, yet he himself is judged of no man. For who hath known the mind of the Lord, that he may instruct him? But we have the mind of Christ."

Notice three things about the spiritual man:

(a.) His identity.

He is spiritual. This means that he has been born spiritually. It means that he is also Spirit-filled. These qualifications fit him with a spiritual capacity.

(b.) His ability.

He "judgeth all things." That is, he discerns spiritual things. He is able to take the Scriptures, which are to be spiritually discerned or examined, and comprehend truths in them that the keenest intellect will consider but foolishness. His is a spiritual ability which transcends the cultures of the wise.

(c.) His immunity.

He is "judged of no man." That is, he is as much an enigma to the world as the Scriptures are. Both are beyond the scrutiny of the common intellect because both have come into being from the same source.

This statement of judging all things yet being judged of no man, has nothing to do with the idea of sitting in judgment on others for the acts which they have committed. It refers entirely to the Christian's appreciation and perception of the spiritual truths of the Bible and of his own inscrutable relation to the Bible.

The secret of all this is found in the last sentence of the last verse, "But we have the mind of Christ." This does not mean the transmission of the actual qualities of the divine mind to us so that we become mental minatures of the Master. It does mean, however, that under the influence of the Holy Spirit, our mental faculties are quickened and enlightened to the point where we can share His thoughts and understand His will and comprehend the revelation of His truth as it is found in these Scriptures.

Now the sum of the matter is this: If we are such as possess the mind of Christ, why should we permit ourselves to be divided by the carnal minds of men? Division and factions, we shall find out, are caused by carnality. If we held to the spirituality of our new lives and followed the unity of the mind of Christ, division and disunity would no longer exist. This is the call of Paul to Corinth. Let it be heard down these nineteen centuries and heeded by the disciples of Christ in this modern day. Yes, "that ye all speak the same thing and that there be no divisions among you; but that ye be perfectly joined together in the same mind and the same judgment."

CHAPTER III

SPIRITUALITY AND CARNALITY

I Corinthians 3

THE THIRD chapter deals with the third phase of the first section of I Corinthians and has to do to a large extent with the subject of carnality and its effects upon life.

I. SPIRITUALITY AND CARNALITY. Verses 1-8.

1. The Nature of Carnality. Verse 1.

> "And I, brethren, could not speak unto you as unto spiritual, but as unto carnal, even as unto babes in Christ."

The closing verses of chapter two and this first verse of chapter three deal with three kinds of men; namely, the natural man, the spiritual man, and the carnal man.

Let us be sure we understand who these three men are. If we do, we shall be able to classify men in their proper categories.

(1) *The natural man is an unregenerate man.*

He is a man *as is*. He is a man Adamically identified. He may be civilized and cultured. He may be educated and improved. But all of this culture and improvement is within the realm of his natural character. What this man needs is to be touched with life from above. This life is spiritual and it comes by a spiritually biological process of birth called the new birth. When one has such a birth, he becomes the second man mentioned here.

(2) *The spiritual man is a regenerated man.*

He possesses not only physical life but spiritual life. He has, in fact, two lives because he has had two births. His first

65

birth was from Adam and his second birth was from Christ. Out of this birth came life. It is the life of Christ in the life of the Christian, for "he that hath the Son hath life." So long as this spiritual life feeds on spiritual food, it will mature and develop according to its nature. Since it is of the nature of Christ, the spiritual man will develop spiritually like Him.

The spiritual man begins as a spiritual infant. He is not born matured any more than a physical person is. But how is he to mature and to grow? It is a twofold matter of energy and exercise. Energy from what he eats and exercise from what he does. Energy from what he takes in and exercise from what he gives out.

To be born spiritually is no promise that we are going to mature spiritually. Spiritual maturity is a matter of individual responsibility. When we fail in it, we become the third man mentioned here.

(3) *The carnal man is a spiritual man with limitations.*

The carnal man is either the case of arrested spiritual development or the case of a Christian living out of character. Both of these explained the Corinthians' carnality.

a. The case of arrested spiritual development.

Paul says in verse one that they were "babes in Christ." They were in a state of spiritual infancy. They had not grown up. Furthermore, Paul says in verse two that he fed them "with milk and not with meat." This indicates their spiritual immaturity. They had to have a diet adapted to babes. They had to be treated as children. Paul had to use childish expressions and deal in the ABC's of spiritual principles.

b. The case of living out of character.

This is revealed in the fact that Paul said they were walking as men. They were, in other words, living out of character. The character into which they were born again was the character of a new manhood but these people were walking in their old manhood. They were walking as Corinthians instead of Christians. They were walking as unregenerate men instead of regenerate men. They were walking as natural men instead of spiritual men. It is true that they were spiritual by nature but they were still natural by behavior. Thus, they were walking out of character, and this means that they were walking in the flesh instead of in the Spirit. The Christian has spiritual life as well as flesh-life, but the secret of his dominance over the flesh-life is to walk in the Spirit.

2. The Capacity of Carnality. Verse 2.

"I have fed you with milk, and not with meat: for hitherto ye were not able to bear it, neither yet now are ye able."

The capacity of carnality is spiritual limitation. It is childish and infantile and it is determined by diet. Paul fed them with milk. They were not able to assimilate adult food. All they could stand were the elementary truths of the gospel.

The reason for this childish capacity may be twofold. It may be either the fault of the individual Christian or the fault of his leaders. Many Christians never grow because the spiritual leaders never feed them on anything more than spiritual elementaries.

It is perhaps true that the spiritual leader is to blame in most cases. When preachers and teachers treat their audiences as children and pass out crackers and milk and get no deeper than spiritual ABC's, what else can we expect? How can we cultivate spiritual maturity unless we give an adequate spiritual diet? If we are in it let us get out of the kindergarten stage.

The other side of the case is the fact that many Christians are parasitic consumers. They have arrested their own development because they have ceased to search for food. They are content to have someone find it for them. They have also ceased to pray, being satisfied with being prayed for. They do no form of spiritual work since they pay their preacher to work for them. This is fatal to spiritual maturity. To be content with outward forms of religion and fail to attend personally to the personal needs for spiritual energy and spiritual exercise will result in arrested development. This makes spiritual parasites who live on others, and spiritual parasites are dead weights.

Paul indicates, when he says, "I have fed you," that they were unwilling to feed themselves. They had to be nursed. They refused to seek their own food. That is what all parasites do. They live off others. The Creator never provides for man's wants in such form that he can simply accept Nature's gifts automatically. He must search for his food. He must work for his food. Thus, he has both energy and exercise.

The spiritual food of the Christian is provided in perfect form but it cannot be of any benefit just as it is found. One must work, think, study, pray, discern, divide, absorb, and digest it. The Christian's food comes by divine furnishing, but its benefit takes personal foraging. Maturity demands activity.

Let us remember that spiritual movement is upward. This requires spiritual energy. This energy is not natural to us. It must be generated by spiritual forces and means and these are twofold. First, the assimilation of spiritual food, in the Bible, and the exercise of prayer. Without these, as conscious and personal efforts, we remain both stationary and immature.

It has often been said in our own day that democracy's greatest dangers are not from without but from within. The tragic dissolution of France before World War II is a point in proof of that.

The same can be said of Christianity. The sinister diseases of selfishness and carnality are more dangerous and destructive than atheism or communism. This danger was one reason for the writing of this Epistle to the Corinthians. It was intended to save the Corinthians from their inner perils. It was intended to save them from stagnation and arrested development. Its corrections and challenge are needed today.

3. The Conduct of Carnality. Verses 3, 4.

"For ye are yet carnal: for whereas there is among you envying, and strife, and divisions, are ye not carnal, and walk as men? For while one saith, I am of Paul; and another, I am of Apollos; are ye not carnal?"

Someone has remarked that great minds discuss ideas; average minds discuss events; small minds discuss people. The Corinthians had ceased searching out the great truths of the gospel and had degenerated to the activity of petty quarreling over men. They spent their energy discussing and defending the virtues of these men rather than the message from God. This is one of the inevitable consequences of carnality. Instead of being united around their Lord, they were divided among their leaders. Instead of unity in the person of Christ, it was division into parties and factions. This sort of thing is a scandal to the cause of Christ. Its correction is in the development of spirituality and the destruction of carnality. It will result in a real Christian front and common action against our common enemy.

4. The Mistake of Carnality. Verses 5-8.

"Who then is Paul, and who is Apollos, but ministers by whom ye believed, even as the Lord gave to every man? I have planted, Apollos watered; but God gave the increase. So then neither is he that planteth anything, neither he that watereth; but God that giveth the increase. Now he that planteth and he that watereth are one: and every man shall receive his own reward according to his own labour."

The mistake was in putting men before the message. Paul argues that, after all, he and Apollos were only servants. Their duty was in one case to plant and in another case to water; but in either case the increase depended on God. It was the investiture of the human vessel with divine power. The man is nothing apart from God. The vessel is nothing apart from its contents. The human effort is nothing unless supported by divine energy.

With all of this careful distinction we feel sure that the sense of this scripture is not to discourage the messenger from as much personal excellence as is possible in both spiritual power and individual personality. It is an undeniable fact that in the actual presentation of the message it often wins its way into men's hearts by the winsomeness of the messenger. We dare not discourage personal improvement nor disparage individual attraction. These enhance the instrument which dispenses the message. What Paul was emphasizing here was the danger of making gospel messengers rivals instead of partners. He declares plainly that "he that planteth and he that watereth are one."

While there is an equality among the laborers, there is no equality in the labor. The labor is according to each laborer's ability. In other words, responsibility is according to ability. In the parable of the talents the Master distributed "to every man according to his several ability." We do not all have the same ability nor the same responsibility. So, likewise, we do not all have the same labor nor the same reward. It will be as Paul says in verse 8, "and every man shall receive his own reward according to his own labor."

In all this let us be sure that we hold up the Master and not the men who represent the Master. They have their responsibility and, consequently, their respect, but the pre-eminent place is to the Master whose message alone has power to transform and remake the men and women of this badly battered world.

"In an Italian city stands a statue of a Grecian maiden of beautiful face, graceful figure, and noble expression. There is a story of a ragged, unkempt, slovenly girl who came face to face with the statue. She stood and stared, and then went home to wash her face and comb her hair. Next day she came again to stand before the statue, and then to return home. This time she mended her tattered clothing. So day by day she changed, her form grew graceful, her face more refined."

So it will be if men and women and boys and girls see the Master; not a dead statue of Him, but a living example of Him and a powerful proclamation of His message. Men and women will not only be mending their clothing and cleansing their faces but they will be mending their ways. This is what the world needs.

There are two things of important interest in these considerations:

(1) *Man's place.* Verse 5.

Paul says of himself and Apollos that they were "ministers." This is not a designation of ecclesiastical rank but rather a description of character. "Minister" means servant. These men were in an engagement of service. They were not concerned with rank or title but rather with production.

Whose servants were they? Were they the servants of men or God? On this point there can be no question. Theirs was a service for God and, consequently, they were the servants of God. You have heard preachers say that they were the servants of the people. If they are, they are in the wrong place. Then they must do the people's will. They must speak the people's mind. The servant of God wears no chains and is bound by no commitments. He does God's will and speaks God's mind.

(2) *Man's part.* Verse 6.

Man's part is to plant and water; to plow and cultivate. God's part is to give the increase. Our part is to plant. God's part is to prosper. But God cannot do His part until and unless we do our part. There is no use for us to sit about indulging in pious wishful thinking. There is no use dreaming of better things. God has promised to empower and prosper the laborer. "There is only one way to make dreams come true; wake up and go to work."

The whole matter of Christian responsibility resolves itself into two things. It is either a matter of duty or mutiny. He said, "Go." If we go it is duty. If we stay it is mutiny.

Now observe that through all the things we have considered from verse one to verse eight we see the distinguishing marks of spirituality. It is a question in these verses of spirituality as against carnality. The major emphasis has been on carnality but through it all there are things that indicate spirituality.

There are three marks of spirituality:

a. Maturity.

The spiritual man has grown into adult capacities. He has developed in spiritual muscle and nerve. He has acquired spiritual wisdom and ability.

b. Unity.

The spiritual man is not a factionalist. His spirituality causes him to walk in the unity of the faith. He has reached the ideal of the Christian which is "in the unity of the faith and of the knowledge of the Son of God, unto a perfect man, unto the measure of the stature of the fulness of Christ."

c. Productivity.

Matured ability and unity plus concentrated effort result in production. Only children play at life. Maturity assumes responsibility and goes to work.

II. WORKS AND REWARDS. Verses 9-17.

1. The Workers. Verse 9.

> "For we are labourers together with God: ye are God's husbandry, ye are God's building."

Here is a new conception of life. It is not an atheistical individualism that considers man his own maker and master. It is, instead, a spiritual individualism in which the individual is linked in life and labor with God. In this conception of life no one says that he will live his life as and where and how he pleases. In this conception it is God's pleasure for our labor. It adds a new dignity to life and it provides withal a thrilling destiny.

It is reported that a "little old lady well beyond her 'three score years and ten,' knocked at the door of her pastor's home. Handing him a basket, she said, 'Here are some things the Lord and I raised.'" Her basket contained an assortment of vegetables, but to her and, undoubtedly, to her pastor they were more. They were fruits of a significant relationship. It was the relationship of "laborers together with God."

In all of this there is the overshadowing idea of production. Life is not merely an inward experience. It is, as well, an outward expression. It is not merely for consumption but for production.

There is in all life the great law of labor. Life means labor as salvation means service. Whoever does not exercise and develop his spiritual abilities will degenerate just as quickly as one will in the physical realm. We are either workers or wastrels.

WORK!

"Thank God for the might of it,
The ardor, the urge, the delight of it—
Work that springs from the heart's desire,
Setting the brain and the soul on fire—
Oh, what is so good as the heat of it,
And what is so glad as the beat of it,
And what is so kind as the stern command,
Challenging brain and heart and hand?
                    Work!

"Thank God for the pride of it,
For the beautiful conquering tide of it,
Sweeping the life in its furious flood,
Thrilling the arteries, cleansing the blood,
Mastering stupor and dull despair,
Moving the dreamer to do and dare.
Oh, what is so good as the urge of it,
And what is so glad as the surge of it,
And what is so strong as the summons deep,
Rousing the torpid soul from sleep?
                    Work!

"Thank God for the pace of it,
For the terrible, keen, swift race of it,
Fiery steeds in full control,
Nostrils aquiver to greet the goal.
Work, the Power that drives behind,
Guiding the purposes, taming the mind,
Holding the runaway wishes back,
Reining the will to one steady track,
Speeding the energies faster and faster,
Triumphing over threatened disaster,
Oh, what is so good as the pain of it,
And what is so great as the gain of it,
And what is so kind as the cruel goad
Forcing us on through the rugged road?
                    Work!

"Thank God for the swing of it,
For the clamoring, hammering ring of it,
On the mighty anvils of the world.
Oh, what is so fierce as the flame of it,
And what is so huge as the aim of it?
Thundering on through dearth and doubt,
Calling the plan of the Maker out.
Work the Titan, Work the Friend,
Shaping the earth to a glorious end,
Draining the swamps, and blasting the hills,
Doing whatever the spirit wills;
Rending a continent apart,
To answer the dream of the master-heart.
Thank God for a world where none may shirk;
Thank God for the glorious splendor of work!"
                                        —Author Unknown.

2. The Work. Verse 10.

"According to the grace of God which is given unto me, as a wise masterbuilder, I have laid the foundation, and another buildeth thereon. But let every man take heed how he buildeth thereupon."

The work is described here as to its character. It is the work of building. We are builders. All of us are lifebuilders.

None of us can escape this implication by supposing it to be some kind of professional religious service belonging to a few. It belongs to all. The special caution is that the builder "take heed how he buildeth thereupon."

Are we careful? Have we given any conscious thought to the greatest task? We are diligent in making a living. What about our life? Of all the life-building agencies the combination of the home and the Bible are paramount. The home holds mother and child for the most formative years of life. Every mother is a wise masterbuilder of life when she moulds the lives of her children in the pattern of this Book.

3. The Beginning. Verse 11.

> "For other foundation can no man lay than that is laid, which is Jesus Christ."

In the previous verse Paul remarked, "I have laid the foundation, and another buildeth thereon." This is a reference to his apostolic mission to Corinth where he laid the foundations of Christianity in the lives of the Corinthians. While the primary teaching of this section deals with Paul's service as a minister, a secondary application can be properly made by all Christians to their own life-building.

This foundation of which Paul speaks was not in human leaders like himself. It was not in human philosophies such as Paul heard discussed at Athens. The foundation he laid was Christ.

This foundation is exclusive if life is to be adequate. It is the statement of Paul that "other foundation can no man lay." There are no ways just as good as Christ the way. Christ is exclusive and our choice of Him imperative. It is the imperative of "Ye must be born again."

Foundations always mean excavations. Men never build on ruins. The new is never founded on the old. Jesus, the great Masterbuilder, said, "No man putteth a piece of new cloth upon an old garment . . . neither do men put new wine into old bottles. . . ." The reason was apparent, and so here foundations must have excavations. There must be a clearing away by confession and cleansing of the old life. The new life must begin in a new setting even if it is on the same old site.

After the great fire in London, hundreds of years ago, it was decided to rebuild St. Paul's Cathedral. Sir Christopher Wren was chosen for the task and was accordingly summoned by Queen Anne for consultation. Out of the tragic ruins it was resolved to erect the most magnificent place of worship in the Empire. Before Sir Christopher made his plans, he inspected the site. It was a dismal heap of ruins. His first task was not reclamation but excavation. An army of men set to work clearing away the debris and excavating an adequate place for its foundation. Then, stone by stone, there arose a magnificent structure which is a symbol of sanctity in that great city. Life, too, must have its excavation before the laying of its foundation. A poorly founded life is as dangerous as an ill-conceived life.

We are dealing with truths that relate to the Christian's responsibility and activity. Their earnest consideration is imperative for their neglect is woefully apparent.

There is, in connection with the United States Post Office department, a Division of Dead Letters. Here accumulates all the mail which has been missent and which has no identification of either recipient or sender. One year nearly 14,000,000 letters, one out of every thousand letters posted, went to the Dead Letter Office. We have a lot of dead letter Christians. They never arrive. They are frustrated messengers of the "good news." They are sent but never go. They have been dispatched but never arrive at the intended destination, and, in consequence, end up in the dead letter state of thwarted purpose.

4. The Materials. Verse 12.

"Now if any man build upon this foundation gold, silver, precious stones, wood, hay stubble; . . ."

A question will present itself to every thoughtful reader of this verse and the subsequent verses of the section. It is this: Do these verses about works and rewards, about labor and testing, refer only to Christian ministers, or do they refer to Christians in general? To explain the verses and answer the question we must go back to verse nine where the context gives the sense of the entire section. Here it says, "For we are labourers together with God: ye are God's husbandry, ye are God's building."

We will notice particularly that it says "we" and "ye" with "ye" occurring twice. The "we" definitely refers to the apostles such as Paul and Apollos. The "ye" likewise very definitely refers to the disciples or the rank and file of Christians of Corinth.

Of the "we" Paul states the fact that their part as apostles and preachers was to lay the foundation of Christ in the lives of these Corinthians.

Of the "ye" Paul speaks of them as a field and a building. Paul planted the seed and Apollos watered the plants in this field of human lives. Paul likewise laid the foundation of that building which was the Corinthian church. He laid the foundation and others would build thereon, but let them have care how they builded.

The other idea advanced here is that of life-building in the individual. The foundation on which we build is Jesus Christ. The next thing is the choice of building materials.

At this point the individual Christian builder is faced with a choice of materials. Paul declared himself satisfied with the foundation. Now the believer-builder must carefully choose his materials. For his building operations a selection of six kinds of materials is offered. They are gold, silver, precious stones, wood, hay, stubble. These six materials fall into two classes of three each. The first class is imperishable material. The second class is perishable material.

Our understanding of exactly what Paul means in this

classification of materials is found in the building customs of Paul's own day. "In such cities as Ephesus, where this letter was written, or Corinth, to which it was addressed, there was a signal difference (far greater than in modern European cities) between the gorgeous splendor of the great public buildings and the meanness and squalor of those streets where the poor and profligate resided. The former were constructed of marble and granite; the capitals of their columns and their roofs were richly decorated with silver and gold; the latter were mean structures, run up with boards for walls, with straw in the interstices and thatch on the top. This is the contrast on which Paul seizes; . . . not, as sometimes the passage is treated, as though the picture presented were that of a dunghill of straw and sticks, with jewels, such as diamonds and emeralds, among the rubbish. He then points out that a day will come when the fire will burn up those wretched edifices of wood and straw, and leave unharmed in their glorious beauty those that were raised of marble and granite and decorated with silver and gold, as the temples of Corinth itself survived the conflagration of Mummius, which burnt the hovels around."

Here the practical reference is to Jesus Christ as the foundation of life and the disciples building a life on this foundation with the materials of both character and conduct.

What concerned Paul most was the fact that it was possible to have a life well laid in Christ, yet to have its superstructure, of character and service, made of materials that would be both inferior and unworthy.

First of all be sure that our life is founded on Christ; that we have had the personal experience of the new birth; that He is the Rock beneath. Then be careful about the selection of materials. Be sure that they belong to the imperishable class, for what we build must pass the inspection of the building laws of eternity. We are building for an eternal duration and only such materials and work as fit the building ordinances of eternity will survive.

Just what do these various materials refer to in acts and deeds of life? The Spirit of God has not amplified with an explanation or an identification in the corresponding matters of our lives. He simply declares their character without stating their kind.

We do observe this fact, namely, that the first class of imperishables, such as gold, silver, and precious stones, are found under the surface of the earth. They are not easy of access. They must be hunted out and dug up. They must be smelted and refined. The perishables, contrariwise, are all found on the surface of the earth. They are plentiful and close at hand. They can be gained with a minimum of labor. So we find it in life: the best things are not the easiest things to acquire. They cost effort and labor. We must sacrifice for them. They must pass through the fires of purification and refinement. On the other hand, the most common things are not the best things. They cost us little. They are no trouble to procure. They may be fitted into life with the least effort. They may be woven into attractive patterns and polished into bright surfaces, but the final test is not the test of appearance but the test of endurance.

We will also find the imperishables are in the minority while the perishables are in the majority. We will find the imperishables in small quantities and in restricted areas while the perishables are found in large quantities and in promiscuous abundance. Think of the contrast between ten dollars' worth of straw and a ten-dollar gold piece. It would take a giant truck, or two or three, to carry straw whose equivalent is represented in a jewel which could be carried in a tiny pocket. The world is impressed with quantity but God is requiring quality.

While we are thinking about the minorities and majorities, remember this: we settle things in our world by a majority vote. Elections are settled that way, yet Abraham Lincoln was rejected by a majority of the popular vote when he ran for President the first time and was put into office only by a providential arrangement of the electoral vote. On the better things the majority is sure to be wrong. Take a vote on the best music, and jazz would win. Take a vote on the best literature, and literary drivel would win. Take a vote on public interest, and a prize fight or a movie would win over the church and the interests of the soul. Yes, the majority is sure to be wrong. But you cannot afford to be wrong. Choose with care. Build with care. "Let every man take heed how he buildeth thereupon."

Few people have the courage to live life with the far view as its goal. It is so much easier to be expedient. The attractions of the moment loom so large that all else is forgotten.

The Bible sets before us the oft forgotten fact that all of life must some day pass the test of divine security. In that case it will be more sensible and more profitable to take the far view. We have this far view in the next verses:

5. The Testing. Verses 13-15.

> "Every man's work shall be made manifest: for the day shall declare it, because it shall be revealed by fire; and the fire shall try every man's work of what sort it is. If any man's work abide which he hath built thereupon, he shall receive a reward. If any man's work shall be burned, he shall suffer loss: but he himself shall be saved; yet so as by fire."

Let us read Arthur S. Way's picturesque and illuminating rendering of these verses. "The Great Day shall make it plain; and the revealing agent is fire. Yes, what is the true quality of each man's work, that fire—nothing less—shall test. If any man's structure, which he has reared on the aforesaid foundation, stands the test, he shall receive his work's wage. If anyone's structure shall be burnt to the ground, he shall thus forfeit his life's work, though he himself shall be rescued, yet only as one who is dragged out through the flames of a burning house."

Several things stand out very clearly here.

(1) *Our life's work reviewed.*

Notice carefully that it says "every man's work shall be made manifest." It is the man's work and not the man which is to be reviewed and tested. Here the fire does not try the man but his work. It is not a question of what the man is but what the man has done. This judgment, therefore, is not a judgment in respect to salvation but in respect to works. Salvation is something received. Works are something rewarded. Salvation is a matter of faith. Works are a matter of faithfulness.

The time when our life's work will be reviewed is described as "the day." And this day is none other than the day of "the judgment seat of Christ," before which we must all appear in order that we may "receive the things done in the body." This judgment seat is a place of review and adjustment. It has nothing to do with salvation, for only Christians appear before it. The purpose of their appearing is to bring about such adjustments as will fit them for the new life upon which they have entered.

So we have "the day." But it also mentions "the fire." Does it mean flames? We think not. Fire is used as a symbol of a revealing agent which will test the quality of every man's work.

Fire is elsewhere used as an emblem of deity—"Our God is a consuming fire." This means the holiness of God. It is used also as an emblem of affliction—"think it not strange concerning the fiery trial." Here it is the revealing agent that determines the quality of life's labor whether it be perishable or imperishable. It is no more a literal fire than the materials of our lives are literal gold, silver, wood, or straw.

(2) *Our life's work rewarded.*

It will be a twofold reward.

a. The reward of gain.

"If any man's work abide . . . he shall receive a reward" (v. 14). This, of course, means our gain. We shall be rewarded for the character of our lives. We shall be rewarded for the quality of our lives. The reward is based upon the kind of materials used in life. In this case they were the imperishables such as "gold, silver and precious stones."

We are rewarded for the kind of materials we have built into life and not for the foundation on which we have built. The foundation represents our salvation while the materials represent our service. Therefore, we conclude that we do not receive salvation as a reward for our works or our faithfulness. Salvation is a gift. We had nothing to do in laying it. It was laid for us by divine grace through the act of faith and we thus become responsible to build upon it. Our reward is the result of what we do because we are saved. Our works are the result of salvation and not the cause of it. No amount of subterfuge can contradict the testimony of this record. We believe it to our gain. We doubt it to our loss.

b. The reward of loss.

"If any man's work shall be burned, he shall suffer loss." The question is, what shall be lost? If in one case one gains and in another case one loses, just what are we to understand them to gain or lose? In neither acse is it a question of gaining or losing salvation. Of the man who loses it definitely says, "but he himself shall be saved; yet so as by fire." He will be saved as a man is saved from a burning building. His life is spared but his labor and possessions are gone. This man loses the fruit of his labor. He has a saved soul but a lost life.

We judge that there would not be much glory in such an end. It will undoubtedly be the end of many, however. The ending will be according to the building. Let us take care how we build. It is what we do today that will be tested tomorrow. We and we alone can determine what it will be. This is not a matter of misfortune. It is something we can choose. We could not choose our birth but we can choose our destiny. We can determine its character. We say today by the person we are and by the manner in which we live and by the things we do whether it will be gain or loss. Let us then begin choosing and living with this intelligent purpose in view.

> "Not what you get, but what you give;
> Not what you say, but what you live;
> Giving the world the love it needs;
> Living a life of noble deeds.

> "Not whence you come, but whither bound;
> Not what you have, but whether found
> Strong for the right, the good, the true—
> These are the things worth while to you."

6. The Temple. Verses 16, 17.

> "Know ye not that ye are the temple of God, and that the Spirit of God dwelleth in you? If any man defile the temple of God, him shall God destroy; for the temple is holy, which temple ye are."

Paul begins now to sum up and conclude his teaching as contained in the first division of his letter. It had to do with the divine origin of Christianity. Because of that origin there was to be a certain order of life among believers. Here it is viewed as a building with the collective believers being considered as "the temple of God."

There are two references in this Epistle to the temple of God. We have the first one here. The other one is in 6:19. "What? know ye not that your body is the temple of the Holy Ghost which is in you, which ye have of God, and ye are not your own?" Here (v. 16) the temple is primarily the collective Christian. There (6:19) the temple is the individual Christian. In the Old Testament God dwelt among His people in a material temple. But the order in the New Testament is different. Here is a body and not a building. In one case it is a body of believers. In another case it is the bodies of individual believers.

The significance of this lies in the purpose of any temple of God. It was a meeting-place for God and man. It was a place of companionship and fellowship. It was a place of worship. Not only this, it was also a place whence blessing would come to the entire world. Such a place, then, must be holy and clean.

No wonder this solemn warning is issued—"If any man defile this temple of God, him shall God destroy." It was a solemn warning against defiling the sanctity of the Christian body of believers. It was a solemn warning against destroying the unity and dividing the individual members of the collective Christian temple into contending and contentious parties. It was a solemn warning against polluting the sacred truth with divisive errors and false beliefs. The temple of believers must be kept clean. It must be kept pure. It must be kept united. And this temple, remember, is that temple which we are—the temple which is the body of collective Christians.

What a solemn responsibility is here laid upon each of us! Assume it with that kind of solemnity which will send you to your daily tasks with resolute purpose and consecrated life.

One of our great educators said: "It is not so important to be serious as it is to be serious about some important things. The monkey has a look of seriousness which would do credit to a college student, but the monkey is serious because he itches." The Christian has an important consideration which challenges his seriousness. He has been warned, as in verse seventeen, against defiling the temple of God which is the body of collective believers. The way in which he may defile the temple is suggested in the closing section of this chapter.

III. Wisdom and Folly. Verses 18-23.

He is warned here against two harmful tendencies. They are tendencies, remember, which will not only react unfavorably to the individual guilty of them but they will also be ruinous to the unity of the community of believers.

1. The False Glory in Human Wisdom. Verses 18-20.

"Let no man deceive himself. If any man among you seemeth to be wise in this world, let him become a fool, that he may be wise. For the wisdom of this world is foolishness with God. For it is written, He taketh the wise in their own craftiness. And again, the Lord knoweth the thoughts of the wise, that they are vain."

Apparently someone or some group in the Corinthian church was trying to unite Grecian philosophy with Corinthian Christianity. They were evidently trying to fuse and weld the two so that they would appear as one. This was tantamount to defiling the temple because it was corrupting divine truth with human wisdom.

In a very true sense, there is no conflict between science and Scripture. There is no disagreement between what science really knows and what Scripture really says. There is wide discrepancy, however, between the probabilities of scientific speculation and the erroneous conceptions of scriptural statements.

While there is agreement between truth in science and truth in Scripture, since truth is truth wherever found, there is something which can never be reconciled. It is what the apostle is pointing out here. He is talking about the wise man becoming a fool in order to be truly wise. He is talking about the wisdom of the world being foolishness with God. When he does so, he is speaking of human wisdom only from the standpoint of its inability to discover and achieve salvation. It is wisdom in relation to salvation which is under discussion.

When Paul says in verse nineteen that, "the wisdom of this world is foolishness with God," what does he mean? Surely God does not mean to ridicule the honest search of man for knowledge. He does not. When man discovers that two parts of hydrogen and one part of oxygen make water, that human wisdom is not human folly. But when the wise try to manufacture God out of their thoughts, when they try to devise a way around the cross, when they discount and discredit the revelation of the Bible, then that wisdom is folly.

As strange as it may seem and as paradoxical as it may be, the formula for real wisdom is this, "If any man among you seemeth to be wise in this world, let him become a fool that he may be wise." This is the first step to the attainment of any wisdom. Whoso seeks to be wise in medical wisdom dares not assault the doors of the medical college and say to its teachers, "I am wise in medicine." He must be as one who knows nothing. And if one is to be wise in divine things he dares not assume the arrogant attitude of knowing it all. It is in the fear of the Lord that wisdom begins.

The largest library in the world is neither in America nor England as one might expect. It is in Moscow and it comprises 12,000,000 volumes. The largest library does not make Russia the wisest nation, however. Her wisdom is her folly because she recognizes a wisdom that does not recognize God. Therefore, it can be truly said of that nation, the wisdom of that nation is foolishness with God.

There were two forces which sought the destruction of Christianity in its early years. They were like the pincers of a military flanking movement converging from two sides with deadly purpose. One was force and the other was intellectuality. It was Roman persecution and Grecian philosophy. Neither succeeded, for Christianity survives to this day.

As for the wise philosophers God took them "in their own craftiness." Their intellectual assaults came to naught. This was so because they were not fighting human ideas but divine truths. As for the bloody persecutions God confused their efforts and brought them to naught. It is true that their fearful operations took a frightful toll of human life; it is also true that the blood of the martyrs became the seed of the Church. This was so because they were not fighting men but God.

2. The False Glory in Human Leaders. Verses 21-23.

"Therefore let no man glory in men. For all things are yours; Whether Paul, or Apollos, or Cephas, or the world, or life, or death, or things present, or things to come; all are yours; And ye are Christ's; and Christ is God's."

This says that the Christian believer's securities do not lie in frail human beings. His strength is not in man but in God. Therefore, he should seek to fortify himself in Christ. He should seek the unity and continuity of the whole community of believers through this common possession of Christ.

There is contained in these verses an inventory of the Christian's possessions. If we could be persuaded of the potential wealth and power of these possessions, it would increase the blessing and improve the behavior of our lives. It was because these Corinthians failed in their understanding of these possessions that they failed in their behavior.

(1) *God's servants are yours.*

They were becoming enslaved to false and faulty admirations of human leaders and failing to see that God had provided these leaders for the profit and blessing of His people. Instead, they were enslaving themselves to fanatical loyalties and jealousies and missing the far greater blessings of Christian experience. The message is always bigger than the messenger.

(2) *The world is yours.*

Here it is the "kosmos" or world arrangement and refers to the vast extent of present things all about us. They have been prepared for us. In this view, the world with its laws and events is not against us because God is for us. If God were not for us, the world would be against us. Because of our new relationship as God's children, God's creation has a different meaning. This will not be actually so until we make it practically so by an active faith and productive life.

(3) *Life and death are yours.*

When does life begin? It begins at Calvary. It begins

with faith. We possess life. We should cash in on our possessions. We possess life in its best aspects and brightest prospects. We possess life eternal. We possess life at its best; see that we live up to the best. Live up to spirituality and not down to carnality. Live it in its new manhood and not in its old manhood.

But death is ours, too. We are not its quarry slave. We are its masters. We are not death's victims. We are its victors. We do not belong to death. It belongs to us.

When Socrates was being put to death he said of his enemies, "They may kill me, but they cannot hurt me." So may a Christian speak of death. It kills but does not hurt. It takes life but cannot keep from life. It is so because his life is "hid with Christ in God."

When it says, "All are yours; and ye are Christ's," it is stating a great and wonderful truth. "All are yours," is your possession. "Ye are Christ's," is your position. Thus, your possession is because of your position.

Let us be encouraged to act upon these great facts and live up to some measure of the possibilities of Christian experience. Let us be masters and not slaves. Let us be victors and not victims. Let us be possessors and not paupers. Yea, verily, let us be what we are.

SECTION TWO

THE DIVINE ORDER IN THE CHURCH

CHAPTER IV
THE CHURCH AND ITS LEADERS
I CORINTHIANS IV

CHAPTER V
THE CHURCH AND ITS MEMBERS
I CORINTHIANS V

CHAPTER VI
THE CHURCH AND ITS CONTROVERSIES
I CORINTHIANS VI

CHAPTER VII
THE CHURCH AND ITS MARRIAGES
I CORINTHIANS VII

CHAPTER VIII
THE CHURCH AND ITS LIBERTIES
I CORINTHIANS VIII

CHAPTER IX
THE CHURCH AND ITS WORKERS
I CORINTHIANS IX

CHAPTER X
THE CHURCH AND ITS TRADITIONS
I CORINTHIANS X

CHAPTER XI
THE CHURCH AND ITS WORSHIP
I CORINTHIANS XI

CHAPTER IV

THE CHURCH AND ITS LEADERS

I Corinthians 4

ENTERING the second phase of the book of First Corinthians we find that it deals with divine order in the
church. If there is a divine origin of Christianity, we are
prepared to find that the church which is the custodian of
that Christianity and the vehicle of its expression, is not
left an orphan in the conduct of its affairs. It is not in the
world to chart its own course. It was handed unsealed orders
on the day of Pentecost. It has both precept and precedent
to establish its message and to shape its policies. Its behavior is not left to its whims. And, of course, if these things
govern the collective body of believers, they automatically
effect the individual members. The behavior of the Christian
is to be judged by the order of the church.

In this order we find a very definite pattern for the conduct of the affairs of both church and Christian. It is presented from chapters 4—11 in a very orderly manner.

There is set forth in this immediate chapter the peculiar
relation maintaining between the church and its leaders.
This union between the leader and the led is a *natural* one.
It is furthermore a *divine* one. It is not something artificially
imposed by ecclesiastical canon, under which there exists an
obedience of fear. It is, instead, an obedience of faith. It is
something which springs out of the normal association of
Christian experience. It is pointed out here that the leadership of the church and the membership of the church represent a common walk and a common bond in Christ. Furthermore, the most healthy, the most virile state of the church
rests upon an understanding of this relationship.

Observe how the chapter deals with the subject under discussion.

I. LEADERS AND THEIR CALLING. Verses 1-5.

Certain facts are apparent in the calling of these leaders. It was not a self-chosen profession; nor was it an ecclesiastically enforced relation.

1. The Leaders and God. Verses 1, 2.

> "Let a man so account of us, as of the ministers of Christ, and stewards of the mysteries of God. Moreover it is required in stewards, that a man be found faithful."

Notice how suggestively it begins to tell us about these leaders. "Let a man so account of us, as of the ministers of Christ, and stewards of the mysteries of God." They were ministers of Christ and stewards of God. This was their first relationship and their initial responsibility. They would be understood and were to be considered in their person and their service in their connection with God. In Corinth the people had lost sight of this fact and were dividing these leaders among themselves as if they belonged to them when, in fact, they belonged to God.

Just where does Christian service begin? Does it begin with a man's ambition to make a living or achieve a place? Does it begin with a man's preparation? Does it begin with a man's ability? It begins with none of these things. It begins, instead, with a conviction. This conviction begins with a call. It, therefore, is something which is the result of God's call rather than our choice.

Unless Christian service begins here and keeps its bearings on these ideals, it will never bear the authority nor accomplish the results that go with it. We must rescue it from the clutches of ambitious place seekers. We must see that it begins with God or it will have its end in man. Rather there be one man who has the conviction that he is sent of God than a thousand who have sent themselves.

You will notice the words used to describe their service:

(1) *They were "ministers of Christ."*

The word "minister" is not merely a name given to a preacher. It is a designation of *rank* and a delegation of *work*. It describes the position of service. It means, literally, an "under-rower." In the ships of that day, wind power was augmented by man power. There were on either side of the ship great oars manned by under-rowers who were under the supervision of a master rower. Such was the position of this minister's service. He was under orders from a higher authority.

(2) *They were "stewards of God."*

This described the character of their service. A steward was a manager intrusted with the management of his master's affairs. In the case of the Christian steward, his was the administration of divine truths, the wise employment of divine power, and the faithful propagation of the message intrusted to his care.

As such a steward there was a supreme concern—faithfulness. "It is required in stewards, that a man be found faithful." It is not required that Christian stewards be found popular or successful in a worldly-wise way. It is required that he be found faithful in relation to the substance and the service intrusted to his management. If this is to become the goal of the ministry then much which now looms large as being important would quickly vanish.

2. The Leaders and Man. Verses 3-5.

> "But with me it is a very small thing that I should be judged of you, or of man's judgment: yea, I judge not mine own self. For I know nothing by myself; yet am I not hereby justified: but he that judgeth me is the Lord. Therefore judge nothing before the time, until the Lord come, who both will bring to light the hidden things of darkness, and will make manifest the counsels of the hearts: and then shall every man have praise of God."

We can explain this no better than by quoting Arthur S. Way's translation: "But, as to my being called to account by you, or at any human bar, that is a matter of perfect indifference to me. Not that I constitute myself my own judge. I am not conscious of any dereliction of duty, it is true: still, I do not on that account claim to be exonerated of blame. But I do say that the only one who has a right to judge me is the Lord. He shall flash light upon the secrets now shrouded in darkness: He shall lay bare the purposes of men's hearts; and then shall the due praise be awarded to each of us from God."

We would spare many a faithful worker a broken heart and ourselves bitter feelings if we were more temperate in our judgments and more charitable in our estimates. After all, Paul is arguing, what does it matter what a fickle public says? The whole manner of one's tenure of office will be reviewed by God and He will judge with equity. It matters little whether men praise or blame so long as God approves. Divine approval is more to be desired than the best of human approbation. Let us have it by deserving it.

We are told to reserve our judgments and wait "until the Lord come." Then the true quality will appear, whether it be wood, hay or stubble, or whether it be gold, silver or precious stones.

It is a tremendous encouragement for every sincere and faithful worker to hear Paul say at the close of verse 5, "then shall every man praise of God." This, of course, means that he shall have the praise he deserves: not necessarily the praise he desires. What we deserve will be according to the measure of our faithfulness.

The estimates which we may hold of ourselves may be due to the narrow and warped view we have of life. Sometimes we need to be thrown into the bold relief of contrast against other lives. Sometimes we may have felt that we had difficulties more numerous than others until our lot was compared with another's.

There had come a feeling to these Corinthian Christians that they were doing very well. They felt extremely self-satisfied. What was worse, they were acting as if they had fulfilled their obligations. In fact, they were acting as though the fight was finished and they were now ready to be ushered into the eternal fruits of their faithfulness. Paul points out how untrue this was. He does so by reminding them of his plight, of his great sufferings, of his bitter struggles.

II. LEADERS AND THEIR FOLLOWERS. Verses 6-13.

1. Their Humility. Verses 6-8.

"And these things, brethren, I have in a figure transferred to myself and to Apollos for your sakes; that ye might learn in us not to think of men above that which is written, that no one of you be puffed up for one against another. For who maketh thee to differ from another? and what hast thou that thou didst not receive? now if thou didst receive it, why dost thou glory, as if thou hadst not received it? Now ye are full, now ye are rich, ye have reigned as kings without us: and I would to God ye did reign, that we also might reign with you."

He begins with "these things." They were the factions and divisions which had grown up in Corinth around their leaders. They had been produced by the rivalries and jealousies of the people. Paul now refers to them in order to teach the Corinthians and us a lesson in humility. He does so by saying, "that ye might learn in us (Paul and Apollos) not to think of men above that which is written." Paul was purposely demoting himself that he might deflate the foolish pride and jealous rivalry of the people. It was the self-effacement of the preacher that there might be spiritual attainment in the people.

2. Their Suffering. Verses 9-12a.

"For I think that God hath set forth us the apostles last, as it were appointed to death: for we are made a spectacle unto the world, and to angels, and to men. We are fools for Christ's sake,

but ye are wise in Christ; we are weak, but ye are strong; ye
are honourable, but we are despised. Even unto this present
hour we both hunger, and thirst, and are naked, and are buffeted,
and have no certain dwellingplace; And labour, working with our
own hands . . ."

These same verses from Way's translation take on illuminated meaning, "It seems to me as if God has exposed His
apostles to public view, like the doomed wretches who close
a triumphal procession—that we, like them, have been exposed in the amphitheatre before the eyes of the world, ay,
of angels as well as of men! We maintain the old crude
absurdities in Messiah's cause; your faith in Messiah is quite
a philosophy. We feel ourselves poor weaklings; you are
strong enough to stand alone; you are men of distinction; we
are abject outcasts. We have never known your privileges:
from the outset to this day we have been suffering hunger,
suffering thirst: we have no decent clothing: we are victims
of mob violence, we are homeless men: we have to toil hard,
working with our own hands."

While the people had been indulging in childish jealousies
and carnal rivalries over Paul and his fellow-apostles, the
apostles had been face to face with the stern realities of life.
So desperate had been the situations they encountered in the
line of duty and in the fulfillment of their commission that
it seemed to Paul as if they had been sentenced to death. He
remarks in verse nine that their lot was compared to that of
condemned criminals. In Paul's day these criminals were a
part of the spectacles enacted in the amphitheatres of the
great cities. There were great gladiatorial contests. At the
end of these spectacles, when the spectators had been sated
with the lesser sights, the condemned criminals were brought
in to fight, unarmed, with wild beasts. There was no hope
for their escape. They "were appointed to death," and Paul
saw himself and his fellow apostles in such a light as that.

This is not all. They were not only like condemned criminals. They were "fools for Christ's sake" while the Corinthians

were "wise in Christ." The apostles were marked for their loyalty to the gospel but the Corinthians had so cleverly presented the Word of the Cross with the wisdom of words that they had lost the stigma of foolishness. It made them appear clever and it made them acceptable.

There is more, however. The Corinthians had won a reputation for wisdom and appeared strong. Whereas, the apostles were made to appear weak and ineffectual. The people received honor. The apostles were despised. Even this was not all. The people were enjoying the security and the plenty of their favored places while the apostles were hungry, thirsty, without decent clothing, the objects of mob violence, without homes, and compelled to keep body and soul together by manual labor. While the apostles were enduring such hardship with such heroism, the people were consuming their energies in selfish and disgraceful rivalries.

Let us be comforted and encouraged if our way is beset by obstacles and hardships. So was Paul's. You will notice that he did not allow a death sentence, taunts and jibes, insults, hunger, thirst, nakedness or hard work to deter him from the object of his goal. The prize is all the more precious for the hardships of the struggle.

A little lad trudging down the road with a basket of blackberries under his arm was accosted by a man who asked, "Sammy, where did you get such fine berries?" "Over there in the briars, sir." "Well, I imagine that your mother will be happy to have such lovely berries." "Yes, sir, she will. She will be happy for the berries but I will never say a word about the briars in my feet." Yes, berries and briars go together. You can not have the berries without the briars and there is a penalty of suffering to pay for every success in this world.

3. Their Attitude. Verse 12b, 13.

" . . . being reviled, we bless; being persecuted, we suffer it: Being defamed, we intreat: we are made as the filth of the world, and are the offscouring of all things unto this day."

Not all the glory accrued to these noble men by *what* they suffered. It came as much by *the way* they suffered it. Men railed; they blessed. Men persecuted; they suffered with magnificent self-control. Men slandered and abused; they entreated and gently pleaded with them. They used these bitter occasions as pulpits to proclaim their Christ. They received stones and gave back bread. They received cursings and gave back blessings. They were hated and returned love. Yes, and what was more, these noble men were treated as if they were the "filth of the world." The significance of their position is not appreciated until we realize that this meant that they were considered as the scrapings and sweepings of the street. What bitterness they bore, yet how magnificently they bore it!

Who of us dare lift our eyes from these words and not feel the hot flame of shame upon our cheeks and the strong lash of condemnation in our conscience? Who of us have endured such as they? Let us dare to bring self-correction to our ways. Let us leave this place of conviction with a new spirit of devotion.

In order to stimulate loyalty and unity Paul does a daring thing. He has witnessed the sorry spectacle of a carnal partisanship which has divided the Christians at Corinth into various parties. He dares now to challenge them to observe his example. He calls them to a new and higher sense of loyalty.

III. Leaders and Their Honor. Verses 14, 15.

> "I write not these things to shame you, but as my beloved sons I warn you. For though ye have ten thousand instructors in Christ, yet have ye not many fathers: for in Christ Jesus I have begotten you through the gospel."

We notice very carefully that Paul does not cruelly criticize these people. He does not parade their iniquity before their shameful eyes. He gently but firmly warns them. "If you would imitate Christ, take sin by the throat and the sinner by the hand." Paul took these erring people by the hand. While he loathed their sin, he loved them. He now suggests that in order to safeguard their spiritual interests they had better take their eyes off the various instructors who have come with their teachings and put them on him.

Paul dares to do this because of his prior claim upon them. He was their spiritual father. He had a deeper interest. Instructors are imparters of light. Paul was a father and fathers are imparters of life. They were begotten by Paul. Therefore, they were to give Paul such honor and such preference and obedience as belonged to one in this spiritual relationship. They were to remember how deeply they were indebted to him and also how extensively they could trust him.

IV. Leaders and Their Influence. Verses 16-21.

1. The Recognition of Paul's Influence. Verse 16.

"Wherefore I beseech you, be ye followers of me."

Was this a contradiction to his previous teaching against choosing various leaders as popular heroes thus creating factions? Not at all. It was the recognition of his singular place in their lives as their spiritual father. It was an emphasis on the part that true spiritual influence plays in Christian experience. He boldly says, "be ye followers of me."

This is not promiscuously thrown out nor thoughtlessly given, for he follows with a second suggestion.

2. The Secret of Paul's Influence. Verse 17.

"For this cause have I sent unto you Timotheus, who is my beloved son, and faithful in the Lord, who shall bring you into remembrance of my ways which be in Christ, as I teach everywhere in every church."

They were to follow him only as he followed Christ. The approval of his leadership would be in his obedience. Paul had been led and now he was able and fit to lead others. He was, therefore, a safe and trusted leader. All credentials of leadership must pass this point. Leaders must be led. Leaders for Christ must be led by Christ. People wish to see as well as hear. They need a demonstration as much as an explanation.

"Have you ever heard the gospel?" inquired a missionary of a Chinese merchant. "No," he replied, "but I have seen it. I know a man who was a terror in this region. He was as fierce as an animal. He was an opium addict. But when he accepted the Jesus religion, he changed completely. Now his wickedness is gone. He is quiet and gentle." Yes, the walk of a Christian is many times a more powerful witness than the talk of a Christian. Paul had *talked* and Corinth had *listened*. Now Paul was *walking* and Corinth was to *watch*.

Paul had brilliantly set forth the facts of their faith in contrast to the hollow philosophies of their age. Now Paul was proposing that they witness the reality of these facts of faith in his life. He was proposing to prove as well as preach.

In the crowded ward of a great hospital for tubercular women, the visiting minister was about to read from the Bible and pray with a young woman patient. She said, "Pastor, please turn around so that the girl in the next bed can hear, too." When he had finished, the minister spoke to the girl in the next bed. During the conversation she said, "When I came to this hospital I thought I was a Christian. Since meeting this girl whom you have come to see, I have decided I am not, but if to be a Christian is to be like her, I want to be one."

3. The Proof of Paul's Influence. Verse 18-21.

"Now some are puffed up, as though I would not come to you. But I will come to you shortly, if the Lord will, and will know, not the speech of them which are puffed up, but the power. For the kingdom of God is not in word, but in power. What will ye? shall I come unto you with a rod, or in love, and in the spirit of meekness?"

It was apparent that this was directed against certain individuals who were discounting Paul's sincerity. For them, Paul proposed an infallible test. Not a test of words but of life, for after all, "the kingdom of God is not in word, but in power." Let each of us solemnly scrutinize our lives under the magnifying power of this scripture. Christianity is not merely a collection of pretty words. It is not a philosophically arranged set of ideas. It is not logic but life. It is not something established by an argument but a completely new arrangement of life which provides us with power. And, in consequence, it is not just a faith you espouse; it is a force that you experience.

Did you ever consider how slight a difference there is in the construction of the words "minion" and "dominion"? Minion means a "servile dependent" while dominion means "to rule." The simple difference in both the spelling and the significance of these two words is the letters "d" and "o." They spell "do." Yes, a minion may have dominion. He may have it in his life and all about him if he will do God's will. It will release both divine power and blessing upon him. Let us dare to do.

I like the daring spirit and searching challenge of Norvel Young's "I Dare You."

> "I Dare You to prove that you are not asleep on the job.
> I Dare You to spend more time reading God's Word than the daily newspaper.
> I Dare You to face your doubts and conquer them.
> I Dare You to brave the snickers of your friends and live in the simple style which will enable you to spend more on Christ.
> I Dare You to talk with your friends about actually living up to their professed religion.
> I Dare You to take Christ with you into the schoolroom, office, and workshop.
> I Dare You to tell the truth in love whenever you speak.
> I Dare You to live above the average standard of morals and be really virtuous.
> I Dare You to be candid with yourself and evaluate the way you spend your leisure time in the light of your love for Christ.

I Dare You to be courageous and willing to accept criticism by trying to start some Christian work in your congregation.

I Dare You to speak out respectfully and yet frankly against those who are stifling Christ in the church.

I Dare You to risk your reputation by rising up in protest at the inertia which characterizes most congregations and members.

I Dare You to throw your whole soul into the worship of God every time you meet for that purpose.

I Dare You to work half as hard to save the souls for whom Christ died as you work for your business.

I DARE YOU TO ACT AS IF YOU BELIEVE THAT JESUS IS THE CHRIST."

Chapter V

THE CHURCH AND ITS MEMBERS

I *Corinthians* 5

A CHIEF reason for the need in our present day of such teaching as is found in First Corinthians is found in the present existence of carnality. In Corinth we have seen the spectacle of factions and divisions. Here are self-satisfied and indifferent Christians, content to listen to their own songs of self-praise while the world-wide work of redemption languishes. Here, now, we are to behold the horrible spectacle of unmentionable sin. We are soon to witness the spectacle of legal contentions, of ill-advised marriages, of promiscuous conduct, and of disorders of worship that scandalize the cause of Christ. Here is reason for shame and reason to flee to the fountain whence flows a cleansing stream.

If there is need for a mission of evangelism to the world of natural men, there is equal need for a mission of correction to the church of carnal men. It is riddled with carnality and First Corinthians should be the textbook of teaching from every pulpit and lectern in America. We will never impress the world with the need of our message until we impress it with the reality and purity of our experience. It seems that in many respects we need the mission to the church more than to the world. If the church were right, the task of persuading the world would be immeasurably simplified.

Here were people boasting of doctrinal excellence. They were boasting and glorying in rival leaders and were filled with complacent pride. Yet there was unmentionable sin in their midst. Shame on them and shame on us when such is true!

It may seem like leaning over backwards but we can forego

a good deal of our doctrinal contentions and get out the antiseptic of divine cleansing and cleanse our lives so that our passionate preaching is supported by persuasive practice.

There are two words which are scriptural Siamese twins. They cannot be separated without fatality to both. One is "orthodoxy" and the other "orthopraxy." One is "straight thinking" and the other is "straight living."

I. SCANDAL IN THE CHURCH. Verses 1-5.

It was not the case of secret sinning but bold, brazen and publicly accepted vice. It was so flagrant that Paul could say "it is reported commonly." And it was such sin as one blushes to mention. It was incestuous immorality involving a son and stepmother.

The almost unbelievable part of this affair is the attitude of the church. Instead of being thoroughly ashamed Paul says, "And ye are puffed up and have not rather mourned." The fact that they were puffed up does not mean that they were actually gloating over this sin, but rather it was meant to be a continuation of the denunciation of their previous controversies over rival leaders. They were so busy in their contentions and so puffed up in their own opinions that they had neither place nor disposition to deal with the awful thing that was eating as a cancer at their spiritual vitals. Their carnality had led them so far into senseless contentions that their spiritual senses were stunted and dwarfed. They failed to see that "the true glory of the Christian Church consists not in the eloquence and gifts of its great teachers but in the moral purity and exemplary lives of its members."

Here was the tragic case of being occupied with trivial and minor affairs and being completely oblivious to the most vital affairs of the church.

Paul speaks up with a justifiable wrath and indignation and declares the course that should be pursued. He tells them to consider him as being among them and, with their concurrence, pronouncing the judgment of excommunication upon this flagrant sinner. He does not usurp the prerogatives of the local church. He does not do the disciplining himself for that belongs to the church. He does not exercise autocratic powers but directs their course of action.

This action was apparently very drastic. In verse five he purposes "to deliver such an one unto Satan for the destruction of the flesh that the spirit may be saved in the day of the Lord Jesus." Here was something of great significance. Paul directs the convening of the church in solemn assembly. Over this assembly both the presence and power of Jesus Christ are invoked. To this was added the special significance of Paul's apostolic authority. After considering the case of the sinning brother he was to be excommunicated. He was to be cast out into the realm of Satan for buffeting and chastisement. This severe punishment was not in hatred nor cruelty, nor an attempt to consign the sinner to final retribution. Back of it were the hope, desire and prayer that it might bring such conviction as to induce repentance and at last to effect the restoration of the offending one.

It was the church which was to do this. It was to be done in the spirit of humility, not for the sake of destruction, but in order to achieve reclamation and reformation. An arrogated authority too often seeks to employ its powers in the wrong way. We have witnessed attempts to so condemn and abuse the offender as to drive him deeper into his predicament instead of extricating him from it. The church has a mission of salvaging the shipwrecks of its sinning members. This can only be accomplished when justice is tempered by love.

We should view this incident in Corinth's church life with deep personal concern. It may be nearer to us than we think. Sensuality is not far from carnality. Here were carnal Christians. They were walking as men instead of new men. They were living out of character. They were following their lower natures. This lead to their jealousies, quarrelings and boastings. It also led to the gross and wicked sin of sensuality that has had to be so severely dealt with. It should constitute a very solemn warning that carnality can very easily lead to sensuality. The only security is to live in the strength and power of Jesus Christ.

There is yet another lesson. The actual act of sin is not a sudden occurrence. Men do not go to pieces suddenly. Behind the act is a period of weakening and inner destruction. When a dam gives way it appears as if the destruction was the work of a few seconds. Back of those few seconds are months and probably years of deterioration and weakening. Either the foundation was inadequate or the construction faulty. But, even so, the weakening and degenerating process went on, sight unseen. Then came the crash and the split-second catastrophe. So with the downfall of a man. The slow process of carnal corruption eating at the thought centers, slowly corrupted character and then came the crash.

Let us be careful of what we think. Let us guard the pools of imagination lest they become reflections of evil. Let us flee carnality. Leave no window of the mind opened, no door to the soul unlocked. Put Christ at every outpost of life. Let the Holy Spirit rule over every thought, desire, ambition, and deed. We shall then avoid the catastrophes of character that overtake so many.

The preservation of the power of the church at Corinth lay in restoring two things. It required the restoration of its unity and the restoration of its purity. Paul has already dealt with the restoration of its unity. He has spoken of the efforts made to formulate a philosophical Christianity that would be acceptable to the current thought of Greece. Now we observe his efforts to restore its purity by putting out of the church those who were perverting Christian liberty by licentious living; and also by maintaining a policy of discipline.

II. DISCIPLINE IN THE CHURCH. Verses 6-13.

Paul has already indicated the course to take in dealing with the particular offender in question. But what shall be done to prevent a recurrence of this scandal? What shall be done to re-establish the purity of the common body of believers?

He begins by rebuking them in verse six, "Your glorying is not good." In verse two they were "puffed up" over their doctrinal attainments and partisan leaders. Here they were exulting in a false conception of liberty. There was a party of Antinomians in Corinth who were polluting the purity of Corinthian Christianity in an open and brazen manner. Antinomian is a name applied to such as claim freedom from all legal restrictions and liberty to live according to personal pleasure. They said that since Christians are under grace, there is no law to prohibit the unhindered exercise of desire. Since there is no law, there is no wrong. This is a perversion of truth. And it is as unchristian as it is untruthful. Grace imposes a higher purity and a higher culture than was ever levied by the law.

The trouble at Corinth grew out of a false attitude to evil. They apparently discounted and disregarded lesser evils. They took a tolerant attitude to sin. Paul points out that the danger of sin is its potentiality. If the oak lies in the acorn, so the flagrant sin lies in the so-called respectable sin. Sin is of such a nature that it multiplies on tolerance.

As an example of what he meant, Paul pointed to the action of leaven. Leaven is the same as our yeast. A little leaven in a lump of dough transforms it gradually into its own nature. The slightest complicity with evil will penetrate into the entire soul of the individual and the body of the believers.

To restore purity to the church, it must cleanse itself of all leavenous members. It must not countenance the least sin or sinner. It must be clean at all costs. Unless it is clean, it will be in no position to minister to the needs of the world. Cleanliness is not next to godliness; it is godliness.

Observe, if you will, the power of evil. Leaven is the Scripture's type of evil. It speaks of "a little leaven" meaning a little evil. In its natural sphere, as it relates to natural man or carnal man in the natural world, evil has more power

than good. Just one drop of foul water will contaminate a
whole reservoir of pure water. Yet, one drop of pure water
does not appreciably improve the foul. A pain localized in
one's tooth makes the whole body miserable. Yet, if pain is
present in all the body save in one place, the painless part
does not appreciably alleviate the painful parts. Why is this?
It is evil's power in its own realm. This is true in the physical
and in the moral realm. The only place it is not true is in
the spiritual. The reason Corinth was suffering the pollution
of its parts was that its members were no longer living in
the spiritual realm but had descended to the carnal, which
is the equivalent of the natural. Watch the sphere of your
life and you have the secret of both the purity and unity of
your life.

The secret of maintaining purity is discipline. It is discipline for the individual believer and for the collective believers.

This discipline has both a past precedent and a present
practice.

1. A Past Precedent. Verses 7, 8.

"Purge out therefore the old leaven, that ye may be a new
lump, as ye are unleavened. For even Christ our passover is
sacrificed for us: Therefore let us keep the feast, not with
old leaven, neither with the leaven of malice and wickedness;
but with the unleavened bread of sincerity and truth."

Since Christ is our Passover Lamb, we should observe the
spiritual equivalent of the passover feast. It was required of
the people that on the eve of this feast all leaven should be
removed from their homes. From that time to the time the
paschal lamb was offered in the temple, no leaven was to
appear on their tables. This suggests the Christian's attitude
to life. He should exclude all sin, anything leavenous, from
his life. Anything that would contaminate the body or the
mind or the spirit should be put away. Ransack the soul as
carefully and religiously as the Hebrew would ransack his
house from cellar to garret for any trace of evil.

2. A Present Practice. Verse 9-13.

"I wrote unto you in an epistle not to company with fornicators: Yet not altogether with the fornicators of this world, or with the covetous, or extortioners, or with idolaters; for then must ye needs go out of the world. But now I have written unto you not to keep company, if any man that is called a brother be a fornicator, or covetous, or an idolater, or a railer, or a drunkard, or an extortioner; with such an one no not to eat. For what have I to do to judge them also that are without? do not ye judge them that are within? But them that are without God judgeth. Therefore put away from among yourselves that wicked person."

In substance Paul is saying this: In a previous letter I warned you not to associate with men like the one just mentioned; but I did not mean that you are to have no relations in the world at large with such men, or with greedy and grasping men, or with idol worshipers; it would be wholly impossible, as you suggest, to avoid all association with such men; in that case you would have to leave the world altogether. What I meant to say, and I now repeat it, was that if a professing Christian is guilty of such sins you should withdraw from all fellowship with him. Do not even eat with such a person. I cannot undertake to regulate the outside world in such matters. I am content to keep the church without reproach, and that is equally your own duty. Our discipline cannot extend to those outside the church. These we leave to the judgment of God. But I have said enough. Excomunicate that wicked man.

Paul is enjoining a state of moral and spiritual isolation upon the Christian in his attitude to those who live in known sin. Here there is to be neither neutrality nor tolerance. We are to be as intolerant as the health officer is when dealing with a case of diphtheria. The danger of contagion calls for the protection of isolation.

In the seventh verse it was the isolation of the sinner so far as collective believers were concerned. In these verses it is the individual attitude. The individual believer is to isolate himself from the offender. He is to protect himself from contamination by isolation from the false-living believer. This isolation is not only from the presence of evil but from the practice of it.

Now these things resolve themselves into a few clear-cut conclusions. The first concerns the church and the second, the Christian. As far as the church is concerned, it must take drastic steps to restore and ensure its own purity. This purity must not only be doctrinal purity but moral purity. It is a travesty to contend for the faith in doctrine while one is unfaithful in life. People have been disciplined because of erroneous doctrines but when have you last heard about discipline for false lives? We guard the truth against doctrinal error while permitting its pollution through carnal living.

As far as the Christian is concerned, he dare give no quarter to carnality. Let him "walk in the Spirit" and he will not "fulfill the lusts of the flesh." Let him remember that the flesh of a believer is not better than the flesh of a sinner. His purity and security rest in the spiritual realms of Christian living.

This matter of life at its purest and securest is only certain with Christ as its center, filling and pervading the whole personality.

Chapter VI

THE CHURCH AND ITS CONTROVERSIES

I *Corinthians* 6

THE CONNECTION between the fifth chapter and the sixth chapter is to be found in the link that exists between their last and first verses. The fifth chapter closes with a reference to the duty of Christians judging those who are within its own borders. Its province of judging embraces its own members and does not include the outside world.

Paul then immediately proceeds to deal with certain matters within the church. This chapter accordingly speaks of two problems.

I. THE CHURCH AND LEGAL CONTROVERSY. Verses 1-11.

Here is an obvious problem and a grievous wrong. It was the problem of disputes among Christians and the wrong of litigation before non-Christians.

Let us be sure we understand the problem correctly lest we err in our conclusions. To begin with, it was a problem which concerned Christians. It sought to compose differences among Christians. It is not a condemnation of civil courts. It is not setting aside regulation by law nor adjudication by legal procedure. It is simply a regulation of Christian behavior in respect to purely Christian matters.

This does not prohibit the Christian from seeking the protection of the law from injustice or from unscrupulous men. But it does speak against Christians airing their differences and settling their quarrels in public courts. This is not only scandalous but sinful. It is descending to carnal methods for the solution of spiritual problems.

111

We notice the reasons why this method of settling Christian controversies is wrong.

1. It Is Contrary to the Destiny of the Church. Verses 1-3.

"Dare any of you, having a matter against another, go to law before the unjust, and not before the saints? Do ye not know that the saints shall judge the world? and if the world shall be judged by you, are ye unworthy to judge the smallest matters? Know ye not that we shall judge angels? how much more things that pertain to this life?"

Here is the lofty destiny of the church. In the day of the kingdom of God on earth the saints are to exercise great powers and prerogatives. They are to hold places of honor and influence. Paul argues that if such will be their destiny, then the settling of difficulties is their duty now.

To do otherwise denies the competency of the church to adjust the differences that arise within itself. This means, as you can readily see, the denial of its very right to exist. If its message has no power over its own members, then how much power can it have over the world?

It is an admission of failure, to go to the world for the solution of inter-Christian controversies. If the church cannot solve the problem of personal relations within its own borders, then it has admitted its incapacity to solve the problems of the world.

2. It Is to be Settled by Christian Arbitration. Verses 4-6.

"If then ye have judgments of things pertaining to this life, set them to judge who are least esteemed in the church. I speak to your shame. Is it so, that there is not a wise man among you? no, not one that shall be able to judge between his brethren? But brother goeth to law with brother, and that before the unbelievers."

The problems involved in these controversies were not intricate questions of law. They did not require super-legal minds. They were personal matters. They arose in the course of community or business life or out of differences of opinion. Their adjustment, therefore, was not dependent upon professional assistance. Paul suggests that even the least esteemed of their company might be of great assistance. At any rate, no matter what the difficulty, it would yield to arbitration. This arbitration is suggested by the words, "Is it so, that there is not a wise man among you? no, not one that shall be able to judge between his brethren?"

To do other than this and to go in carnal indignation to courts of law is to demean the gospel. In the case of the Corinthians it was to set Christians before pagans and say, in substance, that the pagan way of life was better than theirs. In our case it is to take the differences of Christians before the world and say, in substance, we have lofty doctrines but we have neither the grace to get along, nor the government to get together.

This ought not to be. We greatly err and we grievously sin when we do this. If there are no cohesive qualities in the gospel to bind Christians together and save them from divisive factions and erupting contentions, then it is defective. But such is not the case. It is the sin of carnality which causes us to walk as men instead of new men.

3. It is an Evidence of Spiritual Defeat. Verse 7.

> "Now therefore there is utterly a fault among you, because ye go to law one with another. Why do ye not rather take wrong? why do ye not rather suffer yourselves to be defrauded?"

To have won in a legal contest was to lose in a spiritual test. To go to court and ignore the province of the church was a mark of spiritual defectiveness. It meant that they were defective in their character and dwarfed in their stature. This, of course, was precisely so for they were carnal. Carnality is spiritual defectiveness. It is dwarfed Christianity. It is stunted morality.

4. It Is Contrary to the Spirit of Christianity. Verse 8.

> "Nay, ye do wrong, and defraud, and that your brethren."

The very nature of spiritual Christianity is conciliatory. The message of Jesus taught peace, forbearance, unity, and love. What was more, it taught the virtue of losing in order to gain. We like to stand upon our rights and demand justice. But if our selfish standing means the fall of the cause of Christ; and if our gaining justice is at the expense of peace and harmony, it is a hollow victory. Justice before the courts at the expense of unity is injustice. To attain our rights at the expense of a brother's love is a shameful wrong.

We must remember a fact easy to forget, that we dare not sacrifice the spirit of Christ to achieve the letter of Christianity.

5. It Is Contrary to the Nature of Christianity. Verses 9-11.

> "Know ye not that the unrighteous shall not inherit the kingdom of God? Be not deceived: neither fornicators, nor idolaters, nor adulterers, nor effeminate, nor abusers of themselves with mankind, Nor thieves, nor covetous, nor drunkards, nor revilers, nor extortioners, shall inherit the kingdom of God. And such were some of you: but ye are washed, but ye are sanctified, but ye are justified in the name of the Lord Jesus, and by the Spirit of our God."

It is contrary to the nature of Christianity to do anything that would injure another or take advantage of another by legal methods. Any Christian who does this classifies himself with the unregenerate who are to be excluded from the kingdom.

In the conduct of these Corinthians, they were following the very spirit and practice of the world whenever they engaged in litigation against another. This they were now being advised to cease doing. Paul urged them to live and act in their character as Christians. They were once like the unregenerate of the world, but they had been cleansed and set apart to a different kind of life. Let them now go out and live it.

Dr. Campbell Morgan once told of having visited a friend in Scotland. While sitting in the living-room of the home of his host he smelled the most delightful odor of roses. Yet he saw no flowers. He asked his friend how it was that though there were no roses in the room he could smell the unmistakable fragrance of this flower. His host explained that years earlier he had visited an antique shop in the city and had purchased an interesting vase of coarse pottery. Later he bought a small bottle of attar of roses and placed it inside the vase. On reaching home he found to his dismay that the perfume bottle had broken and the vase had soaked up the perfume. He thought that the odor of roses would soon pass away from the vase. "But believe me," he said, "when I tell you that this vase has been giving out attar of roses to this household for more than twenty-five years." Absorbing the spirit of Jesus Christ we are bound to cast His fragrance in life's relationships.

Among the most keenly desired things of life you will find power and influence. These are not easily acquired nor readily achieved. Power and purity go together just as progress and purity do. The church and the Christian cannot go higher until they go deeper. Height, in man as in any well-developed tree, is always in proportion to depth.

The church of Corinth was in a strategic place of great influence. It was surrounded by both culture and corruption. It could exert a tremendous influence but that was unimportant so long as it was not clean. A clean heart means a strong character. A strong character means a fruitful career.

II. The Church and Personal Purity. Verses 12-20.

Here we find purity in its relation to bodily appetites. We find it with a very practical application to common problems. Here are ethics for Christian behavior.

One of the characteristics of popular music is the fact that it unconsciously expresses the native desires of man. Many of the popular songs begin with the same two words, "I want." What man wants and what he gets are, of course, very different. There are human desires that can only be gratified in the spiritual realm and can only be satisfied by the presence of God. The wrong of our modern life is that we seek the gratification of our desires in sensuality rather than spirituality. Peace lies in purity. The end of the trail of human passions is littered with the wrecks of men's fondest hopes.

What the world seeks in sensuality many Christians seek in carnality. It was the sin of Corinth. It is a blind alley of human hopes. It will lead nowhere but to a broken heart and a blank wall of despair.

1. The Danger of Transgressing Liberty. Verse 12.

"All things are lawful unto me, but all things are not expedient . . ."

Paul sets forth a noble doctrine of Christian liberty. In the book of Romans he insisted on the right of Christians in matters of conscience. If it was a question of observing days or of eating food, these were without moral significance and must be matters of conscience. They could be observed or left unobserved, done or left undone, as the individual was persuaded.

Such liberty was not to be used as an excuse for license for no Christian has the liberty to be immoral and impure. Furthermore, no Christian has the right to exercise liberty to the point where conduct becomes injurious to another. Hence, he says, "All things are lawful unto me, but all things are not expedient." That is, while law does not proscribe against them, common sense tells us they are not profitable. The word "expedient" comes from the same root as that from which we derive our word expedition. It carries the sense of helping us on the way. Certain things may be right in themselves but they do not help us on the way. They do not help our expedition of life.

2. The Danger of Moral Slavery. Verse 12.

" . . . all things are lawful for me, but I will not be brought under the power of any."

Every human appetite has a proper purpose. All were implanted for a good reason. Legitimate appetites and proper desires may become our masters and we their slaves. We may be enslaved by good things as easily as by bad things. Drink is an appetite that rules the lives of uncounted thousands. It is unquestionably evil. We do not think Paul had that specifically in mind here. He speaks of the peril of respectable desires. Business is a legitimate thing but its lure fastens itself on some men so that they neglect both God and home. They have neither time for church nor for their families. They are slaves to a legitimate thing, but it is a slavery that is both sinful and evil.

3. The Danger of Desecrating the Body. Verses 13-20.

Here Paul sets forth the appeal which rests on the Christian's relation to Christ. It is not the relation of his soul to Christ, nor the relation of his mind to Christ, but the relation of his body to Christ.

In the first place, he asks us to remember that all uses of the body are not equal. Some uses of bodily appetite may bring pleasure to the senses without harm. They may enhance one's enjoyment of life. But, on the other hand, some uses are sinful and corrupting. Hence, he states this principle to govern us, in verse thirteen, "Meats for the belly, and the belly for meats: but God shall destroy both it and them. Now the body is not for fornication, but for the Lord; and the Lord for the body."

The simple fact stated here is that the body "is for the Lord; and the Lord for the body." What a high conception of life this is! The body is not a machine for moral maniacs. It has a high and lofty purpose. Not only this but it has a glorious destiny because it is destined for resurrection. "And God hath both raised up the Lord, and will also raise up us by his own power" (v. 14). Since this is true, there should be a new significance. It is a significance which is identified with our bodies.

This is established by two facts:

(1) *Our bodies are members of Christ.* Verses 15-18.

"Know ye not that your bodies are the members of Christ? shall
I then take the members of Christ, and make them the members
of an harlot? God forbid. What? know ye not that he which is
joined to an harlot is one body? for two, saith he, shall be one flesh.
But he that is joined unto the Lord is one spirit. Flee fornication. Every sin that a man doeth is without the body; but he
that committeth fornication sinneth against his own body."

Because of resurrection, our body's relation to Christ is
eternal. This denotes our *destiny.* Because of regeneration,
our bodies belong to Christ in this material moment and in
this temporal sphere. This denotes our *duty.*

Since the body has such a spiritual significance, it must
never be allowed the expressions of impurity. To do so is
to take what belongs to Christ and identify it with harlotry.
Thus, Christ is dishonored by the desecration of the body.

(2) *Our bodies are temples of God.* Verse 19, 20.

"What? know ye not that your body is the temple of the
Holy Ghost which is in you, which ye have of God, and ye are
not your own? For ye are bought with a price: therefore glorify
God in your body, and in your spirit, which are God's."

The Corinthians would readily understand what Paul
meant by this statement. There were heathen shrines in
Corinth, each for its special god. Much of their worship was
associated with immoral practices. Here was a new conception
of life. It was—the body as a shrine for God. It was no longer
a sacred building but a sacred body. It was no longer God
isolated to a sacred place but God present in every activity
of life.

These verses reveal three facts:

a. The presence of the Holy Spirit. Verse 19.

The body of every believer becomes, at the moment of
regeneration, the temple of the Holy Spirit. He comes to

indwell us and make of our bodies sacred habitations. For this reason we have been presented with this teaching of purity. God will not indwell temples filled with idols and images of sin. The temple must be clean.

b. The purchase of Christ. Verses 19, 20.

Since we are not our own, we should honor by both piety and purity the One to whom we belong.

c. The purpose of life. Verse 20.

We have here Christianity's unique teaching concerning practical purity. It is not talking about monastery mysticism but practical, personal purity. It is a purity which is not relegated to some intangible spiritual realm but a purity which applies to the body. It refers to habits, practices and customs. It puts the worship of God into a bodily sphere as well as a spiritual sphere. It tells us that our bodies are sacred temples in contrast to buildings.

Here is a new dignity of life. Here is a practical faith that can be translated into daily action through bodily expression. The world needs more of this holiness of body and less of the holiness of buildings. If we practiced this, it would revolutionize the whole realm of Christian experience.

CHAPTER VII

THE CHURCH AND ITS MARRIAGES

I *Corinthians* 7

IN ORDER that we might be oriented to the subject matter dealt with in this chapter, let us be reminded of a few things. First, remember that Paul is dealing with problems created by a new order of life. Here were people emerging from paganism. Mistakes were made. Questions were constantly arising. Problems had to be met. It was, withal, a state of transition from a pagan social life to a Christian social life and it is not surprising that difficulties were encountered. Hence, Paul's letter to these Corinthians is largely a letter of instruction and discipline. He has already dealt with the problems of church unity and social purity. Now he seeks to establish marital sanctity in the midst of paganism and persecution.

This letter was not written with normal conditions of life in view. Two things contributed to the abnormal state of affairs in Corinth. One was their recent conversion from paganism; the other was their imminent persecution by pagans. These two things created abnormal conditions. As a result, a letter had been written to Paul asking his advice on specific questions. Therefore, when Paul writes the advice found in this chapter, he is not treating the general subject of marriage. He is giving advice concerning marriage under certain emergencies which had arisen in Corinth. He is not saying here is what is right or wrong, but what is wise under prevailing conditions.

The abnormality of conditions in that place and at that time led Paul to say as he did in verse seven, "For I would that all men were even as I myself." If this were not interpreted in the light of the Bible's whole teaching marriage, it would mean that Paul was teaching race suicide. Paul's opinion about marriage, however, is given as advice for abnormal times. We must, therefore, not apply it to conditions in general.

Besides this fact, there were those in Corinth who felt that marriage and all other social relations should be suspended after conversion. This was another reason for Paul's particular advice and should be borne in mind as we approach the chapter.

I. MARRIAGE AND CELIBACY. Verses 1 - 9.

In Corinth there appear to have arisen extreme opinions concerning marriage. On the one hand some insisted all should marry and that celibacy was a sin. On the other hand some insisted that none should marry because marriage was unspiritual and carnal. Hence, we find Paul steering a course midway between these extremes in which he defends celibacy for some and marriage for others. In either case it is to be a matter of personal conscience and in respect to general conditions.

1. Celibacy is Honorable. Verse 1.

"Now concerning the things whereof ye wrote unto me: It is good for a man not to touch a woman."

The subject is introduced by referring to a letter received by Paul from the Corinthians. It was at their request and on the basis of both their particular and peculiar problems that Paul gives the teaching of this chapter. We emphasize the words *particular* and *peculiar* when referring to their problems. The same problems may not exist for all people, but wherever the problems do exist the precept is provided by Paul.

Paul is advocating celibacy or the unmarried state, not as the general rule or for common practice. He is stating it in view of two things. First, in view of the opinion of some that all who do not marry are committing sin. To these Paul says it is "good." And, second, in view of the conditions prevailing in their time. To remain unmarried was an expedient and *good* thing for some in view of the present distress of the church in the days of Corinth.

2. Marriage is Desirable. Verse 2.

"Nevertheless, to avoid fornication, let every man have his own wife, and let every woman have her own husband."

There were advantages in remaining unmarried but even these did not outweigh the fact that the general rule was marriage. When it was marriage, it was to be the right kind of marriage. The right kind of marriage is the Christian ideal of one husband for one wife, i.e. a monogamous marriage.

Marriage is to be considered as a sacred institution. It is, therefore, to be entered into with the highest motives and to be preserved with the strictest chastity.

Wherever there have been lax views on marriage, social corruption has always followed in the state. Unless these ideals are guarded and preserved among Christians, they will never be found amidst the world. There is, therefore, a very special obligation resting on the church that it proclaim and preserve the sacred ideals of marriage, the family and the home.

3. Marriage's Mutual Obligation. Verses 3 - 5.

"Let the husband render unto the wife due benevolence: and likewise also the wife unto the husband. The wife hath not power of her own body, but the husband: and likewise also the husband hath not power of his own body, but the wife. Defraud ye not one the other, except it be with consent for a time, that ye may give yourself to fasting and prayer and come together again, that Satan tempt you not for your incontinency."

The rendering of "due benevolence" was specifically enjoined to counteract the views held by some of those at Corinth who were already married. Some of these felt that after their conversion that it was a mark of spiritual merit to cease to recognize the marriage relations. It was their view that where one was a believer and the other a non-believer, it made an unequal and unspiritual union and therefore relieves the believer from the "due benevolence" of marriage.

This, Paul points out, is wrong. The obligations are mutual and they continue after conversion with equal force. They are not to be expected by one party and ignored by the other party. They consist of the mutual recognition on the part of the believing husband to continue to minister to his wife his usual duties of support, protection and personal affection. Also on the part of the believing wife to continue her domestic ministrations and personal affections.

This continuation of domestic ministration and personal affection was urged not only because of the loyalty which should continue to exist between husband and wife in the face of one's conversion and the other's paganism, but also because of the state of social life about them. Corinth was a very wicked city. Its paganism was associated with fornication. Every temple had its religious slave-prostitutes. This condition constituted a peril to Christians and non-Christians alike. If the normal ministrations and affections of the home were not maintained, it might cause an estrangement and lead to temptation from the social and religious conditions all around them. For this reason each Christian man was to keep his wife and each Christian wife her husband, that the home might remain intact.

This principle, after all, is the heart of marriage. It is a mutual relation. If is not a one-sided arrangement provided for the benefit of an overlording husband or an overbearing wife. All its relations and obligations, all its privileges and duties are mutual. It is nowhere or at any time a one-sided affair accruing to one's benefit at the other's expense. If we were to realize this and respect it, we dare say that many, if not most, of our marital difficulties would vanish.

4. Marriage's Expediency. Verses 6 - 9.

"But I speak this by permission, and not of commandment. For I would that all men were even as I myself. But every man hath his proper gift of God, one after this manner, and another after that. I say therefore to the unmarried and widows, It is good for them if they abide even as I. But if they cannot contain, let them marry: for it is better to marry than to burn."

Paul is suggesting two things here. He is suggesting, with his own life in mind, that there is a time when remaining unmarried is expedient and desirable. He is also suggesting the opposite, for he declares the expediency and desirability of marriage. It is to be governed by conscience and conditions.

This is clear by his statement in verse six, "I speak this by permission, and not of commandment." Paul is not less inspired here than he is elsewhere. He is not stepping out of character as an inspired writer. He is as much inspired at this point as at others. What he is saying is that his advice to marry or to stay unmarried is not to be considered as a divine command. Everyone is to act according to his own conscience.

Paul is stating his preference as far as he is concerned and is not giving a blanket commandment to all Christians. To have insisted that all remain unmarried would have been as unscriptural and wrong as for him to have insisted that all marry. In any event, the usual, the natural, the normal, and the Christian practice is marriage.

The Church is the guardian of one of life's most sacred institutions. Let her guard it well. The Christian is the exponent and example of one of life's most cherished unions. Let him cherish it with both faith and fidelity.

II. MARRIAGE AND CONVERSION. Verses 10 - 16.

Paul has, in the first verses of the chapter, spoken to those who were unmarried. Now he speaks to those who, being married, are concerned with the problems that have arisen as the result of their conversion. Remember that theirs was a pagan world. When a man or a woman became a Christian separate from wife or husband, it brought a serious problem to their marital life. It meant a home divided between paganism and Christianity. It was no small matter.

The question had arisen among some of the Corinthian Christians in the case of a mixed marriage, when one party had become a Christian after marriage and the other remained pagan, whether this change of faith and conduct was a sufficient cause for divorce. The question of divorce, remember, had only arisen because of the conversion of one of the married parties. It is not dealing with the general problem of divorce. It applies only to the question of divorce as it relates to circumstances which had arisen from conversion. We must, therefore, confine our consideration to the specific problem.

Now what should one do? In the case of a believing wife and an unbelieving husband, for instance, should she seek a divorce and then re-marry on the basis of her new faith? This is the problem. What is the Christian ideal? It is twofold.

1. The Believer's Relationship. Verses 10, 11.

"And unto the married I command, yet not I, but the Lord, Let not the wife depart from her husband: But and if she depart, let her remain unmarried, or be reconciled to her husband: and let not the husband put away his wife."

The Christian's ideal is very plain. If after marriage one becomes a Christian without the other's conversion, he or she is not to seek separation. This advice was given because of a growing feeling among the Corinthians that conversion made such a difference that divorce from a pagan partner was desirable. In cases where such did seek and obtain separation by divorce, their re-marriage was strictly forbidden.

This was very plain and understandable. Conversion was not to interrupt the usual customs nor disrupt the existing family relationships. The previous marriage was still lawful and binding after the recent conversion and was not annulled by a change from paganism to Christianity.

2. The Believer's Duty. Verses 12 - 16.

"But to the rest speak I, not the Lord: If any brother hath a wife that believeth not, and she be pleased to dwell with him, let him not put her away. And the woman which hath an husband

that believeth not, and if he be pleased to dwell with her, let her
not leave him. For the unbelieving husband is sanctified by the
wife, and the unbelieving wife is sanctified by the husband: else
were your children unclean; but now are they holy. But if the unbelieving depart, let him depart. A brother or a sister is not
under bondage in such cases: but God hath called us to peace.
For what knowest thou, O wife, whether thou shalt save thy
husband? or how knowest thou, O man, whether thou shalt save
thy wife?"

The believer's relationship was to continue as before. But
the believer was now considered under a distinct and important obligation. That obligation was to seek and secure the
unbelieving partner's conversion. It is stated in these words of
verse fourteen, "For the unbelieving husband is sanctified by
the wife, and the unbelieving wife is sanctified by the husband:
else were your children unclean; but now are they holy."

Here is a very wonderful thing. It is the power of a new relationship in which both husband and children or wife and
children, as the case may be, are brought under the beneficent
influence of the Christian life. When the wife becomes a Christian without the husband or the husband becomes a Christian
without the wife, the influence of the Christian wife or the
Christian husband should be directed so as to secure the conversion of the other.

In the person of a believer, Christ is brought into the home.
Into that home and upon that family circle there is then a new
atmosphere. It is not as it once was. Christ is there and since
He is there all the things that are possible through Him hover
over that home. Through a believer's life and influence, the unbeliever should be sought to turn to Christ.

Not only is the status of husband and wife changed, but
the status of the children is changed. It speaks of the children
in verse fourteen with these words, "else were your children
unclean; but now are they holy." This goes back to the previous
part of the verse which refers to the unbelieving husband as
being sanctified by the believing wife. Now, it cannot mean,

in keeping with the rest of the Scripture, that the conversion of the wife automatically produces the conversion of the husband or that the conversion of both mean the automatic conversion of the children. Conversion is an individual matter. It cannot be done by us for either our husbands, wives, or parents. What is meant here is that the Christian wife's conversion sanctifies the marriage relationship to the point where it is to continue as a lawful and binding thing and which is, in all normal expectancy, to secure the conversion of the husband. Likewise, her conversion which sanctifies that continuing relationship means that the children born to that now mixed union are not unclean as if born out of wedlock, nor are they to be considered as belonging to the heathen world. Now, in the case of a mixed marriage, the believing mother's conversion and faith prevent this, and consider such children as clean and holy. They are not clean or holy in the sense that their first birth automatically produces their second birth. This would violate the truth of Scripture and the entire process of the new life. Children become Christians by the same spiritual biology that adults do. They are born the second time spiritually as they were born the first time physically. Since, in the case of a believing mother and an unbelieving father, their status might be ambiguous, they are to be considered as the special objects of the believing mother's concern.

Consider then what a holy and powerful influence we bring into our home and family circle when we become Christians, and, considering it, act on it to the fullest advantage of its truth. Let nothing deter us from fulfilling the high and holy things that God has intended for any believing parent who stands alone.

It is very frankly stated in verse fifteen that if the unbelieving party to a marriage contract seeks dissolution, the believer need not insist on its continuance if the other party is willfully insistent. In no case must the believer seek this dissolution.

The reason given is that where one has made up his mind not only against his wife, but against God, no good cause would be served in maintaining the marriage relation. It would result only in strife, contention, and sorrow whereas "God hath called us to peace." While such separations were allowed under such extreme conditions, the rule was to keep the marriage bonds intact. This, you see, would give the believer partner a great privilege, for Paul argues in verse sixteen, "For what knowest thou, O wife, whether thou shalt save thy husband? or how knowest thou, O man, whether thou shalt save thy wife?"

Many face a modern version of this ancient problem. It is not of their making because they did not deliberately ally themselves with an unbeliever. Consider your problem in the light of this verse and the possibility that a faithful life will result in a loved one's salvation.

A lady who was a follower of Christ, but whose husband was still unsaved sought the advice of her pastor. She told him that she had done all in her power to beseech and persuade her husband, but to no effect. "Madam," said he, "talk more to God about your husband, and less to your husband about God." Both are necessary but in talking to God we may find a greater fitness of life for practical living.

Paul now speaks of marriage in its general relation to the problem of custom. This problem was created by the conversion of people in various walks of life. Should these people change their social status or should they continue where they were? It was the same problem that some found conversion created in marriage. Should the married believer seek to change his marriage relationship by separation?

While Christianity always advocates the principle of *separation* so as to achieve the identity of Christians apart from non-Christians and thus increase their influence as Christians, it nowhere advocates *segregation*. It does not segregate us from our family, our job, or social standing. It does not disrupt existing social customs, but it does set the Christian to the task of transforming the sphere where he lives by the power of his new life. It does not say that Christianity is some peculiar brand of religious life that has to be fenced off from the rest of the world. It does not shut its devotees into special buildings for holy living. It does not *change customs*, by a social revolution, but it does *change life* within those customs by regeneration. It very definitely calls for new lives in old places. It puts Christians into the world as salt to arrest its corruption, and as light to dispel its darkness.

III. MARRIAGE AND CUSTOMS. Verses 17 - 24.

There were some in Corinth who believed that receiving Christ meant that they should dissolve their social, racial, and economic relationships. Paul now tells them that such should not be done.

1. The Principle. Verse 17.

"But as God hath distributed to every man, as the Lord hath called every one, so let him walk. And so ordain I in all churches."

A fine statement of this verse is found in Arthur S. Way's translation. It reads, "Let each member go on living in the same conditions which the Lord originally allotted to him, and in which he was when he heard God's call." The meaning is self-evident. Conversion is not outwardly revolutionary. It is, instead, inwardly regenerative. It does not storm into our national and social life and proceed to create violent changes and adjustments. It is true that changes will occur. It leaves us totally different than what it finds us. It does not require us, however, to make an occidental of the oriental. So the principle is "as the Lord hath called every one, so let him walk." In other words, be what you were when Christ found you. Not, of course, in the manner of your life, but in its sphere.

Paul proceeds to apply this principle to the two great classifications of his day as it is related to the Jew and to the slave.

2. The Principle Applied to the Converted Jew. Verses 18, 19.

"Is any man called being circumcised? let him not become uncircumcised. Is any called in uncircumcision? let him not be

circumcised. Circumcision is nothing, and uncircumcision is nothing, but the keeping of the commandments of God."

Some converted Jews in Corinth felt that they must rid themselves of all national identity. They felt that all identification
previous to conversion must be obliterated. After all, neither
ritualizing nor unritualizing ourselves will save. These things
neither determine nor affect our salvation. It is our relationship
to God's Word that matters. Have we done what God requires of us?

To the converted Jew, therefore, Paul said in substance, "Be
a Christian Jew. Do not try to be a Christian Gentile. Be what
you were, but by the grace of God."

3. The Principle Applied to the Converted Slave. Verses
20 - 24.

"Let every man abide in the same calling wherein he was
called. Art thou called being a servant? care not for it: but if
thou mayest be made free, use it rather. For he that is called in
the Lord, being a servant, is the Lord's freeman: likewise also he
that is called, being free, is Christ's servant. Ye are bought with a
price: be not ye the servants of men. Brethren, let every man,
wherein he is called, therein abide with God."

Three times the principle of practice for the converted person
is repeated. Once in verse seventeen, again in verse twenty,
and again in verse twenty-four. Now it is applied to the social
and economic status.

Christianity does not make all its converts masters or capit-
alists or aristocrats. Christian living belongs to every level of
life. Christians are needed among servants as well as masters,
workers as well as employers, the poor as well as the rich, and
the low as well as the high.

Christianity does not create an artificial greatness but teaches the true greatness of humble places. After all, greatness
does not consist merely in doing great things, but rather in
doing little things in a great way.

There were those at Corinth who had the mistaken notion that since they had been servants, conversion had put them on a social and economic equality with their Christian masters. Some who were slaves felt that becoming Christians required their liberation. Even though the spirit of Christianity is against any system of slavery, conversion, as such, did not mean the upheaval of their status.

Paul proceeds to show these people a superior form of servitude. He points out that although they were slaves to men, they were superior to their masters if they were slaves of Christ. A Christian was, in fact, Christ's bondman. As such a bondman, he was superior to any unchristian freeman on earth. Such freemen were slaves to sin, but Christ's bondmen were purchased out of that kind of slavery and were set free in both mind and morals.

Christianity taught the dignity of lowly places and menial services. While doing this, it did not peg men's lives at low levels of attainment. It did not seek to perpetuate evil systems of slavery. It did not deprecate human attainment nor depreciate human ability. It believed that every man had a right to express his ability and receive the benefits from it. It teaches us today to respect ambition and attainment. If one has the capabilities of a master, let him rise to be one. Christianity does not create an artificial status of society, nor does it teach collective social unrest. Above all, be what God intends you to be. But with this social and economic freedom, Christianity recognizes a higher freedom. It is the freedom of the soul and the mind.

The world is full of men who are abject slaves of passion and habit. They may be monarchs before men, but before God they are menial slaves to sin. To these the message of Christ comes with appeal and power. It would break whatever shackles that bind and make men kingly and women queenly in their lives.

The last word here is this, "Let every man, wherein he is called, therein abide with God." Mother, housewife, teacher, banker, lawyer, or laborer, you are to "abide with God." *Add* God to your life and you will *subtract* all its evils. *Add* God to your life and the new arithmetic will *multiply* all that is worthwhile and lasts longest.

We speak of love and marriage in our common speech in what are very foolish terms. We speak of a person "falling in love." Men fall into ditches and fall down stairs. When they do we say they did it by accident. Do we fall into love the same way? Is the most sacred human relationship to be thought of as an accident? Is it something to heedlessly and thoughtlessly rush into without either advice or consideration? The divorce courts prove by their records that apparently it is an accident to a great many people.

Our youths who choose careers with such forethought should be more careful about life-companions. Good careers are easily spoiled by bad companions. Our wives and husbands are as important as our work.

With these things in view, consider what the Scripture is saying here about marriage. Paul is giving considered advice to the Corinthians. He is not unleashing their emotions and saying, "Do as you like." He is considering all the factors that enter into the marriage relation. He has already considered the problems which conversion from paganism have produced. He has also considered it in relation to the customs of the day. Now he considers it in relation to expediency.

IV. MARRIAGE AND EXPEDIENCY. Verses 25 - 38.

1. Expediency from Parental Viewpoint. Verses 25 - 28.

"Now concerning virgins I have no commandment of the Lord, yet I give my judgment, as one that hath obtained mercy of the Lord to be faithful. I suppose therefore that this is good for the present distress, I say, that it is good for a man so to be. Art thou bound unto a wife? seek not to be loosed. Art thou loosed from a wife? seek not a wife. But and if thou marry, thou hast not sinned; and if a virgin marry, she hath not sinned. Nevertheless such shall have trouble in the flesh: but I spare you."

Just what is Paul saying? It is a very understandable thing. He is speaking, of course, of the case of Christian young women. When such desire to be married, should their parents give them in marriage? Paul speaks of this problem as a fellow Christian and not as an apostle. It was his judgment that under the condition that then existed in Corinth, it was best for these young women to remain unmarried.

Notice that Paul uses the phrase, "this is good for the present distress," in verse twenty-six. Thus, his judgment was for the time then present. It had to do with conditions pertaining to the distress of those immediate people. He is not saying this for all times and all young women. It was advised as an expedient and temporary measure.

When in verse twenty-eight he says, "But if thou marry, thou hast not sinned," he is not speaking of marriage as a sin. There are times when it may be a sin. Such a time was Paul's time. It would have been a sin to have subjected young women to the abuses, privations and hardships of a married life under the persecution and trouble that was pending at that moment. It was because Paul wished to spare unsuspecting young people of trouble that he advised against their marriage. He is only reminding them that marriage under the conditions then prevailing would expose them to unnecessary hazards and troubles.

2. Expediency from the Worldly Viewpoint. Verses 29 - 35.

"But this I say, brethren, the time is short: it remaineth, that both they that have wives be as though they had none; And they that weep, as though they wept not; and they that rejoice, as though they rejoiced not; and they that buy, as though they possessed not; And they that use this world, as not abusing it: for the fashion of this world passeth away. But I would have you without carefulness. He that is unmarried careth for the things that belong to the Lord, how he may please the Lord: But he that is married careth for the things that are of the world, how he may please his wife. There is difference also between a wife

and a virgin. The unmarried woman careth for the things of the
Lord, that she may be holy both in body and in spirit: but she
that is married careth for the things of the world, how she may
please her husband. And this I speak for your own profit; not
that I may cast a snare upon you, but for that which is comely,
and that ye may attend upon the Lord without distraction."

Paul speaks now from the standpoint of a practical expediency. The "present distress" of his times is still in mind. He
had spoken of the complications arising in married life. Now he
gives advice as to their attitude to these conditions as they must
be faced by those who are already married.

In verse 31 he uses the phrase, "the fashion of this world
passeth away." That is, the present situation as he and they
found it in Corinth would not always be. It would change.
While it maintained, what should the Christian husbands'
and Christian wives' attitude be? They were not only married
and with obligations to their partners, but they were Christians
and with obligations to their Lord and the pagan world about
them. Should they let their *marital obligations* obscure their
spiritual obligations? This would be the tendency. Paul states
this in verse 32, "But I would have you without carefulness."
In other words, I would have you without preoccupations. He
is telling them that while they have marital obligations which
must be respected, nevertheless, these must not precede nor
obscure their Christian obligations.

The best explanation of these verses is to read Arthur S.
Way's translation. "It follows, that they who have wives should
be as though they had them not; that they who weep should
be as though they wept not; those who rejoice as though they
rejoiced not; those who buy goods as though they got them not
in full possession; those who enjoy this world's advantages, as
though they never gave themselves up to the enjoyment of
them; for this mere outward show—and the world around you
is nothing more—is fast fleeting away. I want you to be free
from all preoccupation. The unmarried man can be absorbed
in his duties to our Lord: he has but to think, 'How shall I

please my Lord?' The married man is absorbed in duties relating to the world: he has to think, 'How shall I please my wife?' hence, concentration of purpose is impossible for him. So too of the wife and the virgin: —the unmarried woman can be absorbed in her duties to her Lord: she has but to think, 'How may I be consecrated both in body and in spirit?' But the wedded woman must be absorbed in her duties to the world, thinking, 'How shall I please my husband?' I am giving these hints entirely for your own benefit. I have no thought of trammelling your freedom: I want to help you to live a decorous life, a life very near to the Lord, without distractions."

Here you see the relation of marriage to life's obligations. It touches the deeper relations of life. It is something that should be considered in our relation to God. Yet, how few consider it as such. It is a conventional custom when it ought to be considered in its relation to Christian consecration. It is the question of whether one's life is going to be given to one person and God left out or whether, in the light of a Christian consecration, two shall marry in order to unite their lives in a larger service to God and mankind.

Marriage may be one of the most useful unions of life or it can degenerate into the most selfish partnership on earth.

Paul speaks of marriage in relation to the urgency of the times. He says, "the time is short." Two people may utterly waste their lives in a senseless and sensual marriage, or they may make it a most fruitful union. If it is to be fruitful and not senseless, it must be looked at with intelligence and spirituality. Hence, the conclusion—"they that have wives be as though they had none." They were neither to leave them nor ignore them, but be sensible about them in the crisis that existed. In view of the need for Christian service in a world of crisis, they were to be moderate and not consume all their energy and all their affection on either wife or husband.

It was to be the same all the way down life's avenue. "They that weep as though they wept not"—"they that rejoice as though they rejoiced not"—"they that buy as though they possessed not"—"they that use this world as not abusing it." It was to be a policy of moderation in the midst of a world crisis. With the world needing Christ, all our time should not be consumed in pleasing one another or sorrowing over our own misfortune or rejoicing over our personal blessings or enjoying the existing pleasures. *Selfishness everywhere was to be taboo.* It was to be sacrifice and service. Only in this way could a world be won to Christ.

Hence, it is well to consider marriage with all elements in view. Marriage is like falling into a river. It is easier to get into it than out of it. "Marriage is a desperate thing. The frogs in Aesop's fable were extremely wise: they had a great mind to some water; but they would not leap into the well, because they could not get out again."

We would do well to review our ideals of marriage beforehand rather than to view the wreck of mis-marriage afterward. As for Christian marriage, it is to be viewed with consecrated consideration. To this end Paul lends his inspired advice, "And this I speak for your own profit: not that I may cast a snare upon you, but for that which is comely, and that ye may attend upon the Lord without distraction" (v. 35).

The final consideration of marriage problems brings us back to the parents' attitude to marriageable children.

3. Expediency from the Circumstantial Viewpoint. Verses 36 - 38.

> "But if any man think that he behaveth himself uncomely toward his virgin, if she pass the flower of her age, and need so require, let him do what he will, he sinneth not: let them marry. Nevertheless he that standeth steadfast in his heart, having no necessity, but hath power over his own will, and hath so decreed in his heart that he will keep his virgin, doeth well. So then he that giveth her in marriage doeth well; but he that giveth her not in marriage doeth better."

This means, if any parent should consider that in refusing a daughter's hand in marriage, he might jeopardize her future, and if there appear to be good reasons for the proposed marriage, then let him give his consent. It is good that he should do so. Should he consider that the disadvantage outweighs the advantage, then it is Paul's judgment that "he that giveth her not in marriage doeth better." In any case, a wise Christian parent's attitude to a child's marriage is to be considered from the standpoint of the advantages to the persons involved and not from the standpoint of the parent's personal desires.

V. MARRIAGE AND RE-MARRIAGE. Verses 39, 40.

Two Christian principles are set forth. One applies to a Christian marriage and the other to a Christian re-marriage.

1. Marriage Vows and the Wife. Verse 39a

"The wife is bound by the law as long as her husband liveth . . ."

Here is strict monogamous marriage. It is to be observed with strict Christian morality. It must neither compromise with the pagan marriage views of the first century nor with the equally pagan marriage views of the twentieth century. Hollywood may be another Corinth, but Christians are to get their marriage ideals from heaven, not from Hollywood.

This scripture is regulating matters within the Christian community. Paul said in 5:12, 13, "For what have I to do to judge them also that are without? do not ye judge them that are within? But them that are without God judgeth." The particular province of this scripture which is addressed to Christians cannot be expected to be enforced on non- Christians. Nevertheless, God does not condone marriage abuses in any. The point that is made is that the particular and immediate application of this scripture is to Christians.

2. Marriage Vows and the Widow. Verses 39b, 40.

". . . but if her husband be dead, she is at liberty to be married to whom she will; only in the Lord. But she is happier if she so abide, after my judgment: and I think also that I have the Spirit of God."

The matter of re-marriage as dealt with here is not of a *divorcee* but of a *widow*. This section has nothing to say of the re-marriage of divorced people. That is dealt with elsewhere but certainly not here. In the case, therefore, of widows contemplating re-marriage, they should strictly observe one principle. Re-marriage is to be "only in the Lord." The Christian woman is to desire marriage to a Christian man. This was an imperative thing in the pagan world where Christians and pagans were so far apart in both faith and practice. It is equally important in our modern world.

To respect this is to respect a very sacred principle of Christian experience. It will spare many a heartache. It will save much lonesomeness. It will save complication in the rearing of children. It will save embarrassment and cross purposes all the way down life's walk. Would God that this warning and restriction could be heard and heeded by every marriageable Christian in America.

Why is it to be "only in the Lord?" The Scriptures answer elsewhere by saying, "what communion hath light with darkness?" It means that two people with separate destinies, divided ideals and different faiths, should not attempt to preside over the affairs of family and home. A house divided against itself falls. This is true spiritually more so than in any other particular.

If there is any situation or any relation that demands the union of head, heart, hand, and a common faith in God, as well as new life in Christ, it is the home. It must be presided over by a united love: the love of a Christian father and the love of a Christian mother. In the physical problems of the home, it may not seem necessary.

There is urgent need that we restore to American home-life the worship of the old family altar. "Family altars alter families."

What about your home? The old family altar and the old family Bible are any nation's *first line of defense* and first agency for advance.

CHAPTER VIII

THE CHURCH AND ITS LIBERTIES

I Corinthians 8

THERE ARE some things upon which we may differ but not divide. In the church at Corinth there were divisions which had no right to exist. These divisions came because of unnecessary and wrong differences. There are some distinctions that need not cause divisions. All of these distinctions are before us in this chapter.

It reminds us that in some matters there is absolute right and absolute wrong. In others, there is neither absolute right nor absolute wrong. They are matters of moral indifference and spiritual inconsequence. They permit differences of opinion and independence of action.

Conscience forbids doing some things and allows doing others. The great question which Paul now deals with in respect to these things which were in between absolute right and absolute wrong was, how to regulate the conscience.

I. THE TWO MOTIVES OF LIFE. Verse 1.

"Now as touching things offered unto idols, we know that we all have knowledge. Knowledge puffeth up, but charity edifieth."

The question was "touching things offered unto idols." Among these newborn Christians in the early days of Christianity, it meant a solemn thing to be a Christian. They were surrounded by idolatrous paganism. Every home, scarcely without exception, had idolatrous practices in connection with its social functions. The same thing was true in political functions and in relation to civic matters. Meat which had been

139

originally sacrificed in the pagan temple was sold in the public markets and used at social functions. Christians were often placed in embarrassing positions when, as invited guests, such meat appeared on the table of their hosts.

All of this became a delicate and somewhat intricate problem. What should be done? What was right and what was wrong? As it appears in this chapter, indulgence was not a case of absolute wrong nor was abstinence a case of absolute right. Both were a matter of conscience.

Two motives now appear as possible guides for the regulation of our conduct in these matters about which we differ.

1. Knowledge.

The statement, "we know that we all have knowledge," is a reference to enlightened Christians. In their enlightenment, they would have the proper attitude to the question of things offered to idols. They knew that it was a religious question and not a hygienic or dietetic question. Even with such knowledge which would give them the broadest liberty, they were not completely safe.

2. Love.

Arthur S. Way's translation of the words, "knowledge puffeth up, but charity edifieth," is very striking. He says, "This illumination blows up the wind-bag of empty self-sufficiency: it is love that builds up the solid structure of the New Life." Thus we observe that knowledge blows up while love builds up. Knowledge *inflates with conceit* while love *moves us with concern.* Knowledge is selfish while love is selfless. Thus, love becomes the adequate and proper Christian way of life.

Knowledge does not necessarily lead one to be good or to follow the right course of action. Montaigne observed that "many persons, after once they become learned, cease to be good." Love carries with it such promptings of benevolence as to incline always to the good.

This kind of love is identified in verse three as being the love of God in the life of man.

II. THE IMPERFECTION OF KNOWLEDGE. Verse 2.

"And if any man think that he knoweth any thing, he knoweth nothing yet as he ought to know."

Knowledge, at its best, is imperfect. None of us know all things, and it is possible that what we do not know will be the weak link in the chain of our life success. For this reason knowledge, while essential and necessary, must always be accompanied by love.

III. THE PERFECTION OF LOVE. Verse 3.

"But if any man love God, the same is known of him."

Love perfects all human relationships because it is the perfection of the greatest of all relationships, which is man's relationship with God. Love illuminates what knowledge might leave in obscurity.

God is apprehended by the heart more than He is comprehended by the mind. This is why love is put forth as the determining factor on the divine side of salvation and also why our love for God testifies more accurately to our own salvation than any knowledge about God.

In these matters of divided opinion and in all questions that concern a good life, two things are needed above all else.

1. To Know the Will of God.

The will of God will give us the key to the regulation of life. "Work, wakefulness, losses, bereavements, life's burdens and battles are not troubles. They are discipline. While the passions are in healthful play all these things may befall a man and yet he may be wholly untroubled. On the other hand, a man may be surrounded by all that can minister comfort and dignity, and yet be troubled. In the latter case the man's passions are tossed about as the sea is when a tempest is on it; in the other case, they are serene as the lake in the fastnesses of a mountain. The *cause* of all our trouble is the *want of harmony between our wills and the will of God.* Let them accord and then nothing in earth or heaven or hell can trouble us. But when we beat ourselves against the barriers erected by Omnipotence for our safety and good, then there is trouble. Our troubles arise from our want of faith in the rightfulness and paramount authority of God's Law."

2. To Know the Word of God.

The Word of God will give us the revelation of the will of God. It will settle the controversy between our will and God's will.

It is reported that four men were traveling together in a railway compartment. Three of them engaged in a discussion on the subject of faith; they soon realized that they differed in their convictions. Each maintained that his own view was the the only right one. The fourth man, who had taken no part in the discussion, drew out his watch and asked the others as to the time. They at once produced their watches and it was found that their time differed from one another, but each owner insisted that his watch had the right time. It was then agreed to compare their watches with the standard clock in the terminal depot on arrival. This ended the argument and the watches were returned to their pockets. Thereupon the person who had remained silent during the dispute on faith declared: "We have a standard clock also in matters of faith, and you would do well to regulate the watches of your conviction in accordance with it. This standard clock is the Bible, the Word of God."

It is by God's Word that we know God's will.

We are faced with the problem of finding the proper motives to prompt us in our conduct. Lord Bacon reminds us that "the desire of power in excess caused angles to fall; the desire of knowledge in excess caused man to fall; but in love is no excess, neither can man nor angels come into danger by it."

IV. The Regulation of Conduct. Verses 4-13.

We are provided with the Bible's answer for an adequate motive by which to regulate our conduct.

The problem for the Corinthians, you will bear in mind, had to do with partaking of meats offered to idols. This question of the Corinthians was peculiar to them, but it is also ours in a different way. It is not a question of idolatry with us, but forms of social amusement and religious observance. We are baffled at times regarding our own conduct in certain instances. What shall we do? There is no law against it. There are no stated restrictions. The Scriptures do not state the right and the wrong. In that case where the matter is one of moral indifference, it becomes something for the individual conscience. In acting conscientiously, we must consider the effect of our actions in relation to others. It is not the innocence of the act which is altogether the determining factor of liberty, but the effect of the act on others.

The motives of behavior may be twofold.

1. Conduct Regulated by Knowledge. Verses 4-8.

"As concerning therefore the eating of those things that are offered in sacrifice unto idols, we know that an idol is nothing in the world, and that there is none other God but one. For though there be that are called gods, whether in heaven or in earth, (as there be gods many, and lords many,) But to us there is but one God, the Father, of whom are all things, and we in him; and one Lord Jesus Christ, by whom are all things, and we by him. Howbeit there is not in every man that knowledge: for some with conscience of the idol unto this hour eat it as a thing offered unto an idol; and their conscience being weak is defiled. But meat commendeth us not to God: for neither, if we eat, are we the better; neither, if we eat not are we the worse."

To an understanding Christian the problem of idol meat-eating is simplified. He knows that idolatry is an invention of imagination and superstition. Idols are nothing but manufactured gods. They are the crude creations of pagan minds and hands. There were many such gods but they meant nothing. There was but one God in fact, and the fact of that one God was known to the Christian's faith. To a Christian with knowledge idol meats meant nothing.

But what some Christians knew, others were ignorant of. There were many immature believers. There were those lately converted from paganism who had not the same intelligent views. While they knew the difference between paganism and Christianity, they did not have sufficient faith to withstand all of the temptations put before them. These immature disciples therefore might indulge in an innocent and meaningless practice only to have their weak conscience affected.

The strong and intelligent Christian is at liberty to follow his conscience in this matter. To do so is his inviolate right. While it is right as far as the effect of his act on himself is concerned, it might not be right as far as the effect of his act on others is concerned. Shall he then go ahead and exercise his liberty to satisfy himself or shall he limit his activities to help others?

We have faced such dilemmas in our lives. Our intelligence told us that there was nothing wrong in what we were about to do. We refused to be bound by superstition or imagination. Perhaps it was a question of an amusement. Or, on the other hand, it might be a habit, or a friendship, or a business matter. In such cases what must determine the basis of behavior? Where Scripture does not specifically regulate our conduct, what should? The answer is found in the second motive.

2. Conduct Regulated by Love. Verses 9-13.

"But take heed lest by any means this liberty of yours become a stumblingblock to them that are weak. For if any man see thee which hast knowledge sit at meat in the idol's temple, shall not the conscience of him which is weak be emboldened to eat those things which are offered to idols; And through thy knowledge shall the weak brother perish, for whom Christ died? But when ye sin so against the brethren, and wound their weak conscience, ye sin against Christ. Wherefore, if meat make my brother to offend, I will eat no flesh while the world standeth, lest I make my brother to offend."

We are cautioned to behave so that our behavior, while *right* in itself and *intelligent* to us, may be *edifying* to others.

What I do must not only consider *my pleasure* but *another's profit.*

Christian ethics are not based upon selfishness. We are not told to do as we please. If our pleasure is another's hinderance, then our liberty which is good becomes evil.

Christian ethics consider a Christian's example. If our ideas are right and our example is wrong, we should be willing to suspend our ideas and surrender them for the sake of our example.

Paul mentions a hypothetical case in verses 10 and 11: "For if any man see thee which hast knowledge sit at meat in the idol's temple, shall not the conscience of him which is weak be emboldened to eat those things which are offered to idols; And through thy knowledge shall the weak brother perish, for whom Christ died?"

Reduce this Corinthian problem of eating idol meat to modern terms. Reduce it to a current problem. Put it into modern language. You could transfer it into a multitude of conditions. The Scriptures do not mention any of them. Your Christian intelligence tells you they are harmless in themselves, but knowledge of what they are is not a sufficient motive for your indulgence. A Christian is to be moved by love. He must not do anything that would be destructive to another.

Love is to be our prompting motive. Whatever the amusement or the habit, whatever the act or the companionship, it must be accepted or rejected on the basis of love. Knowledge considers our interests, but love considers others' interests. While we may be conscientiously free to act on our conscience, we must never violate a conscience sensitized by love.

Suppose we set out from this time on to live by love. Can we calculate the effect? None of us could approximate the effect of a conduct regulated by a loving consideration of others. It would transform our lives, our homes, and our social contacts. It would sweeten bitter things and make life a more pleasant journey. Many more will join our Christian caravan as a result of the example of love than by the justification of knowledge.

Paul determines in the end to regulate his life by a principle which both reverences God and respects others. He declares himself in these words, "Wherefore, if meat make my brother to offend, I will eat no flesh while the world standeth, lest I make my brother to offend."

To modernize the motive remove the word meat and read in its place anything that constitutes a problem of Christian conduct. Paul is willing that his body suffer instead of his brother's soul. He is willing to enjoy fewer temporal things that his brother may have greater eternal things. He is willing to limit his strength in order to aid his brother's weakness. He is happy to suspend his knowledge in order to aid his brother's ignorance. Thus he comes to a conclusive decision. In all questions of conduct he is willing to regulate his liberty by love. In doing this, is he not going to suffer? Far from it. No Christian suffers who behaves like a Christian. You do not really penalize yourself when you live by love. It may seem so but it will not be so. It will prove the most enriching and the most delightful experience of life.

Chapter IX

THE CHURCH AND ITS WORKERS

I *Corinthians* 9

I T IS recalled that someone once said, "The only possible profit of living is life." There are many illusions abroad. Many think that the only possible profit is riches, fame or luxury. These bubbles will burst the moment we attain them. The only possible profit of living is life. Yes, but it must be God's life. The Bible is the way to that life.

For the Christian worker the greatest profit in living is life. This is abundantly borne out in the teachings of this chapter.

I. THE CHRISTIAN WORKER'S PRIVILEGE. Verses 1-6.

The privileges of the Christian worker are not less or different than the privileges of the Christian disciple. The Christian worker is not required by God to live in some segregated class removed from the common joys and associations of life. As Paul points out here, he is entitled to all the social and family privileges that the common disciples are entitled to.

1. The Worker's Identity. Verses 1-3.

"Am I not an apostle? am I not free? have I not seen Jesus Christ our Lord? are not ye my work in the Lord? If I be not an apostle unto others, yet doubtless I am to you: for the seal of mine apostleship are ye in the Lord. Mine answer to them that do examine me is this."

Paul was an apostolic worker. He occupied a high and exalted place, but no matter how high the place, it had an origin common to all Christian workers and disciples. It began with a factual and actual experience of Christ. He

147

declares he had "seen Jesus Christ our Lord." This fact refers to his experience on the Damascus road. It wrought the
miracle of a great change. It brought Paul from religion into
regeneration. This was the beginning of a chain of divine
providences that set Paul in a place of large usefulness. Apart
from Christ, no one has had so great and wide an influence
in the world as Paul; but the measure of Paul's influence
was the measure of his experience. He had "seen Jesus Christ
our Lord."

Paul's profession is next supported by the production of
his life. It is declared in these words "are not ye my work
in the Lord?" His identity as an authentic Christian worker
is completed by this evidence. We saw his faith. Now we see
his works.

It happens that there were antagonists of Paul in Corinth.
They were disputing his claims to apostleship. This is evident from the second verse where this controversy is alluded
to. "If I be not an apostle unto others, yet doubtless I am to
you; for the seal of mine apostleship are ye in the Lord."
At least these Corinthians knew the authentic identity of
Paul. Others might dispute it, but these had verified the
truth of it. Here are two infallible tests of an authentic
Christian worker: One is *faith*, the other is *fruit*.

Upon these matters Paul was both dogmatic and positive.
He knew what he was and declared it. He knew what he
believed and proclaimed it.

The world has little use for people without convictions.
When diphtheria comes into the home, we will not call a
physician who is open-minded about the matter of disease.
Neither will we send our children to a school where the
teachers are open-minded about the multiplication table.

There is a so-called open-mindedness abroad in our day
which is, in fact no-mindedness. That which believes everything does, in fact, believe nothing. If everything is right
then nothing is wrong. If we were as foolish in our science
and business as we are in our religion, we would ruin our

present world. If all religions are right, then no religion is of consequence.

We notice that Paul's claims rest upon an experience, "have I not seen Jesus Christ our Lord?" He had not merely read a book or espoused a cause. He had passed through an experience. After all, that is what Christianity is—an experience. If you have not had an experience, you have not had anything. Life *has* a definition, but it *is* an experience. If you had not been born, you could not live. Love has a definition, but it is experience. If you have not loved, you cannot know love. Christianity likewise has a definition, but it is an experience. If you have not been born again, you can not know what it is. Its simple, yet conclusive proof is found in these words, "Have I not seen Jesus Christ our Lord?"

Let us be sure to balance faith with fruit and prove faith with works.

2. The Worker's Liberty. Verses 4-6.

"Have we not power to eat and to drink? Have we not power to lead about a sister, a wife, as well as other apostles, and as the brethren of the Lord, and Cephas? Or I only and Barnabas, have not we power to forbear working?"

The worker's identity is verified by his life. This life is now shown to have certain liberties. After all the worker is not some strange creature made inhuman and impractical by his Christian experience.

There evidently were some who were attempting to confine the worker in some narrow sphere of social and family life. This is apparent by what Paul says in verse three, "Mine answer to them that do examine me is this." Paul forthwith defends his right as a Christian worker by being entitled to the same privileges and joys as others. It is true that the immediate comparison is with other workers. It, nevertheless, does not destroy the force of its application to all Christian disciples.

Paul claims the right of free maintenance by those to whom he has ministered. He claims the right to remuneration for spiritual service. More than this, he claims the right of marriage. A celibate clergy is certainly not a New Testament idea. Paul expresses his apostolic rights and further cites the cases of other apostles, the brethren of Christ and also Peter. More than this, he claims the privilege of freedom from manual or mental preoccupation that he might occupy his time solely in Christian service and receive support from the church. All of these are the Christian worker's rights. They are recognized rights which ought to be scrupulously respected by the church in every place and age.

As far as Paul was concerned, we find him renouncing his rights. Both in respect to receiving support and entering into marriage we find Paul stepping aside. He says in verse twelve, "Nevertheless we have not used this power; but suffer all things, lest we should hinder the gospel of Christ." His renunciation was purely personal, and as far as support was concerned, it was purely local. He was not establishing a precedent for all Christian workers.

How refreshing is this policy of Paul. He was not employed as a minister. His was a calling. He was not using his place for profit. He was not demanding his rights. He found greater joy and greater satisfaction in obedience and sacrifice. This is to be found in every life that follows Christ. Pure profit is not always gain. The enjoying of rights is not always pure delight. Loss is sometimes the greatest gain, and renunciation is sometimes the greatest reward.

A large part of the difficulty in modern church life is caused by an ancient problem. It concerns the worker's compensation. It is either the case of his right to it or the amount of it. We will find a worker freely criticized for getting too much but he is rarely championed when he receives too little.

The problem of the worker's wage is caused by the abuse of a scripturally designed policy. The abuse is on the side of the church and the worker as well.

II. THE CHRISTIAN WORKER'S SUPPORT. Verses 7-14.

The entire matter is reviewed in this section under six conclusions. The worker's right to support for his service is defended.

1. Defended by Custom. Verse 7.

"Who goeth a warfare any time at his own charges? who planteth a vineyard, and eateth not of the fruit thereof? or who feedeth a flock, and eateth not of the milk of the flock?"

Paul appeals here to common custom. The soldier, the vineyardist and the shepherd all receive wages for work. Why not the Christian worker? There should be nothing strange about such a contention or conclusion. It is an expected thing and should be followed among Christians without hesitation, for it is not merely the question of a wage but of a spiritual worker's partaking of his work.

2. Defended by Law. Verses 8-11.

"Say I these things as a man? or saith not the law the same also? For it is written in the law of Moses, Thou shalt not muzzle the mouth of the ox that treadeth out the corn. Doth God take care for oxen? Or saith he it altogether for our sakes? For our sakes, no doubt, this is written: that he that ploweth should plow in hope; and that he that thresheth in hope should be partaker of his hope. If we have sown unto you spiritual things, is it a great thing if we shall reap your carnal things?"

The justice of the worker's reward is proved on the grounds of legality. The law protected the oxen. The law prohibited its owner from muzzling it while it threshed the grain as it walked over it. Is God not more concerned with men than with oxen? Indeed so! Therefore, Paul uses this legal citation to defend the worker's rights by saying, "If we have sown unto you spiritual things, is it a great thing if we shall reap your carnal things?" By carnal things is meant the maintenance of the worker by such just competence as would give that worker economic independence.

If there have been instances of the worker's abuse of this principle in taking more than is warranted, one is justified in saying that there have been far more instances of the church's abuse of the same principle by giving less than is proper. If he has been diligent and faithful in his spiritual enterprise, it is the Scripture's teaching that he is as justly entitled to as commensurate a compensation as the soldier for his fighting, the vineyardist for his planting, the shepherd for his caring and the oxen for his threshing. In fact, it is lifted to the place of a material exchange for spiritual service.

They tell of an old Connecticut pastor who declined an increase in salary for substantial reasons. "First," he said to his congregation, "because you can't afford to pay me more. Second, because my preaching isn't worth more than I presently receive. Third, because I have to collect my salary which, heretofore, has been the hardest part of my labors among you. If I have to collect an additional sum, it will kill me."

3. Defended by Precedent. Verse 12.

> "If others be partakers of this power over you, are not we rather? Nevertheless we have not used this power; but suffer all things, lest we should hinder the gospel of Christ."

Let us insert Way's translation at this place. "If others take care to get their share of their rights from you, have I not a still better claim? But—and this is my point—I have never exercised this right of mine. No, I endure every extremity, rather than oppose any hindrance whatever to the spread of the glad-tidings of our Messiah."

The principle is illustrated by Paul's work at Corinth. There were others who labored after Paul left, who claimed their right and received their support. Paul argues his own case with vehemence that if these were sustained, he should have priority because he founded the church, but he preferred to renounce his claims that no hindrance be given to such a newly founded work.

His rights were their responsibility. The responsibility was created automatically the moment they received his ministrations. It was not to be evaded by saying that they did not send for Paul or did not enter into a legal contract. Their responsibility was created the moment they received the spiritual ministrations of the worker. And thus, it continues into our times. If we allow a disparity to exist by what we give, personally or collectively, we are to the proportion of that disparity robbing ourselves of blessing, on our part, and our ministrants of blessing, on their part.

4. Defended by the Priesthood. Verse 13.

> "Do ye not know that they which minister about holy things live of the things of the temple? and they which wait at the altar are partakers with the altar?"

This is an allusion to a common practice in connection with the service of the temple. The priests who ministered in its service were supported by offerings and were allowed portions of the sacrifices used in connection with those sacrifices.

The elevated relation of grace to law and the gospel service to temple service required that the Christian worker be treated with as much regard for his temporal needs as the priestly worker.

While we are considering this matter of the Christian worker's rights to an adequate reward in material things for his spiritual labors, we must not lose sight of the fact that these instructions of Paul were issued to a church newly founded. These people were former pagans. Pagan priests were in the employ of the state. Henceforth, the Christian worker was to live and labor in direct contrast to the pagan worker. One was subsidized by the state while the other was supported by the church. One considered his place a lucrative political job while the other was to labor under divine commission. While his principles were idealistic, his labor was realistic. The law of economic necessity could not be disregarded. To meet the demands that this law placed upon him, he was dependent upon the people to whom he ministered spiritual things.

5. Defended by Jesus Christ. Verse 14.

"Even so hath the Lord ordained that they which preach the gospel should live of the gospel."

Paul now appeals to a word spoken by Christ who declared that a "labourer is worthy of his hire" (Luke 10:7). It has been ordained "that they which preach the gospel should live of the gospel." Nothing could be more plain. The benefits that accrue to the people from the gospel are to be returned in decent and honorable proportion to those human instruments through whom the benefits came.

In all of this we should be careful to make an important distinction. The Christian worker is not a wage earner in the usual sense. His labor is not to be paid for as a wage but recognized as a reward. It is to be thought of in terms of love rather than law. It is to be considered as sowing and reaping. It is to be given out of the fulness of gratitude rather than of the compulsion of duty. It is to be thought of as a thank-offering for blessings received. If this were the case, of the disciples giving and the workers receiving, it would revolutionize our relationships. It is the Bible way and it ought to be our way.

Having addressed itself to the church's responsibility to the worker, the Scripture now addresses itself to the worker's responsibility to the church regarding his motives, both in his preaching and to his parish. If the Christian worker is to expect proper recognition and renumeration from the church, it is the church's right to expect that he shall labor with the right motives, ideals and intentions.

III. The Christian Worker's Motives. Verses 15-18.

These are admirably exemplified in Paul in whom we discover three things:

1. Paul's High Motive. Verse 15.

"But I have used none of these things: neither have I written these things, that it should be so done unto me; for it were better for me to die, than that any man should make my glorying void."

Paul was in a position to waive his rights to a reward for his labor. He did this partly because he had means of his own and partly because he wished to give the gospel's enemies no occasion for charging him with using the gospel as the means of personal gain.

Paul's motive was men not money. It was a far greater satisfaction to give than to get. He saw his life in the light of a passionate service. We dare say that if Paul had considered the money involved in his service, his stature would have shriveled and we would not have heard of him except in passing mention.

2. Paul's Passion in Preaching. Verse 16.

"For though I preach the gospel, I have nothing to glory of: for necessity is laid upon me; yea, woe is unto me, if I preach not the gospel."

The driving force of this man's great ministry was a compelling conviction. It was the conviction that he was God-sent. For him it was a "necessity" to go and a "woe" if he did not go.

For Paul, preaching was not a profession but a passion. Ministers choose their life's work many times as casually as a lawyer does his. They are not in the same category and therefore could not be of the same origin.

An old cleric said to a young man contemplating the ministry, "Don't enter the ministry if you can help it." That was Paul's idea of "necessity."

If the modern ministry is to be adequate to the tremendous days ahead, it needs to be the ministry of a master passion.

Said the great preacher, Charles H. Spurgeon, "The man who says, 'God has chosen me,' can afford to let others think and speak after their own nature. It is his business to take his stand separately, and deliberately, and distinctly to do what he believes to be right, and let the many or the few do as they will."

Speaking about modern ministers, a Christian editor said this: "A man who is forced to preach in order to save himself, always makes a fervent preacher. A man called to the ministry, without a feeling that he is under the compulsion to pit himself against the spirit of his age, will never make a great preacher. Preaching is delivering the soul against something. Heralding is one thing, preaching, another. The first is that of announcing; the second, that of contact and attack. A man cannot preach unless he has something to preach against. If a man is driven of God to be a real preacher, it is because he is first driven within his own heart to resist the spirit of the age which violates his own sense of right. He resists, and, in resisting, cries out against that which he sees is not only ruining others, but threatens to wreck himself. Preachers are made by the developing of their power of moral resistance against the spirit of the age."

3. Paul's Greater Reward. Verses 17, 18.

"For if I do this thing willingly, I have a reward: but if against my will, a dispensation of the gospel is committed unto me. What is my reward then? Verily that, when I preach the gospel, I may make the gospel of Christ without charge, that I abuse not my power in the gospel."

Paul's greater reward was the compensation of joy. It was the joy of giving a life-giving and life-thrilling message without taking selfish advantage of his own rights.

This joy in life can belong to all men and women. It is feared that we rob ourselves of much of the profit of life by our attitude of expecting. We measure service by its gain. It is true that economic independence is the right of the worker, but even this right may sometimes overshadow the altruistic elements of an unselfish Christian service.

IV. The Christian Worker's Adaptability. Verses 19-23.

Briefly stated, the principle Paul is setting forth is the worker's willingness to adapt himself to the conditions and needs of all men so that through this flexibility toward all he might have some.

Three classes of men are mentioned:

1. The Jew Under the Law. Verses 19, 20.

"For though I be free from all men, yet have I made myself servant unto all, that I might gain the more. And unto the Jews I became as a Jew, that I might gain the Jews; to them that are under the law, as under the law, that I might gain them that are under the law."

This adaptability refers to the worker being mobile in his manners and not mobile in his morals. It is a Christian generosity which is willing to make itself flexible to another man's conscience. If the other man's conscience is legalistic, Paul is willing to regulate his social life and respect national custom so as to avoid giving the scrupulous Jew unnecessary offense. By this means Paul hopes to win that Jew to Christ. If he was not flexible and if he brazenly blasted his way through both custom and conscience, he would lose all hope of winning this man.

2. The Gentile Outside the Law. Verse 21.

"To them that are without law, as without law, (being not without law to God, but under the law to Christ,) that I might gain them that are without law."

To this man he became conventionally correct. He respected his ways and ideas. He did not expect him to be regulated by Jewish customs or ceremonies. He sought to understand his background and respect his opinions and be sympathetic with his convictions.

3. The Christian with Scruples. Verses 22, 23.

"To the weak became I as weak, that I might gain the weak: I am made all things to all men, that I might by all means save some. And this I do for the gospel's sake, that I might be partaker thereof with you."

Here was a man who was weak and overscrupulous about many minute matters that were not specifically regulated by Scripture. To this weak man Paul was willing to make concessions and restrict his own intelligent liberty so that he might bring this man into the larger and more abundant sphere of Christian living.

Paul enunciates a principle of being "all things to all men, that I might by all means save some." Does he mean to follow the old maxim, "when in Rome do as the Romans do?" Paul's idea is far from this. He had a flexible conscience when it came to matters that were without moral significance; but a rigid conscience that would not bend nor give quarter to any practice that would violate Christian morality. It was not looseness of life that Paul advocates. It was rather liberty of action with a lofty object. The object was "that I might by all means save some."

Paul's idea was not to sin in order to save. No one ever won another by violating the sacred standards of the Scripture. A flexible expediency is allowable, however. In Paul's case this expediency was not relaxing his standards but sacrificing his own liberties so that he might persuade others to follow his Christ.

Paul's final consideration of the worker's relation to his career puts a very serious responsibility upon all of us. It is particularly so of the worker whose career of service is held in view, but it is equally so of all who would end life in the winner's circle.

V. The Christian Worker's Responsibility. Verses 24-27.

Paul has been setting forth some of the purposes of his life. For instance, he said, "I am made all things to all men, that I might by all means save some." To accomplish so noble a purpose as this Paul was ready to make any sacrifice. He was willing to accommodate himself to the narrow prejudices of men. He was willing to limit his own liberty so as not to transgress another's bigotry. To do this would mean to exercise self-control and to have self-control would mean self-discipline.

The manner by which this discipline and control are to be achieved is set forth in language borrowed from the Isthmian athletic games which were held at Corinth.

1. The Race. Verses 24, 25.

(1) *The object.* Verses 24.

> "Know ye not that they which run in a race run all, but one receiveth the prize? So run, that ye may obtain."

Every two years the Isthmian games were held in a great stadium located in Corinth. Only free-born men could enter the games. These must engage in ten months' preparatory training and be able to certify their faithfulness in training. Moreover, they must keep morally clean, for preceding each contest the contestants were led about the arena by the herald or master of ceremonies while he asked, in a loud voice, whether any spectator could accuse the contestants of any crime, wickedness, slavery or depravity in life and manners. For thirty days before the contests a rigid period of preparation was observed. Each contestant was announced by name and country. In the case of the victor, he was crowned with a garland of victory and returned to his native city with great pomp and ceremony. Here a breach was made in the walls to allow him to enter, and he was immortalized in poetry and verse.

In these races, *all* ran that *one* might win. In the race of life under Christ, all who enter may win. Paul urges, "So run, that ye may obtain."

(2) *The rules.* Verse 25a.

> "And every man that striveth for the mastery is temperate in all things . . ."

There were rules governing the contests. Under these rules the contestants were pledged to observe certain restrictions in diet and certain habits of life. The rules imposed upon the contestants required self-control, not self-indulgence. For this reason Paul was willing to limit himself. There were many things he could do with personal impunity. If his example and service were to be effective to "all men," however, it required discipline and control. This explains why he was willing to be "made all things to all men."

Self-indulgence has never won any victory. The path to any conspicuous success is pain. Pleasure comes best when it has followed suffering. Leisure is best when it follows labor. Whatever is most worthwhile is achieved at a price.

> "The heights by great men reached and kept
> Were not attained by sudden flight,
> But they, while their companions slept,
> Were toiling upward in the night."

Paul recognizes Christian liberty but he also recognizes the restrictions of Christian consecration. The disciple of Christ who declares that he can engage in any pleasure he wishes, indulge in any habit he wants and live in any selfish manner he pleases does not have the spiritual stuff out of which heroic, world-blessing Christians are made.

This is an indulgent age. Its luxury-sated, pleasure-soaked moderns are degenerating our civilization. Along with it we have too many soft Christians. Too many of them play fast and loose with the world. We need more discipline and more sacrifice. The world will never be won to Christ by Christians whose lack of consecration gives them no distinction from the world about them. First century Christianity was disciplined by consecration, denial and sacrifice. Modern Christianity is in desperate need of the same kind.

(3) *The crown.* Verse 25b.

" . . . Now they do it to obtain a corruptible crown; but we an incorruptible."

The master of ceremonies who was both judge and herald stood at the end of the prescribed racing distance holding the victor's wreath in view. In some cases it was a garland of wild olive, in others, ivy, pine or parsley. In any case it was perishable. It faded and lost its beauty. Not so the Christian contestant's crown. It is incorruptible because it is a crown of life.

Let us be sure we understand what is being taught under the figure of this athletic contest. It is not a question of salvation. One does not strive or race to compete for salvation. This whole chapter is the *worker's* chapter. It deals with a servant. Therefore, the crown of the contestant is not an award of salvation but a reward for service.

2. The Contest. Verses 26, 27.

The importance of the Christian worker's application to his task with the utmost seriousness is doubly emphasized by the apostle's reference to another spectacle in these Isthmian games. It was a boxing contest.

(1) *The reality.* Verse 26.

> . . . "I therefore so run, not as uncertainly; so fight I, not as one that beateth the air."

Here is Arthur S. Way's translation of verses 26 and 27, "I am a boxer who deals my blows at anything but the empty air of my rights. Nay, I browbeat my own animal nature (you are inclined to be champions of yours), and treat it, not as my master, but as my slave—lest, by any chance, after acting as the herald of the lists who bids others enter, I might find my own self disqualified from competing."

Paul speaks here of the reality of the contest. He is not shadow boxing. It is not an imaginary antagonist that he engages. In fact, the antagonist is Paul, the man. It is Paul's old man. It is Paul's carnality. It is Paul's human nature. If Paul, the Christian, is to win, Paul, the sinner, must be defeated. If Paul the spiritual, is to transcend, Paul, the carnal, must be put down. Here is spiritual realism.

(2) *The self-control.* Verse 27a.

"But I keep under my body and bring it into subjection . . ."

As the race contestant observes the rules of training, so
the boxing contestant observes the discipline of his body. He
literally fights himself. In this case Paul sees himself constantly engaged in spiritual combat with his lower nature.
He is figuratively bruising and beating his body until it is
black and blue. He is its master and not its slave. He dictates
what it must do; not it what he must do. He leads his body
about as a captive to his will. His body with its carnal appetites and passions does not lead Paul in the pursuit of
vain and foolish things. In other words, Paul, the new man
in Christ, is master over Paul, the old man in Adam.

(3) *The peril.* Verse 27b.

". . . lest that by any means when I have preached to others
I myself should be a castaway."

This scripture is not as difficult as people make it. It is
talking about Paul the worker and not Paul the disciple.
The salvation of Paul is not the thing which is in jeopardy.
The thing which is in jeopardy is Paul's service.

He speaks of himself as having "preached to others." He
had acted as a herald and as such he had summoned others
into the arena. He had proclaimed the good news to multitudes. Paul's peril was the danger of self-indulgence, the
failure to observe the rules of discipline and self-control which
might lead him to a selfish and sensual life and disqualify
him as a contestant for the crown.

It was not a question of his disqualification as a Christian but as a contestant. It was the peril of winning others
but failing to win the prize. It was the danger of aiding
multitudes to find the way of life but failing personally. Oh,
the tragedy of modern castaways, brilliant servants, great
preachers, who failed in self-disipline and are now castaways!

CHAPTER X

THE CHURCH AND ITS TRADITIONS

I *Corinthians* 10

THE EPISTLE to the Corinthians was written to and for Christians who had recently been saved out of the current Christians who had recently been saved out of the current paganism of that day. It was not dealing with mythical problems but with very real ones. It concerned the social life of these people and proposed such social restrictions as would save them from personal and social sins.

For us, the same problems exist in different forms. Ours is not a primitive world filled with pagan idolatry. The same moral problems still exist, however. They are just as real as they were in the primitive civilization of that early century even though now they are supported by automobiles and radios. This fact makes the Bible perpetually modern, and important to every age. We cannot escape the reality of its truths nor live without the support of its life.

Christianity is not something which was the discovery of a day. It has a past as well as a present. It has sacred traditions which are the historical elements of its truth. To these we are indebted for example and precept.

In our sophisticated modernity we discount and depreciate the past. We think that all that matters is what we have discovered today. If we were to take out of our world all that we depend upon which came out of the past, it would be an empty and vacant place. Today is a day made up of a million yesterdays. The Bible is a book filled with the wisdom of yesterday. It is divinely selected facts and truths which have been written for our benefit. For this reason it says in verse eleven, "Now all these things happened unto them for ensamples: and they are written for our admonition, upon whom the ends of the world are come."

Let us *learn* and then *live;* not merely *live* and *learn.* Revelation saves us the expense of experience. The Bible offers us a wisdom that will save us the heartaches that come by learning through experience.

I. The Church and Its Past. Verses 1-13.

1. The Tradition. Verses 1-5.

> "Moreover, brethren, I would not that ye should be ignorant, how that all our fathers were under the cloud, and all passed through the sea; And were all baptized unto Moses in the cloud and in the sea; And did all eat the same spiritual meat; And did all drink the same spiritual drink: for they drank of that spiritual Rock that followed them: and that Rock was Christ. But with many of them God was not well pleased: for they were overthrown in the wilderness."

Paul appeals to the experience of the fathers. While the Israelites were not the church, they were the spiritual soil out of which the church sprang. The Old Testament is the Jewish background while the New Testament is the Christian foreground. Both merge in the cross.

The principle of Christian behavior in view, here, is that of a Christian's right of indulgence in his personal life and in his social life. How far dare he go in indulging his desires in the world system in which he lives whether that system be of the first century or the twentieth century?

Elsewhere he was told that his is the liberty of conscience. He is not bound to legalism with a lot of restrictions around his conduct.

In the first part of this chapter he is told that the indulgence of his liberty may impair his spiritual life and impede his spiritual progress. In the last part of this chapter he is told that the indulgence of his liberty may be a reactionary example that will harm others.

Paul now appeals to tradition and precedent to warn the Christian. The Israelites were not aimless wanderers in a strange and new world. Neither were these Christians. Both had spiritual means of wisdom and strength. The Israelites experienced "the cloud" and "the sea." The cloud meant *guidance*. This means that they were certain of reaching their destination. The sea meant *deliverance*. By this means they were certain of divine aid in their experience. More than this, the Israelites experienced the foreshadowings of baptism and communion. The cloud and sea were the means of exit and entrance. By one they left an old life associated with Egypt. By one they entered a new life associated with Canaan. Through them came the pledge of life and loyalty to their leader, Moses. These are the elements found in Christian baptism.

Following this new beginning was a new sustaining. They were no longer sustained by such food as came from Egypt. They were sustained by "spiritual meat" which was the manna of the wilderness and by "spiritual drink" which was Christ. These are the elements found in the Christian's Lord's Supper.

Despite these new experiences and abundant provisions, many of the Israelites proved unfaithful. Their failure was not due to the fact that the provisions was inadequate. You will remember that it came because of compromise. They had an ample and adequate life, but they looked after the world about them and lusted for what they did not need.

This is the danger of the Christian and Paul specifically states in verse six, "Now these things were our examples." They are models of experience recorded for our benefit lest in our Christian liberties we become too confident and too sufficient and prove unfaithful to the great trust which we hold.

The mention of Christ and His relation to the Israelites reveals that He is not native alone to the New Testament. He belongs to the Old, as well. He is in the Old concealed and in the New revealed. He was a part of ancient life as much as He needs to be a part of modern life. Yes, He is a Rock. He is solid and secure. He is ample and sure.

2. The Application. Verses 6-13.

The application was specific and definite. It applied to them as it applies to us. It is presented in pictures of life to illustrate the principles of Christian experience.

(1) *"Neither be ye idolaters, as were some of them."* Verse 7.

Modern idolatry is the making of gods of the mind as well as the hand. The modern gods of mart and mind are as idolatrous as the golden calf of Aaron.

(2) *"Neither let us tempt Christ, as some of them also tempted."* Verse 9.

By trespassing so close to the borderland of questionable things we may presume upon the forbearance of God and put our lives in jeopardy and peril. Let us not tempt God by presuming on His mercy and goodness.

(3) *"Neither murmur ye, as some of them also murmured."* Verse 10.

Here were people who cast a covetous eye upon the possessions and pleasures of others. It bred a spirit of discontent and brought their own lives into such a false light that the ultimate outcome was defeat and shame.

The sum of the matter is this: If our lives are to be contented and if we are to live to the utmost satisfaction and usefulness, we will find that contentment and that satisfaction within the sphere of a normal Christian experience. All that is necessary for a good life and a great life is to be found in Christ. We need not link arms with paganism, neither ancient nor modern. We need not be half-Christian and half-pagan. Christianity carries with it all that life demands and all that we need. Let us look in and not out. Let us look up and not down.

Benjamin Franklin is reported saying, "We may give advice, but we cannot give conduct." The communication of conduct is indeed a human impossibility. Nevertheless, the Bible is such an adequate book of truth and life that it not only communicates the best advice but it also gives the power of a new life and, consequently, conduct. Here, indeed, is good advice. You can find none better. Do not be content with instruction alone. Let the truth become your life.

In the ensuing three verses you will find some of the richest treasures of Scripture.

(1) *Examples for admonition.* Verse 11.

> "Now all these things happened unto them for ensamples: and they are written for our admonition, upon whom the ends of the world are come."

We must look at Way's very illuminating translation. "Now these things which happened to them should serve as warnings to us. They were, in fact, put on record as admonitions to us, whom the last great days of the world's existence have overtaken."

The traditions of the past are not unimportant items of religious history. "All these things" which the Christian of the New Testament finds in the record of the Old Testament have a pre-written purpose. They are types which serve as warnings. They are events which offer strong persuasions. They have been recorded not merely to serve as events of fact. They have a spiritual value. They also have a personal value. The more we know the Scriptures, the better we know the true manner of life.

The specific intent of these scriptures of the Old Testament was to meet the needs of a certain people. They are those "upon whom the ends of the world are come." Note that it says *the world.* This is not the "kosmos" meaning physical world, but rather the end of a period of time in world affairs. It might be rendered — "who stand at the meeting of the ages — the end of the old order, and the beginning of the new."

They and we stand in the same place: not in point of years for the difference of years between us is some twenty centuries. However, they and we are people upon whom the age hinges. We stand upon the threshold of a mighty moment. It is the time of God's great kingdom on earth. Such majesty of place requires holiness of life. For such a life we have received these admonitions. Let us determine to refuse the mould of paganism and modernism and live our lives as conspicuous examples of disciples of Christ.

(2) *Warning against over-confidence.* Verse 12.

"Wherefore let him that thinketh he standeth take heed lest he fall."

Arthur S. Way's translation again proves valuable, "Therefore, let the man who imagines himself to be standing so securely see to it lest he fall. And you can avoid falling."

Here were people who considered themselves to have excelled in Christian graces. They had been baptized. They regularly observed the Lord's table. They had had some of the most distinguished apostles as their teachers. With all of these, they considered themselves morally and spiritually secure and beyond the danger of misstepping or falling. But it was in such an attitude that lay their greatest peril. Self-confidence without Christ-consciousness is over-confidence and over-confidence is the prelude to spiritual disaster.

It is the thing in which we excel and the privileges we enjoy that constitute our greatest spiritual perils. In these things we become proud, and in pride we are on the brink of spiritual calamity.

The weakest Christian is not in as much peril as the strongest Christian. Our excellencies are our dangers. Our strongest virtues are our weakest parts. Abraham was a man of faith and he failed in unbelief. Moses was a man of meekness and he failed in presumption. Samson was a man of strength and he failed in weakness.

None of us dare be content with ourselves. He who builds walls of spiritual pride about the citadel of his life is doomed to disaster. The secret of Christian security is to go on to higher and greater heights. Perseverance must take the place of personal confidence.

During a military campaign a young captain was recommended to Napoleon for promotion to a higher rank. Napoleon asked, "Why do you suggest this man?" They answered to say that through unusual courage and cleverness he had won a great victory several days before. "Good," said Napoleon, "but what did he do the next day?" That was the end of the matter.

From the divine standpoint our security rests in *our position*. But from the human standpoint our security rests in *our condition*. The position of the Corinthians was excellent. They were "sanctified in Christ Jesus, called to be saints." But their condition was deplorable. They were contentious, divisive, carnal, and compromising. It was their solemn responsibility to see that their condition at least approximated their position. This is the work of grace through the Word of God which the Bible calls sanctification. There is *primary sanctification* by the Holy Spirit. This is before justification. There is *positional sanctification* by the blood of Christ. This is at the time of justification. There is *practical sanctification* by the Word of God. This is after justification.

Instead of being concerned about their practical sanctification, the Corinthians were content with their self-attainments. It created a false confidence which was bringing them to the precipice of spiritual disaster. Let us take heed and have care.

(3) *Assurance of endurance.* Verse 13.

"There hath no temptation taken you but such as is common to man: but God is faithful, who will not suffer you to be tempted above that ye are able; but will with the temptation also make a way to escape, that ye may be able to bear it."

This is a great assurance. It is not against being tempted but rather the assurance of being kept in temptation.

Your attention is directed to the two elements present in this great verse.

a. The human element.

"There hath no temptation taken you but such as is common to man."

Our experiences are common and not uncommon. We may think that we have unusual trials but "there hath no temptation taken you but such as is common." Our problems are not peculiar to us. Our trials are not greater than another's. We live in a world of common experiences.

b. The divine element.

" . . . but God is faithful."

The faithfulness of God is the foundation and promise of our security and victory.

The faithfulness of God will manifest itself in two ways —

(a) Preventive providence.

"Who will not suffer you to be tempted above that ye are able."

The permissive will of God allows situations to arise in our lives that may hurt us, but it is only to help us. "There is some dividend in every difficulty. The smart man is the one who is wise enough to compel his difficulty to pay him that dividend."

"The most valuable year I have ever lived through," said an old man, "was the year I had the most trouble. That was the year I learned to master myself."

(b) Protective providence.

"But will with the temptation also make a way to escape, that ye may be able to bear it."

Before, we saw preventive providence, here we see protective providence. The way God makes in the midst of our temptations is not to escape them but to bear them. God does not shield us but He does sustain us. There is blessing in bearing our sorrows and trials in a noble way. God is not desiring a spiritual race of pampered children. He wants noblemen and noblewomen. Christian nobility is not conferred but is developed in the hardness and the heat of trial. Thank God then for your present lot, that you may make it the place of a great triumph.

The apostle has just pointed out that the past holds admonitions for the present; that over-confidence was the prelude to disaster; and that temptation and trial were not only common but conquerable. What follows in the rest of the chapter is an effort to get the Corinthian Christians and all who follow to apply this wisdom to their present problems of life.

II. THE CHURCH AND ITS PRESENT. Verses 14-33.

What should be a Christian's attitude to the pagan world about him? The answer is found in the scriptures before us. It is stated in terms of Corinthian conditions. For these Corinthians, it was the problem of paganisms and its idolatry. For us it is the problem of a twentieth century world system. The problem is as modern as it is ancient. Whether we write into it words of our modern world or the items of antiquity, the problem is the same. This goes for the solution as well.

1. We Should be Conservative. Verses 14-24.

"Wherefore, my dearly beloved, flee from idolatry. I speak as to wise men; judge ye what I say. The cup of blessing which we bless, is it not the communion of the blood of Christ? The bread we break, is it not the communion of the body of Christ? For we being many are one bread, and one body: for we are all partakers of that one bread. Behold Israel after the flesh: are not they which eat of the sacrifices partakers of the altar? What say I then? that the idol is any thing, or that which is offered in sacrifice to idols is any thing? But I say, that the things which the Gentiles sacrifice, they sacrifice to devils, and not to God:

and I would not that ye should have fellowship with devils. Ye
cannot drink the cup of the Lord, and the cup of devils: ye
cannot be partakers of the Lord's table, and of the table of
devils. Do we provoke the Lord to jealousy? are we stronger
than he? All things are lawful for me, but all things are not
expedient: all things are lawful for me, but all things edify not.
Let no man seek his own, but every man another's wealth."

The sense of this entire passage is found in verse 14, "Wherefore, my dearly beloved, flee from idolatry." This is con-
servatism in conduct. The Corinthians were practicing liber-
alism in their conduct. They were walking as close to the line
of paganism as they dared. More than this, they were abusing their Christian liberty by indulging in certain practices
that were associated with idolatry, notably, the eating of idol
meats. This was not a wise nor a safe thing. It was dangerous
for the indulger and destructive in its example to others. It
left no clean-cut line of demarcation between paganism and
Christianity. Ultimately, one would not know where the one
commenced and the other left off. The safe thing was to keep
as far away as one could from idolatry.

Paul follows by saying, "I speak as to wise men." He was
appealing to their reason and good sense and also to ours
insofar as the problem is ours today. The line of reasoning he
employed compared the Christian's communion service and
the pagan's idol feast. This comparison is found in verses
16-23.

The Christian's identity came as the result of his participation at the Lord's table. This made him one with Christ and
it made him one with the body of believers. It definitely
placed him in a sacred relationship to Christ. If he should then
partake of the table of idols, it would be an act of idolatry.

It was one thing to eat meat bought at a temple market
and another thing to eat such meat in an idol temple with
temple idolaters. Conscience would permit the first but consecration denied the second. It would, therefore, be a mistake to exercise one's Christian liberty to see how strong he

was, and how near he could come to idolatry without practicing it. The wise thing was to flee from it.

For us, the problem is not the idolatry of paganism. It is, instead, the problem of the world in a different form. For us there are personal habits, personal pleasures, and personal practices in relation to the present world system which in themselves may not always be essentially wrong. They become wrong, however, when our practice of them causes us to lose our identity as Christians. They become wrong when on one day we sit at the table of our Lord and on the next day we join ourselves with those who are godless in places associated with sin. To take His Name among His enemies is to insult His deity and our character.

Christians were never intended to be world mixers, rather, world makers. They were to be salt and light. If salt is cast upon the ground, it loses its savour and is good for nothing. If Christians are like everything about them, they lose their significance and are also good for nothing.

The substance of a Christian's policy for his practice is stated in verses 23 and 24, "All things are lawful for me, but all things are not expedient: all things are lawful for me, but all things edify not. Let no man seek his own, but every man another's wealth."

Let us add Way's translation because it illuminates our version beautifully. "All things are permissible for me; but all things are not good for me. All things are permissible; but not all things build up our spiritual life. Let no one make his own interests his one aim, but rather his neighbor's interests."

Many modern Christians are troubled about their relation to modern pleasures and practices. For instance, should a Christian dance, smoke, play cards, drink, and such things? To begin with, there is no scriptural law against them stated with the names of these things. This is so because ours is the economy of grace. In grace there is no law. For this reason Paul could say, "All things are lawful for me." In things

that are not in themselves violations of the moral law and inherently sinful, the Christian has the right to do them. With
the Christian, the highest liberty is not his own rights. What
he may do is allowable but it is not always profitable. It may
be a matter of liberty but not expediency. It may be right but
it is not opportune. It may be good but it is not best. It
may be to his interests but not to his neighbor's interests. It
may be a pleasurable experience but it is not a profitable
example. It may be lawful but it is not fitting.

A bold, brazen Christian liberalist may say, "I will do
as I please!" What pleases may represent selfish interests. To
do this may be lawful but it certainly is not helpful. To the
extent that pleasure is personally selfish, it is also pleasurably
empty. We lose much of our value of pleasure by the motives that prompt it. To deny ourselves the right to do what
we might do is to find a delight and a pleasure undreamed of.

In all of this matter of a Christian's relation to the world
about him, we should remember that it is not a question of
law but love. No law is found against it but much love should
be found that will prompt our behavior to the best interests
of others as well as ourselves.

It is not a question always of a thing being harmful to us
but rather of its being helpful to others. Hence, Paul writes,
"Let no man seek his own, but every man another's wealth."
You say, "I will do it because it is not harmful," when you
ought to say, "I will not do it because it is not helpful."

This idea of helping others by what we do is the most
convincing argument there is for separated and consecrated
Christian living.

In our day we have abused this great principle either by
ignoring it and losing our identity as Christians altogether or
else we have made it legalistic and artificial. In one extreme
Christian liberty has become license. In the other extreme
Christian liberty has become legalistic. Neither is right and
both are wrong. We are under grace and grace means liberty,
but it is liberty under the compulsion of love.

The New Testament does not bind us to an old law. It gives us a new life. That new life, when followed in the light of the Scriptures, will neither impose the law nor violate the law. It will follow a course of love and in its pursuit it will find such happiness and pleasure as could not be found either elsewhere or otherwise.

Cromwell's chaplain was constantly seeking protection of his ruler for others. He never refused to assist any person of merit. Cromwell noticed this and said to his chaplain, "Mr. Howe, you have asked favors for everybody besides yourself; pray, when does your turn come?" "My turn, my Lord Protector, is always come when I serve another." There is always profit in pleasure when the interests of others surmount the interests of self.

The thing that is impressive in these current verses under consideration has been their sensible practicality. After all, the Christian life is not queer and odd and peculiar. It does not make freaks of its adherents. It is our misunderstanding which causes us not only to misuse this scripture but to abuse it.

2. We Should be Conscientious. Verses 25-30.

We discover here that conscience leads to a twofold action. One is positive and the other negative.

(1) *Conscience permits indulgence.* Verses 25-27.

> "Whatsoever is sold in the shambles, that eat, asking no question for conscience sake: For the earth is the Lord's, and the fulness thereof. If any of them that believe not bid you to a feast, and ye be disposed to go; whatsoever is set before you, eat, asking no question for conscience sake."

You will remember that the local Corinthian problem concerned the eating of meat offered for sale in the temple market. It constituted a problem to some because of the association of this kind of meat with idol sacrifices. For us, the problem is not one of meat or idolatry in a pagan form. It is the problem of how far a Christian can go in the participation of the practices and pleasures of the world and retain his distinctive identity and spiritual influence as a Christian. If he throws himself into the social world indiscriminately and makes common cause with Bible deniers and Christ rejectors, he thereby loses his influence and nullifies his purpose.

Paul sets down a practical rule for the Corinthians in their problem. He advises them in these verses to purchase such meat as is sold in "the shambles" or markets without raising any questions to satisfy the scruples of conscience. Consider it from the standpoint of its present purpose and not its previous use. Eat it because of Who made it. Use it and do not think of the abuse to which pagan people put it.

One might be an invited guest and be served such meat as had been purchased at the same market. What then should he do? Should he refuse the food and offend the host? Paul's practical rule suggests that he "eat, asking no questions for conscience sake." This is the prerogative and the principle of Christian liberty. This is the scope of grace. It is the privilege of Christian conduct. This was the case of a Christian sitting down in social life with a non-Christian. Christianity does not forbid such social intercourse. It does not make social hermits out of Christ's disciples. You will be careful to notice that this kind of social intercourse was unlike that which was prohibited wherein a Christian was found eating at idol tables in company with pagan friends. One may be congenial in his relations but he dare not compromise his faith.

(2) *Conscience prevents indulgence.* Verses 28-30.

"But if any man say unto you, This is offered in sacrifice unto idols, eat not for his sake that shewed it, and for conscience sake: for the earth is the Lord's and the fulness thereof: Conscience, I say not thine own, but of the other: for why is my liberty judged of another man's conscience? For if I by grace be a partaker, why am I evil spoken of for that for which I give thanks?"

Before, he was told to eat for conscience sake. Now, he is told to refrain for conscience sake.

In this case the moral and spiritual question has been raised. It may be raised by an over-scrupulous Christian. In that case conscience says, leave it alone. It is not profitable for any Christian to indulge when indulgence might injure another's sensitive faith. On the other hand, this question may be raised by a pagan idol worshipper who is wondering why a Christian should partake of idol-offered meats. In that case, also, conscience says, leave it alone. It is not profitable for any Christian to indulge when indulgence might injure his testimony to an unbeliever. At all costs, he must keep himself free from accusation so the conversion of others may not be hindered.

In this case, it is not his conscience that bothers him for he has understanding enough to know that it can not hurt him. It is the other man's conscience.

As far as the Christian believer is concerned, Paul explains that his intelligent spirituality and his Christian liberty would permit him to partake of such food. It is his right since "the earth is the Lord's and the fulness thereof." It is his right and no one dare rightfully speak evil of him since his eating is sanctified by his thanks to God.

This particular point which Paul makes here is that while it is the Christian's conscientious right, it is not always right to act upon his rights if such action will affect his position as a Christian witness. The Christian's rights are sometimes to be regulated by his responsibilities.

It is to be similarly so in the modern Christian's life. In his habits and his pleasures, he has the right of Christian liberty. If doing a certain thing will compromise his faith or jeopardize his testimony, then his right in that thing is cancelled.

This, mind you well, is not a question of law but loyalty to Christ and love to man. The New Testament nowhere gives us a list of taboos in things that are of moral indifference. It respects Christian liberty based on gospel grace. It also puts Christian behavior on its honor. It charges the Christian with a conscientious regard for his influence on the lives of those about him.

The argument of the pagans in the days of Corinth pointed out that if Christians freely indulged in the doubtful indulgence of idol-offered meats, what actual difference was there between Christian behavior and pagan behavior? The same argument holds true today. If I, as a Christian, participate in all the activities of the non-Christian, what actual difference is there between Christian behavior and non-Christian? If there is a difference in my faith, there should also be a difference in my life. The difference in my life is for the purpose of my influence.

In all these things the apostle was speaking to Christians and was not trying to impose a Christian morality upon a non-Christian world. We do well to remember in our preachment not to try to enforce on the world what is meant for the Church. You can not expect Christian behavior until you have Christian character. After the new birth comes the new order of life with its new ideals.

3. We Should be Considerate. Verses 31-33.

> "Whether therefore ye eat, or drink, or whatsoever ye do, do all to the glory of God. Give none offence, neither to the Jews, nor to the Gentiles, nor to the church of God: Even as I please all men in all things, not seeking mine own profit, but the profit of many, that they may be saved."

The summary of this statement leads to this conclusion. The ideal of Christian behavior is for the glory of God and the helping of man. This imposes a very high principle upon Christians. It takes the common pleasures and makes them sacred privileges. It takes eating and drinking, social contacts and companionship, and makes them noble activities. It tells us that the greatest pleasure in life is not the indulgence of self but the helping of others. Yes, it tells us that our every movement and everyday life can be for the glory of God. The dinner table, the kitchen sink, the school desk, the crafts-men's bench can glow with a glory like Moses' bush in the wilderness.

The keynote is not pleasure that disregards faith and Christ, and seeks selfishness—it is pleasure that is found in pleasing God and helping men.

Sir Bartle Frere was to visit in a Scottish home. The host sent his servant to meet the guest. In order that the dis-tinguished guest might be identified, the servant was told to look for a tall gentleman helping somebody. That's how you identify a distinguished and happy Christian. He is going through life "helping somebody."

Chapter XI

THE CHURCH AND ITS WORSHIP

I Corinthians 11

THE PERPLEXING matters sometimes encountered in our study of Scripture would be more easily understood were we to know the setting and the circumstances in which that particular scripture was written. We go back to ancient Corinth and see the tremendous difficulties and problems of the little colony of Christians lately converted from so vast a paganism and we will have a new appreciation of these people and the scripture which treats of their problems. We see here "the perplexities of domestic life, the corrupting proximity of heathen immorality, the lingering superstition, the rash speculation, the lawless perversion of Christian liberty; we witness the strife of theological factions, the party names, the sectarian animosities . . . We see the picture of a Christian congregation as it met for worship in some upper chamber, such as the house of Aquila, or of Gaius, could furnish." This was the early church within and without. It faced problems and predicaments such as none of us have ever known. No wonder this letter had to be written.

In this chapter we observe the church at 'worship. Two things are discussed.

I. THE PROPER DRESS OF WOMEN. Verses 1-16.

This passage has to do solely with woman's relationship to worship. It is not the matter of her place as a teacher or preacher, but of her conduct and her dress in relation to the assembly and God as a worshipper.

It is assumed, although not rightly so, that this scripture and those elsewhere which speak of woman's sphere in the

church are against her liberties and rights. The Bible is
womanhood's Magna Charta of liberty. No one has done so
much to elevate and liberate woman as Jesus Christ. She
owes a debt of undying gratitude to Christianity for the
honored and exalted place she occupies in Christendom.
Therefore, let no one speak ill of Paul and his attitude to
women as if to say that he was an enemy of their liberties.

It has been said that there are probably more restrictions
attaching to women in the Christian church than in any other
field. If that is so, it is not rightly so. Christianity is womanhood's emancipator and protector. It is not the intention of
the Scriptures, nor of Christ, to restrict her influence or intelligence in her God-given sphere. There is in the Scriptures
a very definite purpose, however, which undertakes to see
that she occupies her sphere. She has her sphere and whenever she occupies that sphere, she brings a benign influence
upon all the world. It is the corruption of her sphere that
nullifies her influence.

So far as we can see, the Scriptures put no restraints upon
the use of woman's intelligence or the exercise of woman's
influence. She is given ample and abundant avenues for their
expression. Proof of this is to be found in the long list of
noble women found, not only in the Bible, but in successive
Christian history.

It is with all of these facts in mind that we look at this
chapter and its teaching about women.

1. The Principle of Women and Worship. Verses 1-3.

"Be ye followers of me, even as I also am of Christ. Now
I praise you, brethren, that ye remember me in all things, and
keep the ordinances, as I delivered them to you. But I would
have you know, that the head of every man is Christ; and the
head of the woman is the man; and the head of Christ is God."

Paul clarifies his own practice before these Corinthians
before he endeavors to instruct them. He challenges them
to follow him as he follows Christ. The words, "of me," and

"as I" link their following him with his following Christ. This indicates the practical and authoritative basis of his teaching. He is not a narrow-minded bigot. He is not a soured critic of women. He is not a woman hater. He is a follower of Christ and he asks others to follow him only as he has caught the spirit and followed the teachings of the Master. Therefore, what Paul teaches is what Christ taught.

The principle upon which this teaching is based is neither custom nor religion. It is a combination of creation and redemption. It goes back to creation and also to the cross. It is expressed in these words: "But I would have you know, that the head of every man is Christ; and the head of the woman is the man; and the head of Christ is God."

The unit of society is the family. The head of the family is the husband. In the Christian version of the family the head of the man is Christ even as Christ is subordinated to God. Here are the checks and balances of justice and equality. To accord to the man the headship of the wife is not to deliver her into the hand of an autocrat, for he is responsible to Christ.

From the creative standpoint they must be considered in their order. In verses 7 and 8 it states that the man "is the image and glory of God, but the woman is the glory of man. For the man is not of the woman; but the woman of the man." Priority in creation gives precedence in the administration of the family. It is God's creative order and should be respected and honored.

From the redemptive standpoint they must be considered in their relation to Christ. If the wife is under the headship of the man, then this is safeguarded from tyranny and abuse and cruelty by the fact that the husband is under the headship of Christ. If she is subordinate to him, he is subordinate to Christ. This balances the family relations. This checks abuses. For, as the husband remembers his relation to Christ, he will exercise his family headship in love and grace.

Something had happened in Corinth to disturb this relationship and particularly as it affected the worship of the assembly. There is a spiritual equality between husband and wife as well as between man and woman, for "there is neither Jew nor Greek, there is neither bond nor free, there is neither male nor female; for ye are all one in Christ Jesus." This is our standing before God. With Him there are no distinctions of race, society, or sex. The distinction between the sexes still maintains in our earthly relations, however, for they are neither liquidated nor equalized.

In Corinth there were some women who were so carried away with the teaching of spiritual equality that they threw away all restraints and appeared in their public assemblies without veils or covering.

The purpose of the veil or covering was purely local. It has no significance to us at all. It was the custom of Corinth for all modest women to appear covered. This covering was in contra-distinction to the idolatrous and immoral priestesses of paganism who appeared with dishevelled hair. It was also a symbol and token of her dependence and submission in the family. To have appeared in Corinth without a covering was not only an immodest thing but an unwomanly thing. As it concerned that age it was distinctly unchristian.

As we have already observed this does not have the same significance for us today. Much of Paul's teaching concerns customs which were local and temporary and do not hold for modern women the same degree of importance.

Let us note Dr. C. I. Scofield's statement on this subject: "Nothing could be more contrary to the whole spirit of this dispensation than to use the casual mention of an ancient custom in a Greek city as fastening a legal and, so to speak, Levitical ceremonial upon Christians in all ages. The point is that 'the head of the woman is the man.' It is the divine order. The angels know this. To them any inversion of that order would be disorder. In Corinth a shorn or 'uncovered' head in the presence of men was a badge of harlotry, and a harlot is not only a woman who sells her body, but she is a woman who has thrown off the restraints of subordination—

of the divine order. In a mixed assembly therefore, a spiritually minded and Biblically taught Christian woman who speaks or prays would do so in a modest and womanly manner, keeping her place in the divine order."

The instruction found here was to insure for the Christian community the modest and decorous conduct of its women in regard to both family and worship.

No one of us will deny that womanhood holds the key to our standards of spirituality and purity. When she fails in these standards, all else fails. May God raise up in our day a generation of noble Christian women who will lift the level of our spirituality and purity to the place where it ought to be.

We have already seen the principle of Paul's instruction concerning women and worship. Let us now detail the next part of this section.

2. The Practice of Women and Worship. Verses 4 - 16.

The practice was, of course, to be based on the principle which recognized the headship of man from both the creative and redemptive standpoints. To begin with, worship was to be conducted with this principle in mind. There were women in Corinth, however, who were actually flinging the veils off their heads to address the assembly. This was a mark of immodesty insofar as local standards were concerned.

The wearing of the head covering by women was not so much a religious sign as it was a matrimonial sign. We unnecessarily burden ourselves with something that does not belong to us when we insist on such a covering today. If we will read the passage with care, we will notice that the covering is a distinctive mark of the wife's relationship to her husband. This relation is both a natural one and a spiritual one. It is in no sense a legal one. Since it was a matrimonial sign peculiarly necessary in the transition age of the church, surrounded as it was by paganism, it does not have the same significance for modern women.

The practice is contrasted as to its use between men and women. In verse four it says, "Every man praying or prophesying, having his head covered, dishonoreth his head." In verse five it says the opposite, "But every woman that prayeth or prophesieth with her head uncovered dishonoureth her head: for that is even all one as if she were shaven." Originally, in the Old Testament, Jewish worship decreed a head covering for men. That covering was a religious sign. It was a sign of sin, shame, and unworthiness in the presence of God, but the man of verse four is a Christian man. He is "in Christ" and his sin, shame, and unworthiness are gone. Its legalism disappeared. Instead, there is a new spiritual order of life without the inhibitions and prohibitions of legal custom.

As for the woman, her behavior is no more legalistic than is true of the man. She is not treated with a superstitious inferiority, but she is required to observe the dignity and propriety of a matrimonial sign to fit the conditions of the age in which she was then living. When the conditions ceased to exist, the sign ceased to be necessary.

The question of women's long hair, short hair or no hair was not a question of law at all, nor was it a regulation to be adhered to by women of all time. In fact, it was for Christian women alone, but only for such times as conditions required.

The significant thing about this question of what kind of hair dress and body dress one wears is its relation to the question of sin and salvation. We are not interested in the legalistic and superstitious requirements of religious regulations. We are interested in the matter from its relation to our very existence as human beings.

To begin with, clothes and fashions have a spiritual significance. The first picture of sin the Bible presents is the picture of man minus clothes. The predominating picture of salvation in the Bible presents us with the figure of man being clothed with the garments of Christ's righteousness.

Clothes were given for three reasons:

(1) *For a covering.* Sin created a human consciousness of shame, and clothes were originally given to cover that shame and give their wearer a sense of fitness and decency in the company of both God and man.

(2) *For a protection.* Clothes are a protective armor against the elements. Heat and cold, dry and wet, create conditions which jeopardize health. Clothes equalize the bodies' temperatures to climatic temperatures and give proper protection.

(3) *For an adornment.* Clothes were an attempt to make up what man had lost through sin. In the Christian life, the Scriptures speak of more adequate adornings than clothing. The Bible speaks of the adornment of character—"whose adorning . . . let it be the hidden man of the heart."

The covering is because of sin's shame. The protection is because of sin's curse. The adornment is because of sin's ugliness.

Why do people dress up? Why is it an intuitive habit to want to appear properly and attractively clothed? It is seldom answered or explained in this connection, but it is a tacit and an instinctive admission that something is missing. We lost something when we fell through sin. Men and women originally had both an internal and an external beauty of person and personality. This made artificial and external beautification unnecessary. To begin with, man was clothed with a magnificent garment of light. It was the effect of a sinless soul. But, losing that original clothing, he must be clothed with something else, hence, the universal inclination to dress up. It is man's effort to outwardly compensate for what is inwardly missing. The first garment God gave to man after his sin was a symbol of salvation, and pointed to Jesus Christ the Saviour.

Yet, fashion has no concern with this aspect of clothing. It is too often interested in encouraging sensuality rather than spirituality. It glorifies the body rather than the soul.

There is no good Christian reason why we should not appear as personally attractive as possible. This is as much the right of the Christian as another. A slovenly Christian is a poor advertisement for godliness. Yet, Christians should recognize the limits of decency in dress. It is equally as possible to be guilty of over-dressing as under-dressing. No decorous Christian will compromise faith with an indecent dress, nor need any Christian make himself ridiculously conspicuous in the other extreme. A sensible, scriptural, spiritual good taste will dictate that kind of propriety which will be both pleasing and becoming.

In natural life below, there is natural beauty in dress, in flower, bird and beast. Their beauty comes from the quality of life within. They are born with it. Among men it is different. His beauty must be put on with his clothes, cosmetics and coiffure. He is not born with it but must be born again to receive a spiritual beauty of soul and personality.

Clothes and coiffure worn for a religious reason can no more add to man's real beauty and attraction than when worn for any other reason. Christian beauty is not put on; it is put in.

This section speaks of "the glory" that is man and "the glory" that is woman. In neither case is it something artificial, created by fashion. It is something associated with God and His gifts.

For the Christian, there is a new glory—the glory of a new character and a new life. Let us not be entangled in either the extreme of religious fanaticism or the extreme of worldly extravagances. Let us fulfill our "glory" as Christians.

Archibald Rutledge relates this story:

"On a day memorable to me, I boarded a tiny tugboat that I used often in crossing a southern river and saw that we had a new Negro engineer. He sat in the doorway of the engine room reading the Bible; he was fat, squat and black, but immaculate, and in his eyes was the splendor of ancient wisdom and peace with the world. As I paused to talk with him I noticed that the characteristic odors that had always emanated from the engine room were no longer there. And the engine! It gleamed and shone; from beneath its seat all the bilge-water was gone. Instead of grime and filth and stench I found beauty and order. When I asked the engineer how in the world he had managed to clean up the old engine, he answered in words that would go far toward solving life's main problems for many people.

"'Cap'n,' he said, nodding fondly in the direction of the engine, 'It's just this way—I got a glory.'

"Making that engine the best on the river was his glory in life, and having a glory he had everything. The only sure way out of suffering that I know is to find a glory, and to give to it the strength we might otherwise spend in despair."

We have here before us one of the most important and valuable portions of Scripture.

II. The Proper Observance of the Lord's Supper. Verses 17-34.

The sacrament of the Lord's Supper is a sensible means of keeping Christ in view.

This sacrament indicates the whole scope of Christ's relationship to us. It indicates *Christ for us* in atonement. It indicates *Christ in us* by appropriation. It indicates *Christ among us* through communion. It indicates *Christ to us* in the Second Advent.

This sacrament is, as its name declares, a supper or feast. It is a Feast in *commemoration* of Christ's death. It is a Feast in *recognition* of Christ's life. It is a Feast in *proclamation* of Christ's coming.

Thus, in all these sacramental elements the Lord's Supper binds the past and the future to the present moment. It is our present communion with Christ which links us to the past as a commemoration of His death and to the future as an anticipation of His return. By these facts it is borne out in our experience, as a provision of divine grace, worthy of our most earnest and serious devotion.

1. Disorder at the Lord's Table. Verses 17-22.

"Now in this that I declare unto you I praise you not, that ye come together not for the better, but for the worse. For first of all, when ye come together in the church, I hear that there be divisions among you; and I partly believe it. For there must be also heresies among you, that they which are approved may be made manifest among you. When ye come together therefore into one place, this is not to eat the Lord's supper. For in eating every one taketh before other his own supper: and one is hungry, and another is drunken. What? have ye not houses to eat and to drink in? or despise ye the church of God, and shame them that have not? What shall I say to you? shall I praise you in this? I praise you not."

Here is a recitation of abuse. Expressed in our words it would read like this: The observance of the Lord's Supper was preceded by a common meal called the "love feast." This common meal was furnished by provisions brought by each member. The poor brought as they could while the rich brought bountifully, and all shared of the common fare. Associated as this common meal was with the sacred supper, it was considered a very solemn affair. But abuses and disorders came into its observance, as Paul states. The Corinthians brought their factional disputes into it and instead of eating it as a feast common to all, it was partaken of in a factional spirit. The rich would eat without regard to others; hence, some were hungry. The sensual would drink without regard to sobriety; hence some were drunken. It was, thereby, debauched into a disgraceful orgy of sensuality.

It was this sort of thing that Paul was rebuking. He was rebuking it because it was not a fitting prelude or preparation to the Lord's Supper. To have engaged in such a feast in this manner of excess was to be ill-prepared for the sacred supper that was to follow.

Out of this story we lift two phrases: out of verse eighteen "divisions among you;" out of verse nineteen, "heresies among you."

(1) *The divisions.* Verse 18.

"For first of all, when ye come together in the church, I hear that there be divisions among you; and I partly believe it."

This was the mark of *wrong living.* It was the case of facing a united paganism with a divided Christianity.

The kind of union which Christianity needs is not ecclesiastical union but spiritual union. It is the union of communion. It is a common union of all in one. It is a spiritual "E Pluribus Unum," or "one out of many." We can think of no place where this is to be most likely achieved than at the Lord's Table. Yet, consider this fact: it is at this table where the church is most divided. We can sing together and preach together but we will not eat together at the Lord's Table.

(2) *The heresies.* Verse 19.

"For there must be also heresies among you, that they which are approved may be made manifest among you."

This is the mark of *wrong thinking.* Thus, wrong thinking and wrong living are natural allies. They are effect and cause.

Heresy is seen to serve a purpose, however. This verse contrasts the approved discipline and the disapproved heretic.

The word heresy means opinion and the verse is translated by Weymouth to read, "For there must necessarily be differences of opinion among you in order to show who are the men of worth among you." Opinions reveal men. Our doctrine is our credential of character. Because this is so, the heresies of Corinth distinguished, by their contrast to the truth, the false heretic from the true believer. For this reason Paul states the purpose of "heresies among you." What was true of Corinth's day is true of our day. The false sects and the false opinions which are constantly present in the church serve at least one purpose. They prove the true by the presence of the false.

In consequence of these divisions and heresies, we see the irregularities of worship and the profanation of sacred things. Let no one say that it matters little what you believe so long as you do right. The soil of our deeds is our creeds. We do what we believe. If Christians were to give careful attention to their faith, their lives would react with a devotion of holiness and righteousness.

2. Order at the Lord's Table. Verses 23-34.

Let us review this section through a series of truths and consequences. Every truth has a consequence. By the same token, every error has a consequence. If we will attentively consider the profound truths of the Lord's Supper, it will produce a consequence that will extend to every department of life.

(1) *Received—Delivered*. Verse 23.

"For I have received of the Lord that which also I delivered unto you, That the Lord Jesus the same night in which he was betrayed took bread."

The truth here is that Paul received the ordinance from Christ. The consequence of the truth was its deliverance to the people. Thus, we see revelation and proclamation. We see also origin and order.

The origin of the sacrament of the Lord's Supper was not in the religious sensitiveness of Paul. He did not conceive or invent this ceremony. It was received by him and delivered through him.

The further fact of origin is that the Lord's Supper is dated. It is not a tradition carried over from a previous dispensation. It is something new and distinct. It dates from the night of Christ's betrayal and, by that fact, is recognized as a distinctly Christian service.

Thus, this sacrament was to be observed as an ordinance from the Lord. It assumed far greater significance than mere ritual. It became a means of grace that multiplied blessing to those who participated in it.

Quite recently an official organ of the Church of England stated this through one of its writers: "Worship is a work of God which of its own nature touches the depth of human feeling. Ceremonial may assist in giving an outward expression, but unless the reality itself is understood, surpliced ceremonial is apt to prove more of a spiritual smoke-screen than a cloud of glory." The purpose of ritualism and ceremonials of the non-scriptural kind is to impress people. It should be expression, and not impression.

In the sacrament of the Lord's Supper, its purpose is to express the significance of the atoning death of Christ. Unless we understand this, it is just a "spiritual smoke-screen" rather than a "cloud of glory" such as filled the Temple with the presence of God.

We see another truth and consequence in the observance of this sacrament.

(2) *Eating—Doing.* Verse 24.

"And when he had given thanks, he brake it, and said, Take eat: this is my body, which is broken for you: this do in remembrance of me."

The significance and importance of what they ate was why they ate. The bread was eaten as a "remembrance." Therefore, the sacramental feast was a memorial, and the elements of bread and cup were not the real body and blood of Christ but rather represented these to them.

The Lord's Supper grew out of the Paschal Supper which was the traditional Passover, kept as a memorial of the ancient Passover night of Egypt. The memorial character of one continues in the memorial character of the other.

The Lord's Supper originated in the midst of the Paschal Supper. Matthew says, "as they were eating," (referring to the Passover) "Jesus took bread," (referring to the new Supper.) In reality, the so-called Last Supper was not the last supper at all. The Passover was the last supper and the Lord's Supper was the first supper. The Passover was the last supper of an old dispensation. The Lord's Supper was the first of a new dispensation.

Jesus instituted the Lord's Supper in the midst of the Passover. The bread He used was the Passover bread. The cup He used was the Passover cup. The bread of the Lord's Supper was administered during the Paschal or Passover Supper, but the wine of the Lord's Supper was not given until the Paschal Supper was finished. It was "when he had supped" that Jesus gave the communion cup.

The meaning is this: since the Paschal Lamb had been a memorial of the Passover in Egypt, so the bread of the Lord's Supper was to be a memorial or "remembrance" of the body of Christ, and the cup, of the blood of Christ. The significance of the one becomes the significance of the other.

What did Jesus mean when He said, "this is my body"? Did His giving of thanks transform the molecules of the bread into the molecules of His body? Some say so. Let us take only God's Word for it.

Upon numerous occasions Jesus said something equivalent to what He said in the Upper Room. In that very room He said, "I am the vine, ye are the branches." Did He mean literally that the vine was He and the branches were they? We all know that He did not. He said, "I am the door," but He did not point to a door and say, "That door am I." Paul says in the tenth chapter of this same Epistle to the Corinthians "that Rock was Christ." Did he mean that Christ was an actual rock, hard and flinty? No, he did not. Christ had the same sacramental relationship to the Israelites in the rock that He has to us in the bread and cup.

One evening, in our home, a guest pointed to a picture on the wall and asked of me, "Who is that girl?" I replied, "Why, that is Marilyn." Did I mean that the picture was the body of my daughter? Of course I did not, no more than Jesus meant that a piece of bread was His own body. In that case He would have had several bodies, the body that reclined at the table and the body that was on the plate.

The whole supper was a representation to the physical senses for a spiritual purpose. Whoever partook of the elements was "showing forth the Lord's death till He come." We do not accomplish His death again but acknowledge His death before. We would not reproduce His body again but represent it in the memorials of the elements.

The Lord's Supper does not indicate the physical person of Christ either in or with the elements, but rather the spiritual presence of Christ. As we partake of what has been designated as His flesh and His blood, we do so by faith. Eating Christ's flesh and drinking Christ's blood are done with the mind and heart and not with the teeth and throat.

When Jesus said in the sixth chapter of John, "Whoso eateth my flesh, and drinketh my blood, hath eternal life," He meant something different from the physical eating and assimilation of physical properties. The ordinance of the Lord's Supper was not instituted until a full year later, and if it meant a physical process it meant that they would have had to wait a year for eternal life. The implication of such an interpretation is both unwarranted and impossible.

Such an interpretation of the Lord's Supper is a contradiction to our reason. "If the real body and blood of Jesus be in the bread and wine, then on the occasion of His instituting the Supper He was sitting and speaking in the midst of the disciples, while yet they were eating His flesh and drinking His blood; or He was both alive and dead at one and the same moment; or He had two bodies, His spiritual body being in the bread, and His natural body reclining on the couch; or His spiritual body was there present, while as yet, seeing He had not risen from the dead, His spiritual body was not in existence. If the real body of Christ be in the bread, then on every observance of the Supper, since they tell us that every crumb contains the whole Christ, His entire spiritual body is within less than an inch, although at His every appearance during the forty days after the resurrection His spiritual body was of the shape and size proper to a man. Then His spiritual body is both larger and less than itself, for every piece of the bread contains His whole body, yet one piece is larger or smaller than another. Then, since, according to some, the substance of bread is not there, where yet all the properties of wine are, the properties of a thing may exist without the thing in which they inhere, so that there may be whiteness without there being anything that is white; and, since, according to the Ritualist, as well as the Romanist, the substance of flesh is there where yet there is not one of the properties of flesh, and the substance of blood is there where yet there is not one of the properties of blood, a thing may exist without the properties inhering in it, as that there may be something white without there being any whiteness" (Bishop Wm. R. Nicholson).

The next time you sit at the communion table to partake of the Lord's Supper, do it with the knowledge of its meaning. Its truth will bring a glad consequence. Its meaning will engulf you with an overwhelming feeling of God's presence.

Look now at another truth and consequence to be found in this sacrament.

(3) *This cup—This do*. Verse 25.

> "After the same manner also he took the cup, when he had supped, saying, This cup is the new testament in my blood: this do ye, as oft as ye drink it, in remembrance of me."

The significance of the statement, "this cup is the new testament in my blood," is the same as attached to the statement, "this is my body." We observe here, however, that the cup is said to be "the new testament" in His blood. It does not say that the cup is His blood but rather that it is a new testament. His blood is the seal of His new covenant. The new covenant is ratified by His blood. Every covenant, testament or will must be ratified by a seal of state. The ratification of the new Christian order of life came through Christ's death by Christ's blood.

Now will you notice that it speaks of a new covenant. It was new in point of time. It was new in nature. It was new in its provisions. It was new in substance. This new scheme of life was brought into existence by Christ. It meant a new life, a new nature, a new destiny, and a new world for all who were beneficiaries of its provisions.

This covenant was ratified upon the divine side by the *blood-seal* of Christ. It is ratified and realized on the human side by the *faith-seal* of the believer. Thus, whenever we partake sensibly of the Lord's Supper, we are partaking spiritually of the provisions of the new covenant.

(4) *As often—Ye do show.* Verse 26.

> "For as often as ye eat this bread, and drink this cup, ye do shew the Lord's death till he come."

The consequence of a faithful and truthful observance of this sacrament would be the manifestation or publication or proclamation of Christ's death. In doing this it would be bearing witness to two things: first, Christ's death; second, Christ's return. Thus, it is a memorial and a prophecy. It is the proclamation of what has happened and the promise of what will yet happen. It is a witness to the twofold ministry of Christ; His ministry as Saviour and His ministry as Sovereign. In the face of this it takes religious chicanery to observe the sacrament of the Lord's Supper while denying the certainty of the Lord's return.

(5) *Unworthily—Guilty.* Verses 27-34.

> "Wherefore whosoever shall eat this bread, and drink this cup of the Lord, unworthily, shall be guilty of the body and blood of the Lord. But let a man examine himself, and so let him eat of that bread, and drink of that cup. For he that eateth and drinketh unworthily, eateth and drinketh damnation to himself, not discerning the Lord's body. For this cause many are weak and sickly among you, and many sleep. For if we would judge ourselves, we should not be judged. But when we are judged, we

are chastened of the Lord, that we should not be condemned with the world. Wherefore, my brethren, when ye come together to eat, tarry one for another. And if any man hunger, let him eat at home; that ye come not together unto condemnation. And the rest will I set in order when I come."

Just what was it that Paul meant by unworthiness in partaking of the sacrament? It was not only personal from the standpoint of the participant's fitness but it was personal from the standpoint of the manner of participation. It was not only those who participated but the way they participated.

As for *the participant,* he would be eating and drinking unworthily when he failed in his personal life and used the sacrament as a cloak of hypocrisy.

As for *the participation,* they would be eating and drinking unworthily when they profaned the sacrament by making it a common feast for eating and drinking.

We are all unworthy in the negative sense of our shortcomings and failures. None of us would qualify for a place at this Table on the basis of virtue. It is not this negative unworthiness that is meant here. It is deliberate, conscious, positive, and present sin that is meant. To fail in these things would be to bring guilt upon us. It would make us "guilty of the body and blood of the Lord." This is the guilt of a fresh crucifixion of Christ.

Every prospective participant of the sacrament should take the preventive measure of examining himself. He is to scrutinize both himself and his conduct. He is to prove himself. This does not mean that one needs to chastise his conscience with all sorts of accusations. It does mean that he is to be able to have the approval of his conscience in respect to both his motives and his conduct.

There is altogether too little of this individual inspection. We partake of the sacrament with a glibness that approximates Corinthian profanation. It ought to be the most solemn moment of our Christian devotions. It ought to be regarded with the deepest personal concern.

Consider here the purpose and object of the Lord's Supper. Its purpose is not to accomplish something in and for the believer. We do not go to the Lord's Table to do something for ourselves. It is not a sacrament for us, but something for Christ. It is to "show the Lord's death till he come." Yet, many people view the Lord's Supper as a means of salvation or as a means of personal fitness. The fitness determines our right to the table. Personal salvation is the credential we have for partaking of its elements. It is a memorial to Christ. Naturally, its proper observance results in blessing to the participant. Yet, we must not lose sight of its object and purpose.

The profanation of the sacrament brings damnation to the guilty one. For the Corinthians, this judgment was very real. The failure to discern the Lord's body brought distress to their bodies. It resulted in physical chastisement, bringing disease and death. Spiritual disease out of their unhealthy souls resulted in physical disease. This was no mere figure of speech. It was actual disease and actual death.

If this judgment of disease and death came to the Corinthians for their profanation of the sacrament, will it also come upon us? The answer is very plain and simple. Yes, but only if and when we are guilty of the same profanation. If and when we make the Lord's Table a place of gluttony and drunkenness, we can expect the same judgment. This judgment does not fall on individuals who may inadvertently come to the Lord's Table with minor faults and failures. There is no occasion for people of tender conscience to feel themselves in imminent peril because it was a punishment applied to a specific kind of sin. It is a kind of sin which is specifically named and easily identified. Until you are guilty of that kind of sin, you need not fear this kind of judgment.

Whenever such judgment came, it was brought for a good purpose. It is so stated in the thirty-second verse, "But when we are judged, we are chastened of the Lord, that we should not be condemned with the world." Chastisement is for correction, not for punishment. God does not punish His people.

He corrects them. Even in the extreme case of premature death, it was to spare them the fate of the world's condemnation. There was a benevolent purpose behind this seemingly drastic action.

With this, we are led to the Lord's Table in the spirit of humility through self-inspection. We shall then leave the Lord's Table under the stimulus of a great inspiration.

SECTION THREE

THE DIVINE OBJECTIVES OF THE CHRISTIAN

CHAPTER XII

THE CHRISTIAN AND GIFTS

I *Corinthians* 12

IN THE ensuing message of Paul, which completes his letter to the Corinthian Christians, the emphasis is not discontinued as far as the church collective is concerned. It has as much to do with the church as before. However, it is more personal so far as the individual Christian is concerned. In other words, it is to the individual Christian in the collective church. This is beautifully expressed in 12:27 where it says, "Now ye are the body of Christ, and members in particular." It does not lose sight of the church but considers the "members in particular." For this reason we speak of the rest of the chapters of the book as containing the divine objectives of the Christian.

If in the previous section we saw the gospel in relation to *church policy*, we see it in this section in relation to *Christian practice*. It is now less a matter of church policy but it is more particularly a matter of Christian practice.

I. THE PURPOSE OF GIFTS. Verses 1-3.

"Now concerning spiritual gifts, brethren, I would not have you ignorant. Ye know that ye were Gentiles, carried away unto these dumb idols, even as ye were led. Wherefore I give you to understand, that no man speaking by the Spirit of God calleth Jesus accursed: and that no man can say that Jesus is the Lord, but by the Holy Ghost."

It is evident that the keynote of this chapter and many Bible chapters for that matter, is to be found in the words of the first verse, "I would not have you ignorant." Ignorance is the breeding place of two vicious extremes, heresy and fanaticism. Both of these had sprung up in Corinth, and both were the result of ignorance. One does not need to be either a heretic or a fanatic. In fact, most heretics are intellectually informed people who are lacking in one of two particulars of knowledge.

Christianity recommends itself to human intelligence. It is a common-sense religion. It is sane and well-balanced. Heretics make it appear to be *unreasonable* while fanatics make it appear to be *unbalanced*. It is neither.

While Christianity is a reasonable faith, we must not lose sight of another fact. There are elements in it which transcend reason. In such places faith carries on where reason leaves off. If this were not so, and if it were understandable in all its parts, it would cease to be a divine system and prove itself to be a human invention. This is its highest recommendation as the supreme truth of God and the superior way of life.

Christianity must not only pass an intelligence test but a spiritual one. This spiritual test is not a mysterious metaphysical thing which is intangible. It is something which every Christian can apply to himself. For this reason Paul reminds the Corinthians that once they were devotees of idolatry; they worshipped dumb idols which could not speak; they were not only inarticulate but they were associated with a vast system of soothsaying and witchcraft. These priests of paganism claimed divine inspiration and supernatural powers, but it was evident that their gods were impotent to help them because they were dumb.

How then could one authoritatively distinguish between the priests of paganism and the apostles of Christianity? How could one prove the falsity of the claims of pagans and the truthfulness of the claims of Christians? How could one show the foolishness of idols and the reasonableness of God? How? By the inner witness which each Christian possessed. Paul states, "I give you to understand that no man speaking by the Spirit of God calleth Jesus accursed: and that no man can say that Jesus is the Lord, but by the Holy Ghost."

Here are two opposing tests. In those days they were the contending cries of two opposing peoples. The one, "Jesus is accursed," was the cry of the pagans, the epithet they hurled at the church. It was the cry of hatred and animosity. The other, "Jesus is Lord," was the cry of the Christians which they hurled back at the pagans. It was faith's reply to unbelief. It was light's answer to darkness. It was heaven's challenge to hell. It meant a line of demarcation between people. Whoever said, "Jesus is accursed," was on the one side. Whoever said, "Jesus is Lord," was on the other side.

To have been on either side was more than a difference of opinion. It meant a difference of possession, a difference of life and character. To have said, "Jesus is accursed," meant that one did not possess the Holy Spirit for "no man speaking by the Spirit of God calleth Jesus accursed." To have said, "Jesus is Lord," meant that one possessed the Holy Spirit, for "no man can say that Jesus is the Lord, but by the Holy Ghost."

This indicated a fundamental difference in life, character, and destiny. It meant that Christians are not identified by names or by creeds or by churches. They are identified by the presence and possession of the Holy Spirit. The Holy Spirit is God present among men. Jesus said, "I will pray the Father, and he shall give you another Comforter, that he may abide with you forever." It is this One who is like Christ that makes the difference between paganism and Christianity. In other words, it is a human being's vital relationship to God in new life by the new birth.

Be sure we understand by this scripture that the Holy Spirit is not one who is received after the new birth but rather at the new birth. It is He in our lives who makes us Christians. We can not even give witness to the Lordship of Christ except by His presence in us. His presence in us makes us Christians. His possession of us makes us both witnessing and working Christians.

This is the significance of the chapter before us. It is the *gift* of the Holy Spirit received *by us* which results in the *gifts* of the Holy Spirit *through us*. We cannot have the gifts without the gift. The gift of the Holy Spirit is something accomplished when we became Christians. The gifts of the Holy Spirit are the result of the Lordship of Christ over us. It is one thing to know Christ as Saviour. It is another thing to know Christ as Lord. The gift of the Holy Spirit comes at conversion. The gifts of the Holy Spirit come through consecration. Thus, one might possess the gift without the gifts. It is the purpose of this teaching to remind us of the individual Christian s place in the plan of God for this age and this world, and then to equip him for that place.

To define the purpose of the gifts is a matter of one sentence. It is to exalt Christ. Whatever the gift we possess, either ordinary or extraordinary, its purpose is to set forth Christ in the majesty of His Lordship. The gifts of Christian ability are never bestowed for the exaltation of their possessor. They are to reflect in him the power and beauty of Christ. It is when we prostitute the gifts for personal aggrandizement that we misuse them.

In considering the various spiritual gifts which were present in the early church, it will occur to some to ask why these same gifts are not present in the same proportion in the modern church. The answer is simply this—the same occasion and the same purpose do not exist.

The occasion for the early gifts was the establishment of the church. The purpose was not only a demonstration of the unique character of Christianity as a divine means of salvation but also an equipment of the early Christians for the quick propagation of the gospel in a pagan world.

It would not be true to say that these gifts have entirely and completely ceased. Wherever an occasion exists for their need, there they may be expected.

In the modern church, faced with the task of maintaining its place in a sophisticated world, we should have the right to expect a reasonable display of the divine presence and power in the propagation of the gospel. The reason why we may not have it lies in the condition of the church. It is divided by disunity and has so professionalized its ministry that its members are merely spectators. Hence, an idle spectator membership has neither need nor place for the exercise of the gifts of Christian service.

Another thing should be borne in mind. The gifts mentioned here were not acquired; they were bestowed. These people did not develop them; they received them. The reason for this is obvious. The emergency demanded their quick bestowment. They were immediately needed in the presence of an overwhelming paganism. Furthermore, these people were without the written Scriptures through which knowledge and ability comes by contact. Hence, they needed what they could not otherwise receive.

It can be readily seen that the same situation does not exist today. We are told to "study to show thyself approved unto God." We are told to "grow in grace and in the knowledge of our Lord and Saviour Jesus Christ." We are told that "all scripture is given by inspiration of God, and is profitable for doctrine, for reproof, for correction, for instruction in righteousness: That the man of God may be perfect, throughly furnished unto all good works" (II Tim. 3:16,17).

We can say, then, that for us in our day it is not the case of receiving universally the gifts in the early church, but rather their providential bestowment for specific cases and conditions; also the enhancing and blessing of the talents and abilities of a regenerated personality by the indwelling of the Holy Spirit through the study and application of the holy Scriptures.

In our day the Holy Spirit operates through the instrumentality of the Scriptures. In the early church the Scriptures were not yet present; hence, the direct bestowment of gifts was necessary for the propagation of the Christian faith. The way for attainment of the modern Christian is "study."

II. THE DIVERSITY OF GIFTS. Verses 4-31.

   1. The Gifts of the Spirit. Verses 4-11.

     (1) *Unity in the source of the gifts.* Verses 4-7.

> "Now there are diversities of gifts, but the same Spirit. And
> there are differences of administrations, but the same Lord. And
> there are diversities of operations, but it is the same God which
> worketh all in all. But the manifestation of the Spirit is given to
> every man to profit withal."

There are many gifts but one Giver. There are various talents but one source.

Here we see the Trinity present in the administration of the Church. In verse four—"diversities of gifts but the same Spirit." This is God, the *Holy Spirit.* In verse five—"differences of administrations but the same Lord." This is *God, the Son.* In verse six—"diversities of operations but the same God." This is *God, the Father.* Thus, we see many human capabilities but one divine source.

There is also to be seen here a unity of purpose in the object for which the gifts are given as expressed in verse seven. Here were gifts for human good. Their object was the good and benefit of man. All men were intended to profit from gifts that might have been given to a few men. These gifts were never intended for the monopoly of their possessors. God gave them for the blessing of all.

     (2) *Diversity in the operation of the gifts.* Verses 8-11.

In these verses you will find three sets of gifts with three gifts in each set.

     a. The gifts of the intellect. Verses 8,9.

They are "wisdom," "knowledge," "faith." They are a perfect triad. Wisdom is given first, knowledge next, with faith, third. Wisdom is the ability to use knowledge to the best advantage. Some have knowledge without wisdom. All need faith to make wisdom and knowledge practical. In this case the gift of faith does not mean a disposition to believe, such as one has at conversion. It means the doing and daring of faith. It means the ability to expect great things from God and attempt great things for God.

George Mueller had such a gift of faith, and what was peculiar to George Mueller none of us should attempt to copy. Not all have the gift of faith. We do not believe that all can have the gift of faith. These gifts were not given to all, but as it specifically states to "one" and "another." In fifty years George Mueller received and disbursed six and one-half million dollars in his great orphanage work at Bristol, England. He received this money without telling a single human being any item of need. It was done through prayer.

A parallel case was that of J. Hudson Taylor who founded the China Inland Mission. He did it without asking for money or telling men of his needs. Yet, God enabled him to send hundreds of missionaries to China. That mission continues as it was commenced.

Manifestly, these were gifts of faith. It would be a mistake, as many have since proved, to try to do Mueller's work without Mueller's faith. This faith belongs to those to whom God chooses to give it and not to those who covet it. Many covet Mueller's faith but do not have Mueller's faithfulness.

You notice that this set of three gifts which apply particularly to reason and intelligence is mentioned first. They lead all the rest. It is so because they are the highest and best of the spiritual gifts. Christianity is best represented by such Christians as have wisdom, knowledge, and faith. It is best promoted under the stimulus of intelligence, reason, and the spiritual power generated by faith.

In spite of this, the Corinthians coveted, not the first and best gifts, but, instead, the last and least gifts. They went into the realm of emotional extravagances. They followed the line of least resistance. They gave expression to their feelings instead of giving exercise to their faith. Because their Christian experience was not lived on the solid basis of a practical, reasonable, sensible spirituality, but on emotional carnality, we account for the shortcomings of the Corinthian Church.

Let us have in our lives the gifts not only in their place but in their proportion. Let there be wisdom for our knowledge. Let there also be faith for our wisdom and knowledge. Intellectuality without spirituality results in carnality. Reason without the counterbalancing of faith will give a cold, calculating Christianity without either warmth or feeling or daring.

The vital part of our Christianity is not altogether what we think about it but what we do about it. Faith puts doing into our thinking.

The gifts of the Spirit are desired far more than the graces of the Spirit. Yet, the graces of the Spirit belong to Christian experience fully as much and, for this age, I believe, more than the gifts.

It is significant that there are nine gifts of the Spirit and nine graces of the Spirit.

It would be a spiritual tragedy to possess the gifts without the graces. These graces are the fruits of the Spirit: "Love, joy, peace, longsuffering, gentleness, goodness, faith, meekness, temperance."

The gifts are for service while the graces are for character. The gifts come by grace while the graces come by growth. The graces consist of sanctified dispositions while the gifts are sanctified abilities. To whatever proportion God may see fit to bestow upon us these gifts, let us be sure that our spiritual growth keeps pace with our spiritual privileges. Let us not be as the Corinthians were, rich in gifts but poor in graces.

b. The gifts of the will. Verses 9, 10.

They are "healing," "miracles," "prophecy." They are the directive and volitional gifts. They demand the exercise of boldness and the projection of our faith.

"*Healing*" is a gift which produces miraculous cures. That there were such cures in the church is a matter of record.

That there can be such cures in the church one dare not deny. That these cures will be affected to the same extent as they once were is open to serious question. In fact, they do not occur as they once did. One has a right to question whether anyone in the modern church has this gift of healing. If we inquire of any who claim to have the gift of healing, we will find that their healing formula requires the sick person first to be a Christian and, second, to possess faith. New Testament healings required neither. The healing was not produced by any virtue in the healed but entirely by the gift of the healer.

"*Miracles*" is a gift which produces "energies of supernatural power." It is something not opposed to natural law, but not accounted for in our present understanding of natural law. The sudden changing of water into wine by a word from Christ was no more opposed to natural law than the gradual changing of soil into grapes by a process of nature. One required an alteration in the usual operation of natural law, but that is certainly not impossible with the Author of the laws found in nature. Who are we to tell God what He can do? It is only our educated ignorance and our religious unbelief that deny this fact.

Miracles are possible when they are necessary. God is the one to determine whether they are necessary. None of us can command a miracle just because we want it. It will come when God wills it. While miracles are possible, they are not probable. That is, they are not to be expected to the same extent as was true in the days when miracles were the credentials of faith and the proof of the truth of Christianity.

While we dare not say that providential miracles have ceased, we are safe in saying that evidential miracles have ceased. Miracles of grace are possible every day while the miracles of the gifts are not probable in our day.

"*Prophecy*" is a gift which produces "inspired oratory." This gift was not the ability to forecast the future. The gift of prophecy was, in substance, the gift of preaching. It was preaching with the compulsion of divine authority. It dared to challenge the oracles of paganism. It did not unravel the future for man's gaze, but it revealed the will of God for man's present duty. It gave with inspired authority, warnings, rebukes, encouragements and exhortations. It was the powerful means through which multitudes in paganism turned to Christianity and found shelter in its fold of faith.

These three gifts were proper in their order to the first three. Whoever possessed wisdom, knowledge, and faith was fitted to exercise the gifts of healing, miracles, and prophecy. Such vast and wonderful power as is represented in healing, miracles and prophecy would be unsafe except in the hands of wisdom, knowledge and faith.

c. The gifts of the emotions. Verse 10.

They are "discerning of spirits," "divers tongue," "interpretation of tongues."

"Discerning of spirits" is a gift which provides "the faculty of detecting the truth or falsity of any inspiration." The gift was particularly necessary in the days of Corinth. There the pagan oracles claimed supernatural powers. These were reproduced satanically among the early Christians as counterfeits. A gift of discernment could detect the spurious from the true. More than this, it could distinguish between the real and imaginary possession of spiritual gifts among Christians. It conducted a spiritual intelligence service. It kept the early church from being overrun with fictitious claimants to spiritual power. It prevented the corruption and pollution of Christianity with all kinds of false and spurious manifestations of spiritual wonder. In other words, by this gift of discernment they kept the ship on an even keel in strange and storm-tossed waters.

"Divers tongues" is the gift which gives ability to speak in varieties of speech. There has been a great deal of speculation and hair splitting about the nature of these tongues. Simplicity, however, is the best solution.

On the day of Pentecost we have the most conspicuous example of this gift. Of what did it consist? Was it some weird, nonsensical gibberish that was both nauseating to decency and insulting to intelligence? The record says, as to the cause, "They were all filled with the Holy Ghost and began to speak with other tongues as the Spirit gave them utterance." The record also says, as to the effect, "The multitude came together and was confounded because every man heard them speak in his own language." These tongues were not unknown languages, for it gives a list of the various people present in Jerusalem.

The gift of tongues, then, was not an emotional gibberish but a genuine linguistic ability imparted to the apostles and disciples of the infant church for the purpose of presenting the gospel in languages they had never learned.

Its purpose, as you can readily see, was unique. The world was without a written Scripture. It needed a quick and speedy evangelization which was made possible through this gift. As far as we know, this gift does not genuinely exist today although a spurious and counterfeit emotionalism makes claims to it.

"*Interpretation of tongues*" is the gift to interpret a language one had never heard, as in the previous gift it was the ability to speak a language one had never learned.

The trouble in Corinth was the abuse of these latter three gifts. They were carried to emotional extremes. They were prostituted for personal satisfaction. In fact, their assemblies became a disgrace, for they were filled with unrestrained orgies of emotionalism and disorder. The use of the gift of tongues became everything it was not intended to be. It degenerated into ecstatic trances in which intelligence was suspended and the speaker poured forth an ecstatic language accompanied by uncontrolled feelings. In no case does any genuine Christian experience put the Christian into a trance or suspend intelligence. Anything that does is counterfeit and false Christianity. That is why the three gifts of wisdom, knowledge, and faith lead the rest. And it was because the Corinthians reversed the order that they became emotionally mired in excesses and extravagances. Let us begin where the Scriptures begin and we shall never end in Corinthian extravagance.

The last verse of this section reads, "But all these worketh that one and the selfsame Spirit, dividing to every man severally as he will," verse eleven. The gifts are not divided to every man but rather to every man severally. All do not receive the same. They are distributed according to divine discretion. In this case all are not expected or intended to have the gift of faith, healing or tongues. It is by divine discretion and not by human desire. The initiating and originating source was this "selfsame Spirit." They were to be desired by all, but they were received only by divine disposal and bestowment. It was according "as He will," and not as we want. If we, as a church, had observed this forgotten fact, we would have saved ourselves much fanaticism and heartache. Let us distinguish between the Pentecostal version of tongues and the Corinthian perversion of tongues.

At Pentecost, people tarried for the gift of the Holy Spirit, but no one ever rightly tarries for the gifts of the Holy Spirit, nor does one ever rightly tarry now for the Holy Spirit. He is here. He has been given. He is a fact and not a promise. Act on what has happened.

The presence of the gifts of the Spirit is followed by an illustration of the place of these gifts and their operation in the collective body of the church. The individual gifts of believers are now shown in their relation to the church as a whole. The church is likened to a body and the believers are likened to members of that body. Thus, the individual member is revealed in his relation to all other members.

2. The Gifts in the Church. Verses 12, 13.

We observe here that the previous gifts have a special application to the Christian as members of the Body of Christ.

They are not given for individual benefit but for the blessing of all. We are not little planets of personality revolving in our own special sphere of privilege but are bound by the laws of spiritual gravitation to a central Son around whom we revolve in unison and precision. Some Christians act like comets blazing a trail of selfish glory across the sky. Comets never last. They soon burn out and are lost to sight, while the planets go on forever.

(1) *The unity of the body.* Verse. 12.

> "For as the body is one, and hath many members, and all the members of that one body, being many, are one body: so also is Christ."

Here we are reminded that the gifts operate in believers as members operate in a body. The hand has one operation. The eye has another operation. The ear has yet another diverse operation, but all the diversity becomes a unity, for the whole body functions as one. The body does not function as many members but many members function as one body.

The apostle makes this observation, "so also is Christ." He links the body to Christ. We are members of Christ when we are members of the body. We function through Christ when we function in the body. There is a grand and imposing unity in the whole Christian system of life. Let us understand it and we shall live and labor more effectively.

(2) *The entrance into the body.* Verse 13.

> "For by one Spirit are we all baptized into one body, whether we be Jews or Gentiles, whether we be bond or free; and have been made to drink into one Spirit."

Here the baptism of the Holy Spirit is described in the present tense. It is declared to be a present fact in every believer. It is not a promise held out to us if we wait long enough and pray hard enough and believe strong enough. Just as the gift of the Holy Spirit is an accomplished fact of history, so the baptism of the Holy Spirit is an accomplished fact of experience.

The Bible declares us also to be born of the Spirit. This is the new birth. Thus, we are not only born of the Spirit but we are baptized by the Spirit. When we are born of the Spirit, the life of God comes into us. When we are baptized by the Spirit, we are put into the Body of Christ. When the baptism of the Spirit is spoken of today people think of it as something that comes into them. That is not so. It is we who are put into something.

Being born of the Spirit gives us a new life. Being baptized by the Spirit gives us a new place. This new place is in the Body of Christ. Both the birth and the baptism are simultaneous but they are not similar. There was a time, however, when there were people who were born again of the Spirit but were not indwelt by the Spirit. Pentecost came to accomplish this, and ever since, one's birth of the Spirit has meant one's baptism by the Spirit.

The result of this baptism is not said here to be speaking in tongues, or ecstatic experiences. It meant a common unity. Jews were no longer Jews as such. Gentiles were no longer Gentiles as such. Slaves were no longer slaves as such. All lost their former standing in the flesh and all found a new standing in the Spirit. There were, henceforth, no castes nor classes. There was a new oneness of life and identity.

A further result of this baptism by the Spirit was not an organization but an organism. It resulted in the forming of a body—the Body of Christ. Our trouble today is the tendency to try to organize life into various religious forms when we should be organisms which impart life by spiritual propagation.

A still further result was unison of life in the one Spirit. They were "all made to drink into one Spirit." That is, through this baptism all become partakers of the Spirit. Here was a new source of life and power. Here was a new attachment. The initial experience of a believer is the baptism by the Spirit. The continual experience of a believer should be the filling of the Spirit. There can only be one baptism. There may be many fillings. There is no place in the Bible where we are commanded to be baptized by the Spirit. Yet, we are commanded to be filled with the Spirit. The baptism gives us our place in the Body of Christ while the filling gives us power and strength to fill that place. It is not the baptism we need to seek but the filling which we may now enjoy.

The result of the baptism was spiritual gifts while the result of the filling is spiritual graces. Spiritual gifts are nowhere, either in Scripture or life, a proof of superior spiritual life. Yet consider how anxiously and eagerly people seek these spectacular gifts while paying scant heed to the graces.

Christians talk of the baptism by the Spirit in terms of emotion. The Bible speaks of it in terms of devotion. We hold no brief for an emotionless Christianity. We believe in the emotions but not out of proportion to their place. We know many people who would rather express their emotions than exhibit a genuine devotion to the real and practical elements of the Christian life. This was precisely the wrong of Corinth. Its Christians were exaggerating the importance of expressional Christianity, while they were failing to display those gifts and graces that would give the best demonstration of what Christianity actually is.

To determine the ultimate purpose of this "baptism" and its consequent and recurrent "filling," we have but to inquire as to the purpose of the coming of the Holy Spirit. It was, as you know, to exalt Jesus Christ. It was to continue Christ's ministry both in us and through us. Our baptism into Christ's body means the Spirit's presence in our body. His presence there is to produce Christlikeness. It is to endow us with gifts and graces that will furnish us with both ability and character for the beautiful life.

The view that is presented to us of collective Christians as a church, is not of a great mechanized organization which has been artificially created and increased by the additions of years and occasions. It is rather the picture of an organism which has had birth and growth, organs, feelings, and functions.

This Church was not the result of religious development. It was not produced by the decisions of men. It came into being by a spiritual process technically called "baptism." Through this process we are joined into one body and become its functional and organic members.

This Church, which is the body, is not the exclusive possession of any particular people. In fact, men have nothing to say about entrance into this body of believers. This is the prerogative of the Holy Spirit. Having once entered the body by birth and baptism, we function in the given sphere of our membership.

The membership spoken of here is not creedal membership but organic membership, for "the body is not one member but many." It is our individual relationship to collective Christianity within the organism of Christ's body.

The membership of this mystical body of Christ is being addressed for the purpose of indicating its inter-related capacities and functions. It is asked to look at itself not as a body alone but as individual parts as well. These parts are to consider themselves in relation to every other part and are to adjust themselves in both spirit and service so that the whole body will function with precision.

3. The Harmony of the Body. Verses 14 - 26.

Two faults are spoken of.

(1) *Envying.* Verses 14 - 20.

"For the body is not one member, but many. If the foot shall say, Because I am not the hand, I am not of the body; is it therefore not of the body? And if the ear shall say, Because I am not the eye, I am not of the body; is it therefore not of the body? If the whole body were an eye, where were the hearing? If the whole were hearing, where were the smelling? But now hath God set the members every one of them in the body, as it hath pleased him. And if they were all one member, where were the body? But now are they many members, yet but one body."

Paul illustrates his meaning by singling out the foot and the ear of a normal physical body and suggests how foolish it would be if the foot, becoming jealous of the hand, should refuse to function as a foot.

The foot being at the lower extremity of the body is in a humble place. It must be covered, and walk over hard sidewalks and stony pavements. It must bear the weight of every other member. The hand, however, is very different. It is more delicately organized than the foot. The hand is a masterpiece. It consists of five small levers suspended to the extremity of the arm by tendons. The thumb faces every one of the other fingers. All are intricately connected with muscles and nerves to perform the most delicate operations. The hand holds the surgeon's knife, the artist's brush and the sculptor's chisel. It is the delicate implement of musician and craftsman. It is always in a prominent place. It is always exposed and in the forefront of action. Suppose now the humble foot, becoming envious of the prominent hand, should refuse to function in its sphere. In that case the function of the hand would be either lost or limited. No, the hand requires the foot.

The same is true of the ear and the eye. Not all the body is for seeing; nor all for hearing. In its various functions the seeing is necessary to the hearing and the hearing necessary to the seeing.

The application of this illustration falls upon individual Christians in their relation to collective Christians. So it is said in verse eighteen, "But now hath God set the members everyone of them in the body, as it hath pleased him." The principle of this placing is "as it hath pleased him." We do not choose our places; we fill them. Here is the solemn truth that follows: if we do not fill our place, no one can do it for us. Others have their place. This they must fill. You have your place. Your responsibility is to fill it or there is a collective loss if you fail.

No one should belittle his place or demean himself. Your place may not be mine, but in relation to mine your place is just as important. It may not be as prominent but prominence is not the issue. It is performance. The most important functional organs of the human body are hidden and never seen. It is undoubtedly true in the spiritual body of Christ. Great names do not always mean the greatest places. Dare to fill your place with a dignity and loyalty that befits one who is a child of God.

At whatever time you are tempted to covet the more prominent places and desire to invade another member's sphere and become inordinately jealous of others' capabilities, think of this: "God set the members, everyone of them in the body, as it pleased him." He has set you where you are. Do not desire to be someone else or somewhere else, but rather to be better and more noble and efficient in the place of His pleasure. There is plenty of room for expansion and promotion and improvement in His place for you.

(2) *Despising*. Verses 21-26.

"And the eye cannot say unto the hand, I have no need of thee: nor again the head to the feet, I have no need of you. Nay, much more those members of the body, which seem to be more feeble, are necessary: And those members of the body, which we think to be less honourable, upon these we bestow more abundant honour; and our uncomely parts have more abundant comeliness. For our comely parts have no need: but God hath tempered the body together, having given more abundant honour to that part which lacked: That there should be no schism in the body; but that the members should have the same care one for another. And whether one member suffer, all the members suffer with it; or one member be honoured, all the members rejoice with it."

Previously, it was the case of the lesser coveting the greater. Here it is the case of the greater. Here it is the case of the greater despising the lesser. The eye dare not despise the hand, nor the head the foot. The prosperity of the whole body depends upon the harmonious co-operation of the lesser with the greater. Eyes cannot get along without hands. Heads cannot function efficiently without feet. If we remembered this dependent relationship, we would have a more charitable attitude to one another.

All parts of the human body contribute a series of interrelated functions. The ear aids the eye and the foot, the hand. The use of speech has resulted in the development of the brain. Without the lips the brain could not make its thoughts known. Without the hands the brain would be impotent. So with the lesser members of the Body of Christ. They are equally important in their place. Therefore, let not the more prominent members despise the more obscure.

Paul speaks of those parts of the body which are "more feeble" as being more necessary. This is so because these lesser members give articulation and mobility to the greater members. The eye could not get along without the hand because the hand does what the eyes sees should be done. The head could not get along without the feet because the feet go where the brain directs. In this sense they are more necessary for they make the execution of the executive operations of the body possible.

Transferring this into our Christian relationships, we need to consider the indispensability of these so-called "feeble" members. They are not feeble inherently but functionally. Their functions appear unnecessary. They discharge their duties only in co-ordination with the rest of the members of the Body of Christ. Your hand is as strong as your head. Your eye is as keen as your brain. Your feet are as mobile as your head. Each of us depends upon the other. No person is so feeble as to be indispensable. It is imperative that we consider ourselves in relation to our place. Our tendency is to think of ourself as individuals. We do not see how necessary we are to carry out the co-operative function of the Body of Christ. Determine to fill your place with faithfulness. Be what you are. Be that thing in the strength of Christ.

The thought conveyed in the immediate verses has to do with the Christian's charitable attitude to fellow-believers who may not occupy such a prominent place or perform such a necessary function. Paul reminds them that in our bodies one member compensates for the defects or disabilities of another member. There is a remarkable adaptation constantly going on in the human body between its various members. This adaptive compensation is entirely automatic. When one half of a thyroid gland is removed, the remaining half increases in volume. Whenever thereafter the body calls upon the thyroid gland for an exceptional effort, this organ will be capable of satisfying the demands made upon it. When the degeneration of blood takes place after a hemorrhage, a remarkable adaptive function is carried on. First, all the blood vessels contract, causing the relative volume of the remaining blood to be increased. This has the effect of maintaining sufficient blood pressure for blood circulation. Immediately thereafter the person feels intense thirst and the blood absorbs the fluids sent to the stomach so as to re-establish its normal volume. Then the reserve red cells escape from the organs where they were stored against such an emergency as this. Finally, the bone marrow begins manufacturing red corpuscles which will complete the regeneration of the blood. For this process the whole body must co-operate and without it, it would suffer.

Notice verses twenty-two and twenty-three. Compare them with Arthur S. Way's translation: "Those parts of the body which we look upon as the more ignoble, these we ennoble with more beautiful clothing. Our ungraceful parts, in fact, are adorned with more special grace, whereas our graceful parts need no adorning."

The thing Paul is saying is this, if there is a part of our body which is disfigured or misshapen or marred, we treat it with special consideration. If it is a malformed ear it is hidden by a considerate hair-dress. If it is a mutilated hand, it is kept covered out of sight. If one hand is atrophied or paralyzed the other hand compensates for its disability. If one eye is reduced in vision, the other eye increases in power.

For this reason Paul goes on to say in verses 24 and 25, (Way): "God in fact has made a composite whole of the body, assigning special honor to the part which naturally lacks it, so that there may be no divided interests in the body and that its various organs may be united in solicitous care for each other's welfare."

The hand is a graceful member of the body and needs no adornment. The top of the head is covered with beautiful hair, soft, silky, and wavy. This is provided because a bald head is unattractive and if hair were not provided, we would look very odd and queer with our shiny pates.

The same consideration should be found in the Body of Christ. Those members which are less comely and seem to be less honorable, whose places or abilities are less attractive and perfected than yours, perhaps, should be regarded with charitable consideration.

Not all preachers are Spurgeons. Not all singers are Sankeys. Not all are masterful musicians and great teachers.

This applies to defects of personality. When the hair lacks order, the hand puts it there. One member covers up the shortcomings of another member. Is that true among Christians? Do we cover up or expose? It is a mark of spiritual perfection to draw the veil of silence where accusation might be made. It is best to treat with kindness the blemishes of another. Let us hide the scars with tears. Let us make beautiful that which may be ugly.

> "Could we only draw the curtain
>   That surrounds each others' lives—
> See the naked heart and spirit,
>   Know what spur to action drives;
> Often we should find it better,
>   Purer than we judge we should,
> We should love each other better
>   If we only understood.

> "If we knew the cares and trials—
>   Knew the efforts all in vain,
> And the bitter disappointments,
>   Understood the loss and gain;
> Would the grim, external roughness,
>   Seem, I wonder, just the same?
> Should we help, where now we hinder?
>   Should we pity, when we blame?"

If our physical instincts teach us consideration and thoughtfulness for our physical members, then our spiritual characteristics teach us their equivalent in Christian relations. We should be constructive and not destructive. Christians of varying attainments and weaknesses have been placed in a spiritual body so that the strong and more self-sustaining members might treat them with consideration.

> "I watched them tearing a building down—
> A gang of men in a busy town:
> With a 'Ho heave ho' and a lusty yell,
> They swung a beam and the side wall fell.
> I asked the foreman: 'Are these men skilled,
> And the kind you would hire if you were to build?
> He laughed and said: 'Why no, indeed;
> Just common laborers is all I need:
> They can easily wreck in a day or two
> That which has taken builders years to do.'
> So I said to myself, as I went on my way:
> What part in the game of life do I play?
> Am I shaping my deeds to a well-made plan,
> Carefully measuring with a rule and square,
> Patiently doing the best that I can;
> Or am I a wrecker—who walks the town—
> Content with the labor of tearing down?"

The intention of such a thoughtful and charitable consideration is twofold.

a. The unity of the body. Verse 25.

"That there should be no schism in the body . . . "

Strife and division appear in the church less because of doctrines than because of personalities. They are, in most instances, the result of personal jealousies and rivalries. They arise out of the promotion of our personal preferences and the minimizing of other's abilities. This, of course, ought not to be and the prevention of it is a charitable consideration of others.

b. The charity of its members. Verse 25.

" . . . but that the members should have the same care one for another."

This is the preventive offered for the previous problem. Do we have the same care for all or special care for some? Many times it is a question of caring at all. The concern seems to be entirely for oneself. The force of Christianity's influence is not centripetal, but centrifugal. It is not selfish and discriminating care for oneself but the same care for all others. Out of this would come an allocation of affection that would be without discrimination and division. It is presented as the ideal of Christian behavior.

Since the functions of the body are bound up in its members, the fortunes of the body are likewise bound up in its members. The good or ill of one member becomes the pain or pleasure of all members. Thus, "whether one member suffer, all the members suffer with it; or one member be honored, all the members rejoice with it." This, of course, is automatic in the physical body. In your physical body an exposed nerve in a tooth produces suffering that is felt in all the body. You cannot localize pain to your tooth so that it is not felt elsewhere. An incontinent and inconsistent Christian brings pain to all the church. The shame that he brings descends on every Christian. The spiritual anatomy of the entire Church feels the pain of broken and sinful sores.

There is also another thought here. It is that of "honoring." Mutual suffering is automatic. Mutual sharing in the honors and success of another is optional. To share in the pain of our fellows is one thing, to share in their pleasures and prosperity is another. We can more easily comfort than we can congratulate. One has said, "to give praise moderately is a sign of mediocrity."

The final and concluding consideration of the chapter deals with the provisions which have been made for the development, edification, and orderly conduct of the Church. The first part of the chapter dealt with gifts which, more or less, concerned the individual sphere of life. Here we see gifts which have to do with official places and capacities. Previously it was the manifestation of gifts. Here is is the administration of the gifts.

4. The Identification of the Body. Verse 27.

"Now ye are the body of Christ, and members in particular."

This identifies the Church. Christians, collectively, are "the body of Christ." Christians, individually, are "members in particular." Thus, Christians appear in their public and personal relationship to Christ. Christ, of course, is the head of the body with each member in a functional place within this great spiritual organism.

This is *the* Church. There are churches. There are great ecclesiastical systems and small Christian assemblies which have grown up during the years since the beginning of the Christian era. Not all the claims are either authentic or valid. It is our relation to this mystical Church of His body which gives all other claims validity and power.

You will notice that the existence of this body is given in its relation to its members. It is done to emphasize both their place and importance. The implication includes all Christians from the most able to the least capable. All have a place, and with that place, responsibility to fill it. The burden of this implication comes to rest close beside our conscience just now. What sort of body members have we been? What have we been doing to fill our places? Answer to be honest and **act to be honorable.**

5. The Responsibilities of the Body. Verses 28-31.

"And God hath set some in the church, first apostles, secondarily prophets, thirdly teachers, after that miracles, then gifts of healings, helps, governments, diversities of tongues. Are all apostles? are all prophets? are all teachers? are all workers of miracles? Have all the gifts of healing? do all speak with tongues? do all interpret? But covet earnestly the best gifts: and yet shew I unto you a more excellent way."

Here are the distributed responsibilities within the ordered operations of the body of Christ.

There is another important distinction we ought to observe between the nine gifts of the first part of the chapter and the eight items listed here. At the beginning it speaks of certain things being "given." Here it speaks of people being "set." At the beginning it was gifts for a people, but here it is people for a place. Thus, the previous gift is a fitting preparation for the appointed place. At the opening of the chapter it speaks of gifts "given to every man to profit withal," but here it is the office in which the gift is to be exercised.

Apostles. The ministry of the apostles, like the earthly ministry of Christ, has definitely ceased so far as its office is concerned. However, the effect continues. It is before us in the Bible. They were the founding fathers of the church. They were the penmen of the New Testament document of the church. We are still under the effect of their ministry.

Prophets. The primary meaning is that of an expounder. They were not explorers of new realms except that in the realm of revealed truth there are vast territories of yet untouched truth. They were to be teachers of the Word which was then in the process of creation. Here is a gift very widely forsaken. Without its exercise, the church suffers from malnutrition. It becomes anaemic, weak and ineffectual in its ministry. It needs to be restored today.

Miracles. Before this office are the words "after that." It indicates that the gifts or offices following are to be considered as lesser ministries. Miracle working is a lesser gift than teacher but far more spectacular. Its office has been largely rendered obsolete by the completion of the Scripture and the authentic establishment of Christianity.

Gifts of healing. Whatever place this gift has in our day, it is most surely not the place it had in the apostolic days. Who dare say it cannot exist? Who dare say it must exist? Here is something at the discretion of the Head of the body. We doubt not that we would have to be a different people were it available to us. Pentecostal preparation would be necessary before we could receive Pentecostal powers. May God grant that whatever His discretion decrees there may be found those who are ready and fit to fill these offices.

Helps. Here is an interesting word. It is a word all can understand. It carries the idea of supporting something. It is, therefore, a more or less obscure office. A steel truss in a building supports its roof, yet it is not seen. Without the truss the roof would be impossible. There are many places in Christian work for "helpers." You can be one. You may not be fitted for a prominent place but you can be a hidden supporter.

Governments. Here is a word with a nautical derivation. It means to pilot or steer. It literally means powers of organization and encompasses a vast territory of activity which looks abroad to the church's task of evangelization. Yes, the church needs spiritual executives, engineers, and scientists who labor under the direction of Christ and in the power of the Holy Spirit.

There may be a closer connection between "helps" and "governments" than is apparent at first sight. "Helps" may refer to the office of deacon while "governments" may refer to the office of elder. In this manner they complement each other and provide a combination of service that edifies the entire church.

Tongues. This is the last and apparently the least in both value and usefulness of all the ministries. Yet notice to what proportion it was sought in Corinth. People wanted prefabricated ability just as people now want pre-digested truth.

Two things remain to be said. The first thing has to do with the source of these ministries. They are divine disposals. To begin with, they have their basis in human abilities. These abilities in a Spirit-filled person become amplified and energized to a place of great fruitfulness.

The other thing has to do with the relation of these ministries to each other. "Are all apostles? Are all prophets? Are all teachers?" No! There has been a wide distribution upon the part of the giver. For this reason service is not intended for a few. Each has some ability intended for consecrated use. These abilities are scattered throughout the entire body and the full functioning of the body requires the faithful operation of each member. All are not Spurgeons or Wesleys. Some are intended to be "helps." All the miracles to be performed are not physical or material. There are the miracles of grace, of kindness, of patience, and of love. All the healings are not in the body. They are in the mind and soul, too. All the tongues are not linguistic. There is the language of love, mercy, kindness and testimony. Yes, God has a place for keepers at home and for sanctified fathers.

Let us recognize the gifts that have been bestowed upon us and fill the place provided for their display and exercise. By all means "covet earnestly the best gifts." Here is legitimate coveting. Do not stop there, however, for "I show unto you a more excellent way." In other words, "I now point you to a path that leads to heights beyond all heights." That path is love. It is something which surpasses both knowledge and gifts. It is the crowning virtue of life. It is the most compelling force in Christian experience.

Chapter XIII

THE CHRISTIAN AND LOVE

I Corinthians 13

IN CONSIDERING the divine objectives of the Christian, there is before us in this thirteenth chapter the pinnacle of personal attainment. Heretofore, in the previous chapter, Paul has been dealing with the gifts of the Spirit. Now it is the crowning grace of the Spirit. It is this grace of love which Paul speaks of in the last verse of chapter twelve, "And yet I show unto you a more excellent way." It is well to be furnished with the abilities that make one useful. It is best to be filled with love. Love gives both composure and complexion to the abilities which we may possess.

There now follows Paul's great "hymn of love." It is a hymn which reaches one of the highest levels in the entire Scripture.

Before examining the details which yield such beauty of expression and content, it would be helpful to read Arthur S. Way's translation of this "hymn of love":

"Though with all tongues of men I speak, yea, of angels,
  And have not Love,
I have become clanging brass or clashing cymbal.
  Yea, though I have utterance inspired,
Though I fathom all mystic secrets, have full illumination,
Though I have utter faith, such as might move mountains from
      their seats,
  And have not Love,
  Nothing am I.
And though I dole away in charity all my goods,
And though I yield up my body to a death of fire,
  And have not Love,
  Nothing it availeth me.

Love is long-forbearing, is all kindness:
Love knows not jealousy,
Love does not parade her gifts, swells not with self-conceit,
    she flouts not decency:
She grasps not at her rights, refuses to take offence, has no
    memory for injuries.
She exults not over wrong triumphant, she shows glad sympathy
    with Truth.
All tolerance is she, all trustfulness, all hope, all strong endurance.
    Love's flower-petals never fall.
    Eloquence inspires—for this there shall be no use:
      Tongues—they shall be hushed:
    Illumination—for this there shall be no use.
Yes, partial is that our illumination, partial our inspiration:
But when cometh the perfect, for the partial there shall be no use.
    When I was a child, as a child I wont to talk;
    As a child I felt, as a child I reasoned;
But now that I am grown to man, outworn for me are the things
    of the child.
Yea, we see as yet the Vision glassed in a mirror—it is a dark
    riddle—
    But then face to face shall we gaze.
Now my knowledge comes from seeing but a part;
But then shall I understand, as fully as I am understood,
    So then these abide unperishing—Faith, Hope, Love.
    These three Gifts alone:
    But chiefest of these is Love."

A large part of the importance of this chapter lies in its contextual location. It is in the midst of Paul's discussion of the gifts. The chapter before it and the chapter after it speak of those gifts. In chapter twelve it is the purpose of the gifts, while in chapter fourteen it is the perversion of the gifts.

Their abuse was largely in the matter of tongues. Paul is here showing "a more excellent way." He is urging that the Christian be dominated by a master passion—love. To be dominated by love is to be controlled by the highest emotion. It is the remedy for all excess and the protection against all error. If we had a genuine experience and expression of

love as found in this chapter, we would have less of the
vagaries of many fanatical movements of our day. Such movements are a prostitution of the gifts of the Spirit and a perversion of the highest principles of Christian experience.

If emotion is carried to the one extreme of fanaticism, as
above, it is also carried to the opposite extreme of formalism.
Love is not a weakness. It gives strength and character. But
it must be love in the right sense—love in its best sense, in
its right sense, and in its highest sense if found here.

Love in the New Testament is translated from a number
of Greek Words. Once it is from the word "philanthropia,"
meaning love for mankind. Once it is from the word "philadelphia," meaning love for brethren. Elsewhere it is from the
word "phileo," meaning love for a friend. Here it is "agape,"
which is used also in John 3:16, and has the meaning of God's
love for us and our love for God. Here we see the intensifica-
tion of love, first for mankind, then for brethren, then for the
friend, and now for God.

Besides these Bible words, there was another word commonly and currently used in those times by the philosophers
and mythologists. It is the word "eros," the name of the god
of love, the son of Aphrodite. This word is found in classical
Greek and speaks of the love between the sexes such as the
love of sweethearts and husbands and wives.

The word "eros," however, is not found in the Bible. This
is very significant. The reason is that its contemporary mytho-
logical use was degrading and corrupting. It was voluptuous
and sensual, hence the Holy Spirit forbade its use in the
Scripture where it would have been out of place and greatly
misunderstood. In its place is found the word "agape," translated "charity;" not charity in the sense of alms, but charity
in the sense of the highest and divinest affection.

Love is not an emotion based upon compassion. It is an
affection based upon the new creation. It is not a frothy,
effervescent emotion that boils over with cheap sentimentality.
It is something born of God. It is the "agape" of God. When

used in the Epistle of John, it is used both for God's love for us and our love for God. It is used in that sense here, which indicates its divine nature.

For humanity you may have *philanthropia*. For brethren you may have *philadelphia*. For friends you may have *phileo*, but for God you must have *agape*. This is an affection of adoration and devotion, based not on human nature, but on the new nature. This means that no one can truly love God until and unless he is born again.

This affection is now extended to encompass human relations. It is not confined to an impractical piety and worship. It is made to live in our homes, our lives, our work, as well as in our hearts. In fact, it is "the greatest thing in the world."

Love is given here, not as a gift of the Spirit, but as a grace of the Spirit. Its immediate importance is to show the Corinthians and all succeeding Christians the way in which the gifts are to be used.

Do not be afraid of this ennobling emotion. Whatever there is that is worthwhile has love as its compelling emotion. Love is the foundation of the home, for affection is the beginning of marriage. It is the foundation of the family, for procreation is the urge of affection. It is the foundation of the nation, for patriotism is love of country. It is the foundation of Christianity, for love is the source of salvation because "God so loved . . . that he gave . . ."

I Love's Preference. Verses 1-3.

> "Though I speak with the tongues of men and of angels, and have not charity, I am become as sounding brass, or a tinkling cymbal. And though I have the gift of prophecy, and understand all mysteries, and all knowledge; and though I have all faith, so that I could remove mountains, and have not charity, I am nothing. And though I bestow all my goods to feed the poor, and though I give my body to be burned, and have not charity, it profiteth me nothing."

Love is a preferred quality of life. It heads the list of our spiritual qualities. We may possess gifts but we must be possessed of love. There follow seven things over which love takes precedence and preference.

1. Eloquence. Verse 1.

To have possessed the eloquence of angels without the affection of love would be like the sound of brass and the tinkling of a cymbal. "Brass" referred to metal castagnettes (our modern castanets) which gave off a clanging metallic sound. "Cymbal" referred to an ancient percussion instrument which gave off more noise than music.

The preference of love over eloquence was a reference to the situation which prevailed in Corinth over the use of the gift tongues. The Corinthians had abused this gift to the point of fanaticism. It led to pride and a false sense of personal excellence and importance. This, in turn, led to strife and division which divided the church. If love had been present, pride, strife, and division would have been impossible. Hence, its importance and preference.

The most eloquent may possess irritable temperaments. The good accomplished through eloquence would thus be dissipated by the devils of a bad temper and a selfish disposition. Hence, love was to be preferred and when possessed, it would bring abilities and gifts to the place of highest usefulness.

William Tyndale had many enemies who persecuted him with a very bitter and cruel hatred. He returned their persecution with a tender charity. To one of these enemies he is reported to have said, "Take away my goods, take away my good name: Yet so long as Christ dwelleth in my heart, so long shall I love you not a whit the less." Tyndale was a man of great eloquence. He is famed as one of our earliest Bible translators. He not only translated the words of the Bible into current language but he personally translated its truth into deeds. To all of us the same challenge comes with great urgency.

2. Prophecy. Verse 2.

Skill in knowing what is going to happen in the future is not as desirable as love in the moments of the present.

3. Mysteries. Verse 2.

To be in a favored circle where the mystic secrets of the divine mind are made plain is not as desirable as love. Love is what God is. Love in us will understand love in Him. Love gives a clearer and better revelation of God than the keenest knowledge.

4. Knowledge. Verse 2.

The wisest men are not always the best. Those who know most about the world sometimes know the least about God. Facts are not the highest goal of the mind. To have an abstract knowledge of God is not enough. We need faith that leads to fellowship.

5. Faith. Verse 2.

The word *all* is employed three times, indicating the extent of the qualities mentioned. All faith is not as important as some love. It does not say, no faith and some love as if the display of affection was the equivalent of salvation. This kind of faith is not saving faith. You must have a saving faith before you can have a surpassing love. This faith is the faith of doing. It is the faith of success and accomplishment. Men are not saved by loving either God or man. It is not the affection of our love to God but rather the extension of His love to us that saves. Love is the consequence of faith. Nevertheless, faith without love puts its possessor in the minus column. He is nothing. He is not something less than he might be, but nothing. There is nothing less than nothing. You cannot get below or behind nothing.

To be proficient in the productive abilities of Christian service and activity such as eloquence and prophecy and mysteries and knowledge and faith, and to be deficient in love, is to be nothing.

6. Charity. Verse 3.

Philanthropy is a noble virtue but even this may be used as a selfish thing to purchase for ourselves peace of mind. We toss a coin to the beggar because we wish to get relief from the sympathetic feelings his plight has aroused. Or, perhaps, we wish to be known for our generosity. Subscribing to the Red Cross and the Community Chest may be as selfish as buying an unneeded luxury. These acts of charity may only be acts of selfishness. Without love, charity "profiteth me nothing."

7. Martyrdom. Verse 3.

To have died in sacrifice for one's friends or in testimony to one's faith would be a noble thing in any language, but the act must have a motive. Martyrdom may be endured because of fanaticism. Then it is nullified. The Bible is saying that to live for one's faith and one's friends is greater than to die for them.

Many martyred missionaries lie in the sacred soil of faraway places. They sealed their faith in their blood. Many times, to live and love in living is a greater martyrdom than to die. Henry Drummond said, "In the heart of Africa, among the great lakes, I have come across black men and women who remembered the only white man they ever saw before—David Livingstone; and as you cross his footsteps in that dark continent, men's faces light up as they speak of the kind Doctor who passed there years ago. They could not understand him; but they felt the love that beat in his heart."

Here are seven great things, but love is greater. Here are things greatly to be desired, but love the most of all. Without love their possession is prostituted by selfishness and thus nullified. Without love their profession is a pretense and a sham. Without love none of them can be perfected in our personalities or career. Therefore, not to love is, in the deepest sense, not to live.

II. Love's Properties. Verses 4-7.

> "Charity suffereth long, and is kind; charity envieth not;
> charity vaunteth not itself, is not puffed up, Doth not behave
> itself unseemly, seeketh not her own, is not easily provoked,
> thinketh no evil; Rejoiceth not in iniquity, but rejoiceth in the
> truth; Beareth all things, believeth all things, hopeth all things,
> endureth all things."

Love has been contrasted. It is now being analyzed. It has
been contrasted with seven things. Now its analysis reveals
twice that many properties. We shall see that while "love
may be difficult to define, it is not difficult to discern."

1. Love "suffereth long"—Patience.

The normal state of love is placid, calm and composed. It
has poise. There is an absence of that petulance which piques
and disturbs us. Its poise is beautifully apparent under the fire
of misunderstanding and disapproval.

2. Love "is kind"—Kindness.

An elderly Scotch minister upon hearing his people censure
each other with merciless criticism said to them, "Remember,
if you are not very kind you are not very holy, because holiness and kindness cannot be separated."

One may be patient without being kind. Patience is passive
endurance while kindness is active service. Patience is love's
endurance of ill and evil while kindness is love's activity in
good. Patience is love waiting with folded hands while kindness is love working with busy hands. Patience is being good
while kindness is doing good. It is possible to be passively
good without being actively kind.

3. Love "envieth not"—Generosity.

This is not the generosity of alms but generosity of thought.
It is lack of jealousy toward another's good work or prosperity.
If love is kind in what another lacks, it is also happy in what
another possesses. If one possesses better gifts and greater
wealth, our attitude is to be one without irritation.

4. Love "vaunteth not . . . not puffed up"—Humility.

"Love does not parade her gifts, swells not with self-conceit" (Way). This is love in modest retreat. It does not push itself into public notice or aspire for the limelight, nor does its eagerness for place and position cause it to crowd out others. Here is an excellence of personality that wins respect and never ceases to progress and go higher. In Christ's kingdom one stoops to rise and shrinks to grow.

Love is not arrogant toward inferiors nor is it in vain in its accomplishments. This had a very pertinent meaning to Corinth, for they were gloating and exulting over their gifts and successes. It is peculiarly fitting as a rebuke to Christian ministers and lay workers alike. Preachers boast of crowds and converts and sound like a noisy hen boasting as if she had laid an asteroid instead of an egg.

This does not mean that love retires one's usefulness, or sets one aside. It does not create a false inferiority complex. It does not refuse obligations by excusing itself through inability or false modesty. Love may be modest, but it is not lazy. It may be humble, but it is not humiliating.

Most of us aspire to obtain something when we should aspire to be something. Our desires are usually translatable into things. We want to procure instead of become. The Christian version of this perversion of life was found in Corinth. They wanted gifts but lacked the grace to use those gifts properly. Hence, love is being pointed out as the sum of all desire and aspiration. This is for us as well as for them.

5. Love "doth not behave itself unseemly"—Courtesy.

Love contributes that fine and noble sense of gentlemanliness and womanliness. Love softens the hard lines and smooths the sharp edges. It is neither rude nor boorish, neither hard nor harsh. It gives a sense of Christian fitness. In this it fashions us to the pattern of the Master who possessed a finesse of manners that was perfect.

This highest attainment does not come through literature, but love. It is not *put on* but *put in*. It is more than etiquette. It is another sense.

If love is a fine sense of gentlemanliness, then remember that a gentleman is just a "gentle man—a man who does things gently with love." This is not a mark of unmanliness or weakness. It is the higher kind of manliness and womanliness. It is real strength, for it is love.

6. Love "seeketh not her own"—Unselfishness.

This verse tells us that love does not grasp for its rights. The most natural and human thing is to stand up for one's rights. That is justice. That is the law. Here, however, is an unnatural thing. It transcends human feelings and reactions. It declares itself willing to surrender rather than determined to possess. Has love no protection against the unscrupulous and the designing? Does this mean a passive resistance to all aggression? Indeed, love has an adequate defense. Love is its best defense. It has the defense of character. This is not the thing in view here. It refers more directly to the selfish grasping for things. Life will never be found in things but it will be found in love. This means that the secret of living is not concentrating on oneself. It is looking *out* instead of *in*. It is found in gratuitous service rather than selfish gain.

7. Love "is not easily provoked"—Good natured.

It is marked by an absence of temperamental explosions. Love is not a prohibition. It is a contribution. It gives us a good nature.

A puritan once said, "I am determined so to be angry as not to sin; therefore to be angry with nothing but sin." Henry Drummond said of ill temper that "it is the vice of the virtuous."

One of the commonest faults of church, social and family life is bad temper. It is one of the most baneful things among us. Temper is as necessary to strong character as it is to good steel, but an unleashed temper spoils life. There is a secret

to its control. That secret is Christ-control, not self-control.
Your temper is yourself. It is the cause of incompatibility between the Christian's higher nature of spirituality and the
lower nature of carnality. To be mastered by this love is the
same as being mastered by Christ. To possess His mind is to
display His love.

8. Love "thinketh no evil"—Charitableness.

This is another evidence of love's charity of thought and
opinion. We need this as much as the charity of benevolence;
much more than we now have. We are too often benevolent
with our money while being penurious with the charity of
opinion. We hoard good opinions and think the evil.

Love provides a delightful frame of mind to live in. It is
crediting people with the best possible motives. It is exercising
the grace of charity in extending to friends, associates and
fellow-believers an understanding attitude.

> "If I knew you and you knew me—
> If both of us could clearly see,
> And with an inner sight divine
> The meaning of your heart and mine,
> I'm sure that we would differ less
> And clasp our hands in friendliness;
> Our thoughts would pleasantly agree
> If I knew you, and you knew me.
>
> "If I knew you and you knew me,
> As each one knows his own self, we
> Could look each other in the face
> And see therein a truer grace.
> Life has so many hidden woes,
> So many thorns for every rose;
> The Why's of things our hearts would see,
> If I knew you and you knew me."

In birds, there is a great difference between a dove and a
raven. Noah first sent out a raven but it never returned, for
it lived on the carrion of the yet unabated flood. Then Noah
sent out a dove. Being a clean bird, it quickly returned, for

it found only uncleanness in the wake of the flood. Carnality is raven-like. It flies over the clean and beautiful but delights in evil. Spirituality is dove-like and "thinketh no evil."

In all our proper insistence on what a person believes we must not think lightly of how that person lives. Pious professors may be good actors. Public appearance may present a notable parade of piety but the backstage life may be a travesty on truth.

There is another meaning in this statement. The love that "thinketh no evil" is the love that "has no memory for injuries." It does not keep an account book of evil things. It does not wait a day of reckoning so as to balance the budget of ill-will. It has a charitable forgetfulness.

9. Love "rejoiceth not in iniquity"—Sincerity.

This is love without a mask of pretense. It does not go behind the scenes and gloat and laugh over others' misfortunes, failures and mistakes. It is a transparent sincerity that concerns itself with another's well-being. It is the recognition of the spiritual unity of all believers in the Body of Christ. Here the fortunes and misfortunes of one become the same for all.

This kind of love is "never glad when others go wrong." It "finds no secret satisfaction in discovering the moral weakness or the hidden wickedness of a rival, is not eager to spread an evil report, glories not in the triumph of wrong."

Although love is all this, it is not guileless to the point of tolerance with sin, no matter where it is found. Love is charitable but it is not foolish. It sees good but it is not blind to willful, premeditated and hidden evil. Its charity will cover up the mistakes of a penitent but it will never childishly close its eyes to sin being hugged to the bosom of a hypocrite. Love has a good sense of proportion. It is proportionately charitable and proportionately critical.

10. Love "rejoiceth in the truth"—Goodness.

This is the inherent goodness of love. It means the genuine

gladness of goodness. It rejoices not so much in the truth, as a set of ideas, but with the truth as a means of living life. Love genuinely rejoices in the victory of truth. That victory may be outside our particular church communion. It is the importance of truth that counts and not the opinions of sectarianism. It is gladdened "when suspicions are proved unfounded, when wrong is vanquished and right prevails."

Here is a generosity of goodness that marks a high level of life. Here is a generosity of goodness that marks a nobility of life. Here is life that really lives because it loves.

11. Love "beareth all things"—Graciousness.

It is not the bearing of our own faults in the spirit of martyrdom but the bearing of others' faults. It is overlooking others' faults by putting a mantle of kindness over them. Whenever fire breaks out in the forest and leaves the black scar of a ruthless burning, nature soon hides its ugliness with a mantle of green. The lesson of nature should be the lesson of life. Let us put a mantle of gracious charity over the scars of another's life.

12. Love "believeth all things"—Confidence.

Love is full of trust. Trust, however, is not necessarily credulity. It is not a sentimental guilelessness that makes one gullible and an easy prey for charlatans. Love, to the contrary, has a keen sense of discernment. Here it is the disposition to accept one another without the suspicion and distrust that is found so often in the world. Even when cause for trust may be gone, love remains love. It does not turn to hate to rend limb from limb. It may tearfully acknowledge defeat but it will cheerfully pursue its course. It will be intelligently confident.

13. Love "hopeth all things"—Assurance.

Love believes in its cause so deeply that it possesses the assurance of ultimate victory. Here is optimism. It hopes for the best in the face of every adversity. All of us should be optimists of this sort. A pessimist has been described as a person who blows out the light to see how dark it is. Love has no affinity to such an attitude of life. It is optimistic, hopeful, expectant and forward looking.

14. Love "endureth all things"—Endurance.

Here is the last property of love. How fitting! It endures. What good is patience, kindness, generosity, humility, courtesy, unselfishness, good nature, charitableness, sincerity, goodness, graciousness, confidence and assurance unless they continue? Most of us can be kind for a day but love is kindness that endures. Most of us can be patient for a while but love is patience that endures.

Love's endurance is of itself. It contains in its own nature the strength of continuance and stamina against fatigue. Yes, love endures.

Love endures not only because of what it is but because of the One whom it reveals. Love gives eyesight to faith. It gives us the sight of God. It reproduces in us what it produced for Moses—"By faith he forsook Egypt, not fearing the wrath of the king: for he endured as seeing him who is invisible." Love reveals the invisible and saves us from the inevitable.

III. Love's Permanence. Verses 8-13.

Love is not an optional virtue whose effect is some emotional experience that exhilarates for the moment and is gone forever. Love is indispensable. It is needed to tone and temper all the other qualities of life. Besides this, love is immortal. It is not a passing emotion. It is not something to be felt and forgotten. It leaves behind it a strength and beauty of character that all of us need.

We are now to be told that the purpose for which the gifts were given is to change and with its change the use of the gifts is either to cease or be definitely limited. Whatever ceases or whatever else is limited, "love never faileth." Here is a quality that continues to be necessary today as always. It is the highest goal of Christian attainment. It is the greatest possession of Christian experience.

Three things appear:

1. That Which Passes. Verse 8.

The statement "love never faileth" literally means, "love's flower petals never fall." Here is something whose efficiency never ceases. It never loses its place.

There are things that do lose their place:

(1) *Prophecy.*

Prophecy will not fail in the sense of a breakdown in its fulfillment. "Fail" here means "to make useless." The prophetic gift was rendered useless by the written word. When the body of Scripture came into being, the verbal gift ceased its necessity.

(2) *Tongues.*

"Whether there be tongues, they shall cease."

Just as we have had no prophets for centuries, so we have no evidence that there are men today who have the ability to intelligently preach in languages never learned. Tongues as signs ceased when the necessity for them ended. The need for these tongues was the preaching and rapid spread of the gospel.

(3) *Knowledge.*

"Whether there be knowledge, it shall vanish away."

This knowledge which vanishes is to be distinguished from knowledge as an intelligence. This is knowledge in the sense of illumination. It is knowledge as a gift of discernment. It was the knowledge of illumination which resulted in inspiration. When the written word came into being and form, the need for this special illumination ceased.

Did it ever occur to you to ask why this beautiful hymn of love was not only written by Paul but why the sequence of truths puts it in this particular place? Love is presented in this setting of the gifts between the twelfth and fourteenth chapters of the book to indicate how these gifts are to be used, also to show that love is greater than any gift. The strongest testimony for Christianity in our day is not one who has the gift of prophecy, tongues or knowledge; but one who loves.

During the last war a report came from London that had to do with the devastating German air raids on London. These raids were not on military objectives such as arsenals, airfields and factories, but on hospitals, museums, churches, and homes. In the face of this wanton destruction, it might be expected that the public would demand reprisals in kind. From the Christians of England, at least, there was almost a unanimous insistence that the R.A.F. was not to bomb Germany as Germany had been bombing England. One church paper in stating its case said, "The reason why, even to win the war or to win it quickly, this country cannot adopt the methods of the jungle is simply that it does not wish the world to be a jungle when the war is finished . . . The allied nations are dedicated to the cause of Christian civilization . . . There are some steps they cannot take without abandoning the standards for which they are fighting." That was a noble decision. If more of it were abroad in our hearts and in our world, this would no longer be a charnel house of destruction. Let us see that love whose "flower petals never fall" is in our hearts.

Life is an investment. The manner in which we invest our lives is far more important than the way we invest our money. The quality of life determines the quality of its investment. Love is being revealed to us as the determining quality of life; a quality which will govern the soundness of our investment. In other words, *loving is living life at its best*. Love is the life of the Christian because it is the very nature of the life he has received of God. In this kind of life love is not merely the way we feel but the way we act. In Christianity love is life and life is love.

2. That Which is Perfect. Verses 9-12.

In these verses will be found two contrasts and two comparisons:

(1) *The contrasts.* Verses 9, 10.

Here Paul contrasts the partial against the perfect.

a. The Partial. Verse 9.

> "For we know in part, and we prophesy in part."

We must not lose sight of the perspective of this chapter or else we shall be amiss in the understanding and application of the truth of the chapter. Its truth applies to life at this moment. A far-away day is not the time which is in view.

The partiality of knowing and prophesying was true of the day of Christianity's beginning. That day was a day of growth and development. The time would come when the partial would be supplemented by the perfect. That time was not the distant time of heaven alone but the time when the Scriptures would appear in their final form and life would mature and love would perfect.

b. The Perfect. Verse 10.

> "But when that which is perfect is come, then that which is in part shall be done away."

This perfection is the perfection of maturity. Paul speaks later of being a child and becoming a man. Therefore, the things of the early age of Christianity's immaturity would be supplanted by the things of Christianity's maturity. He deliberately states that the partial shall be done away. This means that there will no longer be any use for them. They will have served their purpose. They will fulfill the time of divine intention. Moreover, these things which shall be done away are specifically identified in a previous verse as prophecies and tongues. These were special and spectacular gifts needed in the apostolic age for the quick and rapid spread of the gospel. To a large extent, the absence of these gifts is explained by the presence of the Scriptures. We would not be presumptuous and say that we cannot have any of the gifts today. However, the manner of their possession would be different. Then they came by direct divine bestowal. Now they would come through the blessings of native abilities by the Scriptures and the Spirit.

(2) *The comparisons.* Verses 11, 12.

These comparisons reveal the Christian in the light of a child and a mirror.

a. A child. Verse 11.

"When I was a child, I spake as a child, I understood as a child, I thought as a child: but when I became a man, I put away childish things."

Here the Christian is compared as to childhood and manhood. Each of us has a physical, mental, and spiritual childhood. This comparison is not concerned with the physical and mental, however. It is the spiritual childhood that is emphasized. In that childhood one thinks and acts in terms of immaturity.

His activities are trivial. His thoughts are limited. His desires are selfish. There is in every normal life a transition period. It is the time when one passes from adolescence into maturity. During this time, what is the outstanding thing? It is the awakening of love. Intellectually, emotionally, and organically, the life is prepared for the one outstanding characteristic of manhood and womanhood. That is the ability to love. Children do not love; they cannot. They are not mentally, emotionally or organically supplied with the faculties which create love. Oh, yes, they have infatuations but we facetiously call these "puppy loves." They are capable of affection but it is an affection confined to the family.

When love comes, it becomes the controlling and dominating factor of life. It means that the childish things are outworn. The activities and desires are now very different. When this kind of spiritual maturity comes to a Christian, love very definitely pegs the level of our spiritual experience. Corinth's Christians were in the immaturity of carnality—hence, their childish bickerings, their silly differences, their foolish quarrelings and their small-minded activities. When love comes, it will lift life to the level of greatness and a goodness we never dreamed possible. This is probably the most important item in Christian experience, all other things being equal.

Do we really love both our Father and our brother or are we emotionally exercised with pious feelings that may be as false as a child's infatuations?

b. A mirror. Verse 12.

> "For now we see through a glass darkly; but then face to face: now I know in part; but then shall I know even as also I am known."

The Corinthians would understand this comparison because their local art had developed a means of polishing metal to a fair degree of reflection. Their homes and buildings were full of mirrors, but they were imperfect mirrors. They were not like our mirrors with their silvered backs. Looking into them he saw himself "darkly." So it was with gifts of prophecy, tongues and knowledge. They were imperfect reflections. When love came, it would be the perfect mirror because love is the most perfect, the most honest, and truest of all life's qualities. Whosoever saw himself in the light of love saw all there was to see. It gave an honest and a final verdict.

You have undoubtedly noticed the use of the words "now" and "then." Now we see and now we know, but then we shall see face to face and know as we are known. This may have reference to heaven when it will be God's face and my face. We believe it comes *now*, when love will reflect a perfect image and reveal a perfect knowledge. Love will show one what kind of a face we have and love will tell one what kind of a man we are.

3. That Which is Permanent. Verse 13.

"And now abideth faith, hope, charity, these three; but the greatest of these is charity."

Notice the stability of these three leading words—"and now abideth." All through this chapter we saw vanishing and passing items of character and furnishings of ability. There was a veritable parade of the passing and transitory. Here are the permanent virtues. Here are three immortal qualities.

FAITH abides because it is "the substance of things hoped for, the evidence of things not seen."

HOPE abides because it anticipates the fulfillment of what faith expects. As long as there is true faith, there will be real hope.

LOVE abides because it is the very nature of the new life. It is the last and greatest of the three things that survive time, death and disaster. Enriched in these things, you can afford to be poor in everything else. Possessing these things, you possess the dimensions of eternity.

It is not enough to love life. Only when we live love can we know life at its best. May we feel the tremendous challenge of this mighty fact and read this chapter until it has saturated our souls. If we do it and live it, life will be transformed both inside and outside.

To face this great document on love is to face one of the most thrilling challenges of life. In a world gone mad with greed and war, we must dare to give it the antidote of love. In a church life of petty partisanship, we must dare to exhibit the cardinal virtue of our faith. The strictest creedal faith cannot be sufficient in any life unless it is accompanied by the excellence of love.

CHAPTER XIV

THE CHRISTIAN AND TONGUES

I *Corinthians* 14

CHRISTIAN experience follows the normal channels of human expressions. We express ourselves as normal human beings through our thoughts, our emotions, our speech and our deeds. The salvation of the gospel regenerates the processes of these expressions. Then, as a normal spiritual development and growth take place, these expressions are both sanctified and amplified. We have already taken note of the fact that there have been times in history when God heightened the use of men's faculties for a divine purpose. This was done, as in the growing years of the church, by the bestowal of various gifts. Among these gifts there was the gift of tongues. As that gift was displayed at Jerusalem on the day of Pentecost, it accomplished a gracious result. Many heard the gospel in their own languages by the lips of men who had never previously spoken that language. As that gift was abused at Corinth, it produced an unfortunate effect. It resulted in revolting excesses and brought shame upon the name of the church.

We are now to consider the Scripture message concerning this gift.

We have found the gift of tongues dealt with in chapter twelve and chapter fourteen. In chapter twelve we have spiritual gifts in their relation to the collective church. In chapter fourteen we have spiritual gifts in their relation to the individual Christian. In chapter twelve the gift of tongues is mentioned as a lesser and least desirable gift. In chapter fourteen the gift of tongues is referred to in connection with

248

its abuse by the carnal Christians at Corinth. These Corinthians were the first examples of a modern travesty on spirituality. That travesty is the modern abuse of tongues. It was done at Corinth and significantly enough it was done by carnal, immature Christians. In my personal experience, I have seldom known spiritually mature Christians becoming involved in this abuse of the tongue gift. If such did, they soon recovered their spiritual equilibrium and repented of their folly.

Apparently, the employment of the gift of tongues had not entirely ceased in Paul's time. He declares, "I thank my God, I speak with tongues more than ye all," and concludes the chapter by adding, "and forbid not to speak with tongues." Let us keep our bearings by remembering that Paul's statements here are dealing with the abuse of a declining gift and not with the use of an ascending gift.

The presence of tongues at Corinth is not a justification of their use in our times. In fact, we do not believe that there is any scriptural evidence or any practical evidence to support the claim that this gift genuinely exists at all. There are various movements which profess it, but a fair and impartial investigation of these movements will reveal this so-called gift either a delusion or a form of hysteria. Further than this, you will find out that it is practiced by people who may be classified as emotionally impressionable. They are people who, while their sincerity cannot be questioned and while their Christian faith cannot be doubted, belong to a temperament level where this sort of thing thrives.

The Corinthian version of tongues was not the Pentecostal version at all. It was a *perversion.* It was an erratic and ecstatic expression of unintelligent and unintelligible speech. It was not a language in the real sense but a jargon of speech. When Paul mentions his experience and says "forbid not," he was not speaking of the Corinthian perversion but the Pentecostal version. From the lack of bonafide evidence, we must conclude that this gift has served its purpose and that

present representations are an unhappy recurrence of the
Corinthian perversion.

I. PRIORITY OF THE GIFTS. Verses 1-25.

With all the Corinthian excitement about tongues and with
all the claims of our modern movements as to the importance
of tongues, it is a significant thing that the Scriptures nowhere
tell us to seek this gift. Even in Paul's day he told them to
desire prophecy or inspired preaching, as preferable to anything else among the gifts.

In the priority of the gifts, tongues is never first. In the
priority of the Scriptures, it is never first. Outside of the books
of Acts and Corinthians the gift of tongues is mentioned only
once in the New Testament. It has been elevated entirely
out of proportion to its place and importance.

It is claimed today that tongues are a sign of the believer's
baptism with the Holy Spirit. This is a perversion of
Scripture which declares it to have been a sign to unbelievers
and not to believers. In verse 22 it says, "Wherefore tongues
are for a sign not to them that believe, but to them that believe not, but prophesying serveth not for them that believe
not, but for them which believe."

It is claimed today that tongues will be the possession of
all believers when they are spiritually right. This, too, is a
perversion of the Scriptures, for it says in I Corinthians 12:30,
"Do all speak with tongues?"

It is claimed today that the experience of tongues is a mark
of high spiritual attainment. This, also is a perversion of the
Scriptures, for the Corinthians were described as childish and
carnal Christians. Paul said of them, "And I, brethren, could
not speak unto you as unto spiritual but as unto carnal even
as unto babes in Christ." It was their spiritual immaturity
which led them into the abuse of an otherwise legitimate
Christian experience. This will largely explain the modern
abuse of the same gift. It is found among people who, for
the most part, are genuinely sincere, but they are apparently

emotionally unstable. It is a constitutional psychological weakness and because they have not developed sufficient spiritual maturity, they become involved in this emotional excess.

When we say this, we speak kindly and charitably. We have no purpose to despise any fellow Christian. We deplore the abuse that some of them are making of the Scriptures and speak with the utmost earnestness in desiring its correction.

The Bible is very plain in its explanation of the legitimate use of the gift of tongues. Its wonderful use on the day of Pentecost was not an emotional orgy that brought shame on the infant church. It had been promised that "ye shall receive power, after that the Holy Ghost is come upon you: and ye shall be witnesses unto me both in Jerusalem, and in all Judaea, and in Samaria, and unto the uttermost part of the earth."

First, it was the power of a personality indwelling and possessing us for it was to be the power of the Holy Spirit. Then, this power was for the purpose of witnessing. It was not to be an emotional exploitation of a divine gift. In fact, it was for them all. Through them it was to result in a witnessing to others. It says, "ye shall be witnesses *unto me*." It does not say witnesses unto the truth or unto the gospel, but unto Christ. Until the personality of the Holy Spirit is resident in us and His power manifest through us, we may be witnesses to the truth but not actually unto Christ. Because there is so great a difference between witnessing to Christ and witnessing to the truth, we can explain why so much good preaching accomplishes so little.

Pentecost did not give the unrestrained privilege of emotional hysteria. It gave power. It was power to live Christlike. A witness to Christ is more than a mouthpiece. He is a demonstration. He is a demonstration of Christlike forgiveness, goodness, and love. Pentecost meant more than an emotion; it meant devotion to a new order of life and a new world task. Until we see the world aspect of Pentecostal blessing, we shall continue our personal perversion of a great truth.

There is much in the Bible which transcends our understanding. That fact is one of the Bible's most compelling credentials. Yet there is nothing in the Bible which transgresses our intelligence. It is intelligent to subscribe our faith to a book which transcends our minds. It is intelligent to believe in a God we cannot comprehend. This intellectual integrity not only applies to the great things of the Book but to the little things of life.

The Bible will never lead us into experience which will shame a Christian's intelligence. It will never betray your trust. This is particularly appropriate to the matter in hand. It concerns the gift of tongues.

In this first section of the chapter we have Paul's teaching set forth in a twofold light:

1. The Effect of Tongues on Believers. Verses 1-19.

(1) *Paul's advice.* Verse 1.

> "Follow after charity, and desire spiritual gifts, but rather that ye may prophesy."

In view of the emphasis the Corinthians placed on spectacular gifts, it is important to notice Paul's advice.

First, "follow after love." Linking the first word of the fourteenth chapter to the last word of the twelfth chapter, we have an added emphasis. The last thing Paul said in the twelfth chapter was, "yet shew I unto you a more excellent way." This "more excellent way" of life is love. They are now advised to "follow after" it. Love is a quest. It is not a gift bestowed upon us. It is true that love as a principle is implanted in the new birth. It is equally true that love as a practice is a growth. We must seek it. We must develop it.

Second, "desire spiritual gifts." Love is developed and gifts, desired. As originally true these gifts were divine bestowals. Now, since we possess the Scriptures, they are undoubtedly the improvement of our natural abilities. As we become filled with the Spirit our abilities are sanctified and sharpened.

In this desiring of gifts, one is singled out over the rest. It is the gift of prophecy or the inspired use of speech. Tongues was speaking in another language while prophecy was speaking in one's own language. It was the enhancing of the ability to speak the gospel both conversationally and publicly.

(2) *Paul's argument.* Verses 2-6.

"For he that speaketh in an unknown tongue speaketh not unto men, but unto God; for no man understandeth him; howbeit in the spirit he speaketh mysteries. But he that prophesieth speaketh unto men to edification and exhortation, and comfort. He that speaketh in an unknown tongue edifieth himself; but he that prophesieth edifieth the church. I would that ye all spake with tongues, but rather that ye prophesied: for greater is he that prophesieth than he that speaketh with tongues, except he interpret, that the church may receive edifying. Now, brethren, if I come unto you speaking with tongues, what shall I profit you, except I shall speak to you either by revelation, or by knowledge, or by prophesying, or by doctrine?"

The argument Paul advances for the advantage of prophecy over tongues is very simple and plain. Prophesying has wider benefits. It is calculated to reach many and thus extend the benefits and blessings of the gospel to their intended proportion. Contrary to this, the Corinthians were conforming their use of tongues to personal advantage. They were becoming wrapped up in their own abilities and selfish spiritual superiorities.

The very nature of the gospel requires its propagation. We cannot keep it to ourselves and enjoy its richest benefits. It was intended that each possessor of the gospel become a preacher of it. We have isolated it and professionalized it to the detriment of all concerned.

"There are two seas in Palestine. One contains fresh water, and there are many beautiful fish in it. Slashes of green adorn its banks. Trees spread their branches over it, and stretch out their thirsty roots to sip of its healing waters. Along its shores the children play, as children played nineteen centuries ago. The River Jordan sends its sparkling waters from the hills into this Sea of Galilee, and it laughs in the sunshine. The men build their homes near it, and the birds their nests; and every kind of life is happier because it is there.

"The River Jordan flows on south into another sea. Here is no splash of fish, no fluttering leaf, no song of birds, no children's laughter. Travelers choose another route, unless on urgent business. The air hangs heavy, and neither man nor beast nor fowl will drink.

"What makes this mighty difference in these neighbor seas? Not the River Jordan, for it empties the same good water into both. Not the soil in which they lie; nor the country round about. This is the difference: the Sea of Galilee receives, but does not keep, the Jordan. For every drop that flows into it, another drop flows out. The giving and receiving go on in equal measure. The other sea hoards its income jealously. It will not be tempted into any generous impulse. Every drop it gets, it keeps.

"The Sea of Galilee gives and lives; the other gives nothing. It is called the Dead Sea. There are two kinds of people in the world, just as there are two kinds of seas in Palestine. One kind gives and the other kind keeps. One kind is flowing and growing; the other is stagnant" (Bruce Barton).

(3) *Paul's illustration.* Verses 7-12.

"And even things without life giving sound, whether pipe or harp, except they give a distinction in the sounds, how shall it be known what is piped or harped? For if the trumpet give an uncertain sound, who shall prepare himself to the battle? So likewise ye, except ye utter by the tongue words easy to be understood, how shall it be known what is spoken? for ye shall speak into the air. Ye shall be a barbarian unto me. Even so ye, forasmuch as ye are zealous of spiritual gifts, seek that ye may excel to the edifying of the church."

One illustration is of a musical instrument, the other of language. Unless there is an intelligent use of a musical instrument according to the notes of the musical scale, its playing is useless. Likewise, unless our language is intelligible according to the use of speech, its employment is meaningless. Neither music nor language have any value unless there is a means for their interpretation. This applies to tongues. Their value is according to their utility and helpfulness. On this basis, prophecy is much more valuable than tongues. It is the intelligent and understandable gift of utterance that will bring the larger and wider benefit to mankind.

(4) *Paul's preference.* Verses 13-19.

"Wherefore let him that speaketh in an unknown tongue pray that he may interpret. For if I pray in an unknown tongue, my spirit prayeth, but my understanding is unfruitful. What is it then? I will pray with the spirit, and I will pray with the understanding also. I will sing with the spirit, and I will sing with the understanding also. Else when thou shalt bless with the spirit, how shall he that occupieth the room of the unlearned say Amen at thy giving of thanks, seeing he understandeth not what thou sayest? For thou verily givest thanks well, but the other is not edified. I thank my God, I speak with tongues more than ye all: Yet in the church I had rather speak five words with my understanding, that by my voice I might teach others also, than ten thousand words in an unknown tongue."

You will notice the frequent use of the word "understanding." It is emphasized as an attribute to worship and is to be preferred over unrestrained and unintelligent emotionalism. The use of the emotions, we must understand, will always attend real worship, but when emotions supplant intelligence, worship has lost its significance. Worship is intended to produce lasting and beneficial effects upon our character. The effects of emotions are transient. When emotions and understanding are concurrent, then the effect is continuous. In Corinth they were not observing this and were allowing their worship to be tumultuous and superficial.

2. The Effect of Tongues on Non-Believers. Verses 20-25.

"Brethren, be not children in understanding; howbeit in malice be ye children, but in understanding be men. In the law

it is written. With men of other tongues and other lips will I
speak unto this people; and yet for all that will they not hear
me, saith the Lord. Wherefore tongues are for a sign, not to them
that believe, but to them that believe not: but prophesying
serveth not for them that believe not, but for them which believe.
If therefore the whole church be come together into one place,
and all speak with tongues, and there come in those that are
unlearned, or unbelievers, will they not say that ye are mad? But
if all prophesy, and there come in one that believeth not, or one
unlearned, he is convinced of all, he is judged of all: And thus
are the secrets of his heart made manifest; and so falling down
on his face, he will worship God, and report that God is in you
of a truth."

The very first sentence of this section is a challenge to
spiritual sanity. It says, "Brethren, be not children in understanding." The Corinthians occupied the spiritual position of
babes and were, consequently, living in the spiritual conditions
of immature children. These people of spiritual immaturity
are challenged to become manly and womanly in faith and
life. In other words, they were expected to grow up. When
they became mature and developed, they would not be spend-
ing their time in emotional utterance. They would be using
the intelligent utterance of prophecy. This intelligent utterance of the gospel's message would have a saving effect on the
non-believers. Paul argues this from verses 23-25.

The appeal of the gospel is intellectual, emotional and volitional. It takes the mind, the affections, and the will to become a Christian. To carry on emotionally as the Corinthians
did would result in the charge that they were mad. That is
exactly what happens today. However, to listen to an intelligent appeal of the gospel supported by the warmth and feeling supplied by the Holy Spirit will lead to a decision of will
for Christ. Emotional converts are unstable and insecure.
Converts who know what they believe and why they believe
it, with reason and revelation as the basis for their faith, have
a solid experience.

It is our earnest and assured conviction that modern Christianity needs to review the pattern of its faith as found in the Scriptures and to set its house in order according to that pattern. We shall continue to be afflicted with fanaticism on the one hand and formalism on the other unless we determine to think and live according to this Book.

A news item in a Canadian paper reported the effects of a recent storm which had swept over the town. "We are glad," said the item, "to announce that the wind storm which blew down the Congregational Church did no serious damage to the town." The church was of such little consequence that its destruction was not a loss. The church should be and must be of tremendous consequence to every town. It can be if it will observe the things that give it spiritual power. Its New Testament pattern is laid in such plain outlines that there is no excuse for its inconsequential existence.

II. Proprieties of the Church. Verses 26-40.

Certain proprieties of order and dignity are given to the church. Any well-regulated home observes rules of decency. Should less than this be true of God's house? In this we often find ourselves in the throes of extremes. In one case it is the confusion of fanaticism with its uncontrolled pious rowdyism. In the other case it is the frigidity of formalism with its stilted and oppressive ritualism. It seems that neither of these conditions should exist. After all, the church is our Father's house. There is no reason why we cannot have a reverent friendliness there as well as in our own homes. God is not impressed with people who act like pious icicles when they worship Him. By all means, let us have reverence, but with it the freedom and liberty of the Spirit, for "where the Spirit of the Lord is, there is liberty."

1. Tongues and Interpretation. Verses 26-28.

"How is it then, brethren? when ye come together, everyone of you hath a psalm, hath a doctrine, hath a tongue, hath a revelation, hath an interpretation. Let all things be done unto edifying. If any man speak in an unknown tongue, let it be by two, or at the most by three, and that by course; and let one interpret. But if there be no interpreter, let him keep silence in the church; and let him speak to himself and to God."

Having been regulated so long by law or confined by the ritualism of paganism, it was easy for the early Christians to fall into excesses. They often carried on their meetings without restraint or order. Paul describes this confusion in the twenty-sixth verse where he recapitulates a service in which one would sing a psalm, another would speak in tongues, another would interpret, another expound a doctrine, and someone give a revelation. All of this would be going on simultaneously.

The most frequent offender was the tongues speaker. Upon him was put the regulation of interpretation. He should not speak in any such manifestation unless he could interpret. This points out to us that these manifestations of tongues were to be definite languages which might be understood. Its interpretation was to be given for the benefit of all who heard. This regulation of interpretation for edification was the fundamental principle of all the gifts. They were to be spiritual utilities. They were not mystic wonders or metaphysical demonstrations to impress people. It was not impression but expression that determined their right of use. This intelligent and wise regulation would put an end to the disgusting vagaries of our own day.

2. Prophecy and Revelation. Verses 29-36.

"Let the prophets speak two or three, and let the other judge. If any thing be revealed to another that sitteth by, let the first hold his peace. For ye may all prophesy one by one, that all may learn, and all may be comforted. And the spirits of the prophets are subject to the prophets. For God is not the author of confusion, but of peace, as in all churches of the saints. Let your women keep silence in the churches: for it is not permitted unto them to speak; but they are commanded to be under obedience, as also saith the law. And if they will learn any thing, let them ask their husbands at home: for it is a shame for women to speak in the church. What? came the word of God out from you? or came it unto you only?"

The impressive thing about both of these gifts and their regulation is the fact that they are under the control and regulation of the will. No genuine Christian experience will ever cause its participant to lose control of himself either emotionally or volitionally. Anything that causes an emotional or volitional release that is not under control is not spiritual but Satanic. It belongs to the realm of that borderland of mysticism and metaphysics that is both diabolical and dangerous.

The item that interests us considerably in these verses has to do with the women's place in public worship. There are a great many people so rabidly fanatical on this point that they are more concerned about women's place in the church than that sinners are on their way to destruction. To them we pay scant heed. We are not interested in their prejudices or opinions. What we are concerned about is, what does this and kindred scriptures say about the matter?

There is grave danger of interpreting the Scriptures according to our desires, dispositions, personal circumstances, modern conditions and wishful thinking. It is argued that woman's large place in the modern world is her credential to the same place in the spiritual world. Then there is the other extreme of denying her any place but the place of inferiority.

The Scriptures will never be inconsistent. If it is true that wherever the gospel has gone, it has raised the status of womanhood, it is equally true that, having lifted her, it will not deny her a proper place.

Before you make up your mind about this matter, consider the following facts:

At Pentecost women were included in the one hundred and twenty who were filled with the Spirit and proclaimed the gospel (Acts 1:14).

They were included in Joel's prophecy (Acts 2:17, 18).

Women were companion laborers with the Apostle Paul (Phil. 4:3).

Women were on a new basis. It was the basis of the New Testament principle of "neither male nor female" (Gal. 3:28).

In the very first verse of this chapter women are automatically included in its admonition, "Follow after charity and desire spiritual gifts, but rather that ye may prophesy." It is quite impossible to suppose that women must keep the "love" clause and refrain from the "gift" clause.

In I Corinthians 11:5 it speaks of women praying and prophesying, which were privileges undeniably accorded to them.

On the other hand, yet us remember these other things.

Paul says in I Timothy 2:12, "I suffer not a woman to teach, nor to usurp authority over the man, but to be in silence." That is very plain and quite drastic.

In the light of all these scriptures, what does this scripture mean when it says, as in verse thirty-four, "Let your women keep silence in the churches: for it is not permitted unto them to speak?" Neither prejudice nor preconceptions must hinder us here.

One of the first laws of interpretation is to interpret according to the context, which means the verses which go with the text in question. These verses speak of the order that should be observed in their worship services. The thirty-first verse declares that "ye may all prophesy one by one, that all may learn, and all may be comforted." There is no exclusion of women from these instructions. They belong in the "all." Whatever part woman was to have in the benefits and blessings of public worship was to be observed in the light of verse thirty-four. How could she be one who prophesied and yet remained silent? This is either a glaring contradiction or else theirs was a local problem which made it necessary for her to exercise care and caution in the use of her gifts. There was a local condition. Greek women were kept in almost Oriental seclusion and it would have created a tremendous scandal to have exercised their Christian liberty by appearing in the public assembly in such a manner. Woman's privilege was to prophesy, learn and be comforted, but this privilege was to be limited to meet the problems of her age. She, indeed, was to learn, but not to take part in the confusion of Corinthian abuse and interrupt those who were giving Spirit-filled messages.

Suppose we were to observe this regulation in the same sense that it applied to Corinthian conditions. It says, "if they will learn anything, let them ask their husbands at home: for it is a shame for women to speak in the church." How much would any modern women be able to learn of spiritual matters if they had to depend on their husbands? It is the women who are predominantly informed in spiritual matters. Then suppose she did not have a husband. Should she remain ignorant or get married in order to be informed? Or suppose she was a Christian and her husband was a pagan. You can easily see that these would be pertinent problems.

The problem here was entirely Corinthian. In the days of Corinth there was scarcely a woman who could read or write. Under these conditions, it would be much better for her to ask her husband at home about whatever concerned her. Moreover these were days when slavery debased womanhood to a low degree. She lacked the opportunities and advantages of modern womanhood.

We do not believe that this scripture was intended to discriminate against woman or to restrict her activities necessarily. We do believe she has a sphere, both in the home and in the church. The point of this particular scripture is to regulate her public appearances for the sake of propriety.

If it was "a shame for women to speak in the church," what kind of a shame was it? An immoral shame? Yes, that is what it meant under Corinthian surroundings. It was an indecent, a disgraceful and a base thing, simply because of conditions which prevailed; conditions which made it both immodest and disorderly. The wrong was not inherent in the

act but in the circumstances. If it was right for her to prophesy
and pray, what made it wrong to ask questions in public?
The only answer you can give is the circumstances that maintained in that day.

Womanhood was emerging out of the restrictions and de-
basements of paganism into the new liberty of Christianity.
Let Corinthian Christian women observe the proprieties of
the church and they would best suit themselves as an uplifting
spiritual influence.

We have already considered it in the light of Corinthian
problems. Elsewhere Paul said, "I suffer not a woman to
teach nor to usurp authority over the man, but to be in silence."
Here it is not a question of custom but sphere. Christian
women have a sphere just as Christian men have a sphere.
Many things might be interchangeable but two things were
rigidly set. In one case she was not to "teach" and in the
other she was not "to usurp authority over the man."

In the light of this, what place can Christian women legiti-
mately occupy in the sphere of Christian service? There is
Dr. C. I. Scofield's very comprehensive summary of this whole
matter. "There is no verse which says woman must not preach.
Three things are forbidden to women: (1) They must not
interrupt meetings where the Holy Spirit is at work, by asking
questions (I Cor. 14:23-35); (2) A woman must not 'teach.'
The word 'didaskein' here means, as defined by Thayer, 'to
deliver didactic discourses'—that is, to teach doctrinally by
authority—as we would say, dogmatically. It is the same word
used by the apostle of himself in I Timothy 2:7. A woman
must not set herself up as an authority in matters of doctrine,
like an apostle (I Tim. 2:12); (3) A woman must not be put
in a place of authority in the church, such as the office of
elder would be (I Tim. 2:12, 13). The ordination of women
is an abomination. It should be remembered that two great
principles govern the relation of subordination in marriage
(Gen. 3:16; I Tim. 2:13) . . . The wife is to be in subjection
to her husband 'as the church is unto Christ.' It is obvious that

I Corinthians 14:34, 35 relates to married women, as also do I Timothy 2:12 and Ephesians 5:24. The prohibition to 'teach' is, however, general. 'I suffer not a woman to teach (authoritatively).' So far all is negative. What a woman clearly may do is (1) to 'prophesy' (I Cor. 11:5, Acts 21:9). The gift of prophecy is not exclusively nor even chiefly foretelling, but forthtelling—speaking to edification, and exhortation, and comfort (I Cor. 14:3). Such speaking, therefore, is permissible to women . . . It will be obvious, therefore, that, within the limits expressly fixed, and with the spirit of modesty and subordination, a Christian woman may exercise a wide and varied ministry. (2) She may teach, in any sense not involving dogmatic declaration of doctrine; (3) She may speak 'to edification and comfort;' (4) she may also pray (I Cor. 11:5); and, (5) since 'him that heareth' is commanded to say 'Come,' she may evangelize."

This presents the wide sphere of activity which Christian women enjoy. Wherever she is restricted, it is not to slight her gifts nor to set aside the great value of her service. It is to keep intact the order of God in the management of both home and church. There was a governmental headship vested in man which God foresaw to be necessary. Let us be wise enough to observe it.

Besides these scriptural things there is a biological reason for this restriction of sphere which we seldom consider.

Let us summarize a statement made by Dr. Alexis Carrell in his famous book, "Man, the Unknown." In speaking of the physiological differences that exist between the sexes, he states that these differences are of a very fundamental nature. The very structure of the tissues declare these differences. Then he says, "Ignorance of these fundamental facts has led promoters of feminism to believe that both sexes should have the same education, the same powers, and the same responsibilities. In reality, woman differs profoundly from man. Every one of the cells of her body bears the mark of her sex. The same is true of her organs, and, above all, of her nervous system. Physiological laws are as inexorable as those of the sidereal world. They cannot be replaced by human wishes. We are obliged to accept them just as they are. Women should develop their aptitudes in accordance with their own nature, without trying to imitate the males. Their part in the progress of civilization is higher than that of men. They should not abandon their specific functions."

There is a spiritual equality between men and women. There is also a social equality. But God help us to see that there is a constitutional and functional difference. It is our failure to recognize this in both the church and the world that is destroying the effectiveness of modern womanhood.

We are out-and-out for masculine men and feminine women. The trend to masculinize women is one of the dangers of civilization. To support what we say, let us quote a recent article by Will Durant in which he describes the gradual process which has been disintegrating our civilization: "Women ceased to be women, longing to be men; the masculinization of women was the correlate and result of the demasculinization of men; intellect without character unsexes either sex. The ancient authority of the husband over the wife was replaced by a soul-searing tug-of-war called equality, in which each partner struggled for years to win dominance over the other, and peace came only with the surrender of one or the exhaustion of both. Women ceased to be mothers, and became fragile, expensive toys; men played with them, spent fortunes on them, but did not respect them; education lavished itself upon them, but the more knowledge they collected the more superficial they became. Powerful instincts, formed for the care of offspring, fretted in frustration. Man did more and more for woman; but since he could not bear children, and she would not, fertility fell, the race lost the will to live; and as the best bred least and the worst most, western society began to die at the top, like a withered tree."

The Scriptures assign but one office to woman. It is that of deaconess. Besides this, no ecclesiastical office was open to her. Temperamentally and otherwise, she is best suited for this. It will give her an outlet for her rare and God-given qualities of sympathy and understanding.

As we have already seen, she was assigned the right to use gifts such as prophecy. She could "speak to edification and exhortation and comfort." This did not mean didactically, but it gave her liberty to do all that any Christian woman ever needs to do or say.

As one has said, "God did not mean woman to rule, but to love, suffer, and help. Her heart, and not her head, should be put in the ascendant. Her yieldedness is strength; her gentleness is her scepter. She is not called to exercise ecclesiastical authority, or take her place in the ordained ministry and government of the church; but in the ministry of testimony and teaching, both in public and in private, and in every office of holy love consistent with principles of Christianity, she has boundless right and freedom."

Surely a great honor has been placed upon womanhood. Her feet have indeed been set in a large place. She lacks no useful opportunity. The manner in which she has filled this place in the church is a glory-studded record. In Sunday school and missions she has held a place which is largely responsible for the advance of the cause of Christ. It has been said that the church is "sustained by dead men and living women," referring to the bequests of rich men and the sacrificial service of women.

To sum the matter in a brief statement we may safely believe and know that these are not restrictions upon the ordinary abilities of women. When Scripture says "be filled with the Spirit," the effects of such a filling in service are equally to the woman as to the man. When Scripture says, "let the redeemed of the Lord say so," the right of such testimony is equally to her as to the man. Even the Great Commission is hers to share. However, it would be out of her sphere to take the place of man in the prophetic office so as to usurp the official sphere of spiritual leadership. This is denied her. Let us reverently remember it and obediently respect it.

3. Decency and Order. Verses 37-40.

> "If any man think himself to be a prophet, or spiritual, let him acknowledge that the things that I write unto you are the commandments of the Lord. But if any man be ignorant, let him be ignorant. Wherefore, brethren, covet to prophesy, and forbid not to speak with tongues. Let all things be done decently and in order."

Someone is going to be troubled with the thirty-eighth verse where it says, "But if any man be ignorant, let him be ignorant." It would be an abuse of this scripture to apply this to intellectual ignorance because it has no reference whatever to such ignorance.

In the previous verse Paul speaks of his apostolic authority. If there were those who were jealous of Paul and vainly and stubbornly ignorant of that fact, so that they rejected his authoritative teachings, then let them remain in their self-chosen ignorance and bear its consequences.

There is much self-chosen ignorance. Atheism is such, and we can as contemptuously say of atheists as Paul said of his enemies, "if any man be ignorant, let him be ignorant." We have many other current forms of ignorance. The everyday ignorance of the Bible is a self-chosen ignorance. Opportunities abound on every hand for information. May God help us to utilize them.

The concluding word is both an admonition and a regulation—"let all things be done decently and in order." To put it in different language, we might say, respectably and by arrangement. The "all things" unquestionably refer to all the things discussed in the chapter. They include the operation of the gifts and the administration of the functional work of the church. To do these things respectively does not mean with an unspiritual formality. It does mean to avoid the extravagances and emotional excesses that surround Corinthian tongue speaking. To do these things by arrangement does not mean with an unspiritual mechanics. It does mean order and purpose.

A decent and consistent observance of this admonition would change many of our modern churches into attractive places of worship. It would save them from becoming places of commonplace importance. It would make them desirable as a refuge for world-weary souls for quiet and helpful meditation. God give us such churches.

CHAPTER XV

THE CHRISTIAN AND THE RESURRECTION

I *Corinthians* 15

THE RESURRECTION is a cardinal fact of the Christian faith. It is a double fact holding to the physical resurrection of Christ and holding out the prospect of the bodily resurrection of the Christian.

Paul begins this teaching by saying, "I declare unto you the gospel." This was pointed especially at certain members of the Corinthian church who had followed the philosophical denial of the resurrection. The particular point of their denial was to deny the actual and historical resurrection of Christ. Paul expands their argument to say that if Christ is not raised then the whole Christian gospel collapses.

Paul had lately come from Athens where he had engaged the Grecian philosophers in controversy on this subject of the resurrection. He finds this thing to have filtered into the church and as a result of his discovery we have this magnificent document on the resurrection, both of Christ and the church.

None of these pagan Grecian philosophers denied the idea of immortality. All of the religions of antiquity believed in the survival of life after death. Christianity, however, is the first to teach the resurrection of the body unto eternal life. Judas had immortality but not the same kind as Jesus. There is an immortality which is eternal death and an immortality which is eternal life. Here is advanced the fact of an immortal body for an immortal soul.

The resurrection is dealt with in three ways:

I. THE PLACE OF THE RESURRECTION IN THE GOSPEL. Verses 1-11.

In these verses we have the two facts of Christ's death and resurrection.

1. The Gospel and Christ's Death. Verses 1-3.

(1) *Its declaration.* Verse 1.

"Moreover, brethren, I declare unto you the gospel which I preached unto you, which also ye have received, and wherein ye stand."

The gospel is about to be stated in fresh terms so that there may be no mistake as to its essential parts. It is to be stated with special reference to the Christian's future life.

The gospel is something personal. Here were people who did two personal things with the gospel. They received it and were standing in the provisions of life which it provided. Even so, there were some who needed a better understanding of all its parts. For this reason the old gospel needs a new emphasis. The facts of our faith do not change but our faith changes by a better appreciation and fuller understanding of the facts. Let us have more of the facts and faith will become a fuller and greater force in our lives.

Christians' greatest weakness is the weakness of their faith. They are weak in faith because they do not know the facts of the gospel message. Know, and you will grow.

(2) *Its salvation.* Verse 2.

"By which also ye are saved, if ye keep in memory what I preached unto you, unless ye have believed in vain."

The gospel is a means of personal salvation. This personal salvation was conditioned upon a personal faith. This personal faith was not some religious shibboleth that was to be repeated, but a vital act of life by which the sinner identified his life with the Saviour.

This salvation is not a conditional one. When Paul says, "by which also ye are saved, if," he is not making faith dependent on works. He is not saying that they were saved so long as they remembered certain things. He was telling them that their continuance in the faith was the proof of the reality of their faith. This is stated here as a solemn reminder that men may give a mere mental assent to the gospel. When they do, they are believing in vain. A saving faith requires not only a mental but an emotional and a volitional faith.

There are four conditions of life described by the word "vain."

In verse 2—"vain" believing.
In verse 10—"vain" grace.
In verse 14—"vain" preaching.
In verse 14 and 17—"vain" faith.

It is possible in these conditions to possess all the outlines and semblances of Christian reality and yet be without the genuine elements of Christian experience. We do well to inspect our own hearts to be sure ours is not a vain faith.

(3) *Its revelation.* Verse 3.

"For I delivered unto you first of all that which I also received, how that Christ died for our sins according to the scriptures."

The historical gospel is the effect of a cause. Paul delivered what he received. He did not conceive or invent the gospel. It was not the production of mind or the evolution of time. It was not the outgrowth of circumstances or the result of superstition. It is our satisfaction to be confident in our faith because of its origin. The hope of men rests in the help of God and this is offered us in the simple facts of the gospel.

Three facts are stated here as to the nature of Christ's death.

a. It was *actual*—"Christ died."

Rationalistic critics have endeavored to point out that Christ's death was only a swoon. The scriptural evidence is of such a nature as to make this claim preposterous. More than this, the repeated emphasis which the record puts on the actual death of Christ points to it as the focal point of His redemptive career. The Scriptures do not say that we are saved by the words of Jesus, by the works of Jesus or by the life of Jesus. Salvation rests on the death of Jesus. It is so because death released His life to us and its transmission is by the act of faith. It was as much a biological necessity that Jesus die as that He should have been born. His birth was God's life come down to our level. His death is God's life available for our life.

b. It was *sacrificial*—"for our sins."

The career of Christ was not merely an ethical appearance. It had a definite mission. That mission was laid deep in the needs of the human race. The Scriptures set it forth in promise and prophecy, in type and in symbol. It was of a sacrificial nature.

c. It was *scriptural*—"according to the scriptures."

The death of Christ was neither an incidental nor accidental event. It was according to a pre-determined and pre-written plan. That plan was conceived "before the foundation of the world." It was not an afterthought but a forethought.

Jesus could point to an Old Testament scroll and say, "they are they which testify of me." In accordance with this Old Testament pattern we have the New Testament facts of His death.

The question is often asked, what is the gospel? There are numerous items in the gospel but all are reducible to two things: the death of Christ and the resurrection of Christ. The one produces the redemption of our soul and the other produces the resurrection of our body. Up to this moment, redemption extends to the soul but it will later include the body, thus making redemption a complete and inclusive remedy for humanity. Until now, none of us has experienced the redemption of the body. It is yet to be.

A man once arose in a religious service to say that he already had the redemption of his body and no longer needed a physician to attend his physical needs because he would never be sick again. An elderly Scotch lady sitting nearby noticed the old fillings in his teeth and exclaimed, "Aye, but who is your dentist?"

A Christian's life begins in Christ's death. It is limited now to a physical order but it will possess a new and better expression. This is associated with the resurrection.

A great man once said, "You may bury me if you can catch me." My body is not I. It is only the vehicle of my personality. The body is more than a machine to be thrown into the grave of dissolution to resolve into its elemental dust. In the Christian scheme it will be raised. This was and is a thought foreign to paganism and modern materialism.

The body will have an eternal identity; not to its present sin-form but in a future Christ-form. Man was originally made in "the image and likeness of God." The body is more than dust and it will have more than a destiny of dust. It has been redeemed and it will be resurrected in a form which will conform to Christ's resurrection.

It is this which Paul forcefully declares to the Corinthians in the midst of paganism and to us in the midst of materialism.

2. The Gospel and Christ's Resurrection. Verses 4-11.

(1) *The fact of the resurrection.* Verse 4.

"And that he was buried, and that he rose again the third day according to the scriptures."

Thomas Jefferson was a great American statesman and a religious rationalist. He edited a Bible of his own choosing entitled "The Life and Morals of Jesus of Nazareth." He had no belief in the bodily resurrection of Jesus and thus ends his Bible, "There laid they Jesus, and rolled a great stone to the door of the sepulchre, and departed." The end of the story, thank God, is not a sealed tomb. To depart from such a place into life is to enter a hopeless world.

The resurrection of Christ, like His death, was "according to the scriptures." It is depicted in the Levitical feasts and in the typical persons and is declared in the prophetical statements of the Old Testament. In each of three great ages of the divine economy are to be found foreshadowings of the resurrection. It is found in Enoch in the patriarchal age; in Elijah in the Levitical age; and now its great phototype, the resurrection of Christ in the Christian age.

The use of the phrase "according to the scriptures" with both the death and resurrection of Christ is not a casual literary statement. These two events are fundamental facts of redemption. Their appearance and execution are deliberately declared to be in connection with the Scriptures. The death of Christ is the judicial aspect of redemption. The resurrection of Christ is the justifying aspect of redemption. It is said of Christ that He was "delivered for our offences and raised for our justification." Thus, His resurrection becomes the historical proof and testimony of the efficacy of His sacrificial death. One is complementary to the other; both were "according to the scriptures."

(2) *The proofs of the resurrection.* Verses 5-11.

"And that he was seen of Cephas, then of the twelve: After that, he was seen of about five hundred brethren at once; of whom the greater part remain unto this present, but some are fallen asleep. After that, he was seen of James; then of all the apostles. And last of all, he was seen of me also, as of one born out of due time. For I am the least of the apostles, that am not meet to be called an apostle, because I persecuted the church of God. But by the grace of God I am what I am: and his grace which was bestoweth upon me was not in vain; but I laboured more abundantly than they all: yet not I, but the grace of God which was with me. Therefore whether it were I or they, so we preach, and so ye believed."

Here is assembled a series of indisputable historical facts concerning the personal and physical resurrection of Jesus Christ. These facts plus those found in the resurrection accounts of the four Gospels and Acts make an unbreakable case for the resurrection of Christ.

In the first place, the risen Christ was seen by all kinds of people. At one time He was seen by one person; at another time by two people, at another, by eleven, and at another, by over five hundred people. These numerous witnesses could not have all been guilty of an hallucination.

Furthermore, what these people saw was under all sorts of conditions. It was from so many angles as to make its imagination impossible. Some saw Him in a garden, others in a room, others on a road, others by a sea and others on a mountain. Some saw Him at the dawn, others during the light of day, and yet others, at night. This diversity of circumstances and evidence puts the truth and reality of the resurrection beyond successful disputation.

Beyond all this, the account of the resurrection was circulated while most of the witnesses were alive. No one in that day denied it save dishonest and designing ecclesiasts who purchased the testimony of false witnesses. It was boldly preached as the chief subject of their discourses, both to Jew and Greek. In synagogue and temple its truth was proclaimed. To defend it, they were ready to suffer the loss of all they possessed, endure the most painful sufferings and even die. To deny it they could not be bribed by ease, wealth or fame.

To this array of massed personal testimony, Paul adds his own. He speaks of himself as "last" and "least." But the testimony he submits is not merely the testimony of an eyewitness or of a casual spectator of a notable event. He speaks of it as a life-changing, as well as a world-changing, event. It had a profound effect upon Paul's life. It was the turning point of his career. He came to it as Saul of Tarsus and went away from it as a preacher. He came to it in religious profession and went away from it in personal regeneration. He came to it hating and went away from it loving. He came to it doubting and went away from it believing.

The resurrection is more than a fact. It is a force; but the reality of the force is in the reality of the fact. This fact has been the means of changing the course of history and the face of civilization. To it more than to anything else can be attributed the profound effects of Christianity. It was admitted by the historian Gibbon that the fact of the resurrection was one of the chief reasons for Christianity's conquest of the pagan Roman world. Is it any wonder that it accounts for the conquest of bigoted Saul of Tarsus and made him a colossus of grace?

We find in verse ten the simple autobiography of a soul, "But by the grace of God I am what I am: and his grace which was bestowed upon me was not in vain; but I laboured more abundantly than they all: yet not I, but the grace of God which was with me." This is Paul's brief account of himself. It is the story of an origin, for he came into being "by the grace of God." This man of such a magnificent ancestry and such a brilliant religious record did not claim self-salvation. It is not only the story of origin but of a process, for His grace "which was bestowed upon me was not in vain." Saul did not remain Saul. He became Paul. He was changed and transformed from the narrow version of a religious bigot into the ample proportions of a world-apostle. He stepped out of his provincial environment into the place of a world-maker.

This autobiography of a soul contains the secret of a great life. When Paul mentioned his extensive labors, he added "yet not I but the grace of God which was with me." Here is the secret of his dynamic life and effective ministry.

The indisputable fact of Christ's resurrection became the unanimous testimony of its early apologists and the unanimous belief of its early disciples. Paul states, "so we preach and so ye believed." What they preached and believed was the most obvious fact of their faith—the resurrection. It was so notorious and so conspicuous that any flaw might have been easily exposed. Instead, every item was confirmed. Today, it is our Christian hope because it is our Christian faith.

Luther Burbank was buried under a giant redwood in his garden at Santa Rosa, California. It was his expressed wish for he said, "I should like to feel that my strength was going into the strength of a tree." It is not where we are buried but how we have lived that will measure the contribution of our strength. To live in the power of the resurrection is to transfer one's influence world-wide. It is to live so that one never dies.

The resurrection of Christ is set forth in relation to our resurrection. It seems that there were some in Corinth who, while not doubting the existence of a continuing life, were doubtful regarding the bodily resurrection of the Christian. It is likely that some of them had been influenced by the pagan philosophies which denied any kind of resurrection. These philosophies, like many in our own day, readily conceded that the personality of man persisted after death, but as for the body, they held its total annihilation through the chemical dissolution of the grave.

II. The Plausibility of the Resurrection of Christ. Verses 12-34.

The bodily resurrection of Christ and the bodily resurrection of the Christian are placed in sequence. The plausibility of one is the plausibility of the other. Proof has already been presented to establish the resurrection of Christ. If He has been raised, then His resurrection argues for the resurrection of the body of the believer. Therefore, the simple argument is stated in verse twelve, "Now if Christ be preached that he rose from the dead, how say some among you that there is no resurrection of the dead?"

If they believed in Christ's resurrection, they could not logically disbelieve in the Christian's resurrection. Whatever resurrection they believed in must be a bodily resurrection, for there cannot be a spiritual resurrection if the spirits do not die; and if they cannot be buried they cannot rise. Whenever the Bible uses the word "resurrection," it uses it of the body, meaning that the bodily manifestation of the individual is raised. It is, therefore, very foolish to argue for any resurrection unless it be a physical one, for there is no other.

Three things are presented in this section:

1. The Denial of the Possibility of a Resurrection. Verses 12-19.

To deny the possibility of a resurrection involves:

(1) *A denial of Christ's resurrection.* Verses 12, 13.

"Now if Christ be preached that he rose from the dead, how say some among you that there is no resurrection of the dead? But if there be no resurrection of the dead, then is Christ not risen."

The two resurrections are tied together as cause and consequence. To deny the impossibility of a bodily resurrection is to say that Christ is not raised. This is mental suicide, abject infidelity, and historical blindness, because the resurrection of Christ is a fact so indisputable as to put it beyond any reasonable doubt.

Two distinguished Englishmen, Lord Lyttelton and Gilbert West, were contemporary skeptics in the eighteenth century. That century was the darkest period, religiously, in all the history of England. It was the age of agnostics, rationalists and unbelievers of all classes and descriptions. Both West and Lyttelton belonged to this group. Lyttelton was a member of Parliament and West, a barrister. Both men rejected Christianity. Being fully persuaded that the Bible was a fraud, they determined to expose it. Lyttelton chose to expose its fraudulency by showing the conversion of Paul to be false. West chose his espose in the resurrection of Christ. Both men went to their respective tasks with great confidence. They came together by pre-arrangement and to their great surprise each found the other converted, as a result of their investigations. Instead of exulting over an exposure of Christianity, they both lamented their previous folly and felicitated each other on their joint conversion. Such is the power of the resurrection.

(2) *A denial of Christian truth and faith.* Verses 14, 15.

> "And if Christ be not risen, then is our preaching vain, and your faith is also vain. Yea, and we are found false witnesses of God; because we have testified of God that he raised up Christ: whom he raised not up, if so be that the dead rise not."

Apostolic preaching is a fabrication of historical inaccuracies and personal lies if the resurrection of Christ is not a fact. This involves the believers of this preaching, for if the preaching is false then the faith which resulted from this preaching is a baseless fabric.

Two things are described as being "vain."

a. The apostle's preaching.

They preached the deity of Christ, which was untrue, if the resurrection was not true. Christ made the resurrection a test of His deity. They preached the redemption of Christ, which was ineffectual, if the resurrection was not true, because the resurrection was the proof of His vicarious death.

b. The disciple's faith.

They believed the truth of these doctrines and evidenced it by a new day of worship and a new way of life. As for the new day of worship, it was the first day instead of the seventh day. The Old Testament set the Sabbath as the seventh day. Nowhere is that changed except by the resurrection. The Christians automatically and naturally worshipped on the first day because that was the new day, the day of resurrection.

As for the new way of life, we find the believers immediately changing their mode of living. Both the new day and the new way are wrong if Christ is not risen.

(3) *A denial of the efficacy of salvation.* Verse 17.

> "And if Christ be not raised, your faith is vain; ye are yet in your sins."

The Christian's salvation involves not only the cancellation of the penalty which was upon us for our sins, but it also involves a new contribution to us; the contribution of a new life, a new righteousness and a new standing. The cancellation of the old came by Christ's death while the contribution of the new came by Christ's resurrection. So says Romans 4:25, "Who was delivered for our offences, and was raised again for our justification." Therefore, if the resurrection is not true, salvation is not true and we are yet in our sins. This cancellation was of no effect if Christ was not raised. What good is a negative salvation? What good is a salvation that deals with the past but does not deal with the future? This is the kind of salvation we have if Christ be not raised.

(4) *A denial of hope for the dead.* Verses 18, 19.

> "Then they also which are fallen asleep in Christ are perished. If in this life only we have hope in Christ, we are of all men most miserable."

If Christ is not raised, then the believing dead have perished. They have been annihilated. In this case "we are of all men most miserable." But we hold the hope of a continuing life. We proclaim that hope by an observance of the first day. We set it forth in sermon and song. In our rites for the dead as we stand by the grave we tell of our faith. All of this is a mockery if Christ be not raised. Easter is a foolish festival. Funeral and committal services are meaningless. Yes, the whole thing is a useless and meaningless superstition if Christ is not raised.

Evidently, from all of this, the doctrine of the resurrection, His and ours, is not an empty and unimportant hope. It is something which is vital to the whole structure of Christian faith. If the resurrection is not true, then our house of faith and hope crumbles like a building made of sand.

There is no middle ground here. We either believe it or we deny it. We either accept it or we reject it. Upon the reality of its truth rests the validity of our faith.

The doctrine of the physical resurrection of Christ is not an incidental item of the Christian faith, but one of its most important doctrines. It is not a question of holding an optional opinion about it any more than a chemist may be optional in his belief about certain chemical formulas. There is a formula of faith in Christianity which is necessary to its experience. The resurrection is one item of that formula. There is no redeemed life in us unless there is a risen life.

The hope of the future breathes instinctively in the human breast. Even an avowed agnostic like Ingersoll said, as he stood beside the bier of his brother, "In that night of death, hope sees a star and listening love can hear the rustle of a wing." Christ's resurrection is the historic answer to that hope.

2. The Pledge of our Resurrection in Christ's Resurrection. Verses 20-28.

In the verses immediately previous to these, Paul has stated the impossible position into which a denial of Christ's resurrection places the Christian. Now he states the manifest consequences of that resurrection as they affect the Christian.

(1) *The historic pledge.* Verse 20.

"But now is Christ risen from the dead, and become the first—fruits of them that slept."

Here is a fact positive. It is stated so because it can be proved true—"but now is Christ risen." The ample proofs have preceded in the apostle's argument.

The result of this proven fact is the pledge which Christ's resurrection brings concerning our resurrection. He had "become the firstfruits of them that slept." This was a very understandable thing. Every Jew knew what the "firstfruits" were. They were the farmer's first sheaf of ripened grain presented to the Lord as the pledge of the ingathering of the whole harvest. This procedure was in connection with the third of seven Jewish feasts known as "The Feast of the First-Fruits." On the first day of the feast, selected delegates marked out the spot in the grain field from which the sheaf would be cut. On the second day the sheaf was cut and brought into the sanctuary. On the third day, corresponding to the day of Christ's resurrection, this sheaf was presented to the Lord as a pledge, sample or guarantee, that the remainder of the harvest would be brought in.

According to this previous type, the present fact is that Christ, as the firstfruits raised from the dead, is the sample, pledge and guarantee that all Christians will be raised from the dead. Prove Christ's resurrection and you prove the Christian's resurrection. It has been proved and its proof is our certainity.

(2) *The divine remedy.* Verses 21, 22.

> "For since by man came death, by man came also the resurrection of the dead. For as in Adam all die, even so in Christ shall all be made alive."

The divine remedy for our human predicament is set forth in terms of Christ's incarnation. The tragedy came through a man—Adam. The triumph of resurrection comes through a man—Christ. This involved humanity and necessitated incarnation. Christ must be of our kind to provide our remedy. He, therefore, became the man who felt our death and produced our resurrection.

There are two "alls" mentioned in verse twenty-two. We must not inter-mix them or we destroy their meaning. "All" in Adam die while "all" in Christ will live. The relation to Adam is natural while the relation to Christ is spiritual. Both relationships are biological since both mean life through birth. Our natural life through Adam came by the first birth; our spiritual life through Christ came by the second birth. One is by nature and the other is by faith. To be "in Adam" means to be a member of the human race. To be "in Christ" means to be a member of a new race. One is the progeny of the flesh and the other the progeny of the Spirit.

We are being told here that the "all" who are in Adam must pass through the inevitable process and penalty of death. We are also being told that the "all" who are in Christ escape the penalty of death, pass through the process of death, but through the resurrection they will be made to live. These two "alls" are not interchangeable. They are fixed classifications. Our place in these categories is not altered by wishful thinking. It is only by the biological change of birth. Being born into the dying "all," we must be born into the living "all."

(3) *The future order*. Verse 23.

"But every man in his own order: Christ the first-fruits; afterward they that are Christ's at his coming."

The resurrection is as orderly as creation except that it is in reverse order. In creation it was the lesser and the greater. In resurrection it is the greater and the lesser. Christ first—this is past; Christians following—this is future.

There is an order here. It is "every man in his own order." This order is that of a military rank. It is to be in military precision. The resurrection is not going to be a mob movement. It will be like the organized movement of a regiment. The order that is suggested here does not distinguish between people but rather is to indicate the orderly and military manner of the resurrection.

The "afterward" is the interim between Christ's resurrection of His first coming and the Christian's resurrection at His second coming. It is distinctly stated that our resurrection is to be at Christ's coming.

(4) *The final consummation*. Verses 24-28.

"Then cometh the end, when he shall have delivered up the kingdom to God, even the Father; when he shall have put down all rule and all authority and power. For he must reign, till he hath put all enemies under his feet. The last enemy that shall be destroyed is death. For he hath put all things under his feet. But when he saith all things are put under him, it is manifest that he is excepted, which did put all things under him. And when all things shall be subdued unto him, then shall the Son also himself be subject unto him that put all things under him, that God may be all in all."

Following our resurrection is His reign, for "He must reign."

Why must He reign? It is in order to "put all enemies under his feet."

The order of these momentous events as described here is as follows: First, Christ's resurrection, which is past; then our Resurrection at His return, which is future. After His return and our resurrection will come His reign. This is His earthly reign. The reign of His second coming complements the redemption of His first coming. We have spiritual life as a result of His first coming. We shall have physical life, which is eternal, as a result of His second coming. Concluding His reign is the destruction of the last enemy, which is death. This will mean that with the destruction of death He will have "put all things under His feet."

Here we see "the end" and the advent. They are not simultaneous. At the advent will occur the resurrection of the Christian. Following this resurrection will be Christ's reign and the ultimate conquest of death—Then cometh the end when he shall have delivered up the kingdom to God, even the Father; when he shall have put down all rule and all authority and power."

This putting down of all rule, authority and power will be the achievement of His reign. A new order will come into being on the earth. The autocracy and militarism which have made earth a charnel house will be gone. The ravages wrought through disaster, disease and death will be past. The recurring collapses of civilization will be over.

Today men despair of our civilization. And well they might, though not of our future. Dr. Millikan recently intimated that modern thinkers are revising their former opinion that his present breed of mankind is able, of intelligent thought and of human reason.

This scripture gives in sequence three great "musts." Christ *must* rise. This is past. Christ *must* return. This is future. Christ *must* reign. This is imperative to the rehabilitation of civilization. All of these are links in a chain of great events, the consequence of which will alter the whole scope of life.

The Emperor Alexander of Russia, when in England, ordered a very intricate watch to be made. It was a watch which would combine the features of several notable ones of that day. He was told that if such a watch were made, it would be of such intricate construction that no one in his dominion could repair it. Nevertheless, he insisted on its making. It was eventually finished and sent to Russia. As is inevitable with all watches, something happened to it, and, as its makers had said, no one could be found to repair it; it was returned to England to its original mechanical creators who knew the watch, not only as a piece of jewelry but as a child of their own conception and execution. Who is there to be found who can set right what is wrong in the human mechanism? It is an intricate combination of physical, mental, moral, and spiritual movements. He only who first taught this human machine to move in its divine image, who is acquainted with all the springs and pivots of human action. Some day we shall see this human mechanism once more in the hands of its Maker and by those hands it will be restored to its original precision.

The argument for the resurrection of the body turns next to the everyday problems which the Christian meets.

3. The New Incentives Through the Resurrection. Verses 29-34.

Two questions are asked in their relation to the resurrection:

(1) *Why baptize for the dead?* Verse 29.

"Else what shall they do which are baptized for the dead, if the dead rise not at all? why are they then baptised for the dead?"

The exact meaning of this baptism is quite obscure and is consequently open for various interpretations. We present two; one which is impossible because it contradicts the entire scheme of redemption, and one which is entirely probable.

The first view considers baptism a saving ordinance and suggests that this scripture advocates that living people be vicariously baptized on behalf of dead people who died unbaptized and unbelieving. This kind of baptism of the living for the dead without their consent or knowledge and as a vicarious sacrament is practiced in our very day. Any consistent treatment of divine Scripture will forbid such a practice. Salvation is something we choose for ourselves. It cannot be imposed upon us or accomplished for us by another. It is a matter of the individual will. The desires and wishes of others cannot change our destiny.

The exact meaning of this verse is expressed by Arthur S. Way's translation, "Again, what object will be attained by those who get themselves baptized by proxy for relatives who died before they had such an opportunity for themselves?" It is apparent that this kind of proxy baptism was being erroneously practiced in Corinth. Paul argues, what good does it do them if the dead rise not? He is not advocating such proxy baptism but merely calling attention to its futility apart from the resurrection.

There is a thought here that is worthy of merit. The statement of verse twenty-nine is linked with the conviction of verse nineteen. In verse nineteen Paul said, "If in this life only we have hope in Christ, we are of all men most miserable." Now in verse twenty-nine, "Else what shall they do which are baptized for the dead, if the dead rise not at all? why are they then baptized for the dead?" To be baptized for the dead meant to be baptized in place of the dead. It is not to be baptized on their behalf, you understand, but to be baptized in order to take the place they left vacant when they passed away. Thus, each time one is baptized, he takes the place of one who left his place vacant in the ranks of disciples at death.

This second view is the more probable. In either case no kind of baptism was of any use, if the dead rise not.

(2) *Why stand in jeopardy?* Verses 30-34.

"And why stand we in jeopardy every hour? I protest by your rejoicing which I have in Christ Jesus our Lord, I die daily. If after the manner of men I have fought with beasts at Ephesus, what advantageth it me, if the dead rise not? let us eat and drink; for tomorrow we die. Be not deceived: evil communications corrupt good manners. Awake to righteousness and sin not; for some have not the knowledge of God: I speak this to your shame."

Paul is speaking of the daily dangers with which he and contemporary Christians were faced. It was a momentary hazarding of life. It meant facing death every time they ventured to speak for Christ. If there was no resurrection, what was the sense of enduring such jeopardy?

Paul illustrates what he means by mentioning an experience at Ephesus. Here his life was threatened by the beast-like pagans of the cult of Diana. Paul gladly faced the threat of death there because he believed in the resurrection. He knew that if his life was ended under such violent circumstances, it would be resumed in another world. If the resurrection were not true, then what advantage was there in living so dangerously? Why should he or any other Christian give up the ease, fame and pleasure of the world to live at such a sacrifice if this life ended all? Why not live "after the manner of men" and enjoy oneself with every kind of selfish indulgence? The world said, "let us eat and drink; for tomorrow we die." Sometimes they used other words and said, "Let us have a good time while we live, for we are going to be a long time dead." If death ends all, why not get all we can out of life? Why make the sacrifices of a Christian, if there is nothing to gain?

Death does not end all! The apostle warns them of such a false philosophy. He tells them to beware of the wrong company because it means the corruption of good characters. These Corinthians were associating with cynics and skeptics. It was a mistake because "ill company doth mar good characters."

Goethe once remarked, "Tell me with whom thou art found and I will tell thee who thou art." Proverbs 13:20 says, "He that walketh with wise men shall be wise: but a companion of fools shall be destroyed."

Men are more susceptible to example than precept. Wisdom and folly are contagious. Our companionships affect our thoughts, habits and acts of life.

No wonder so few are endowed with overcoming convictions. Their whole sphere of life is in the midst of the world which either consciously or unconsciously acts as if this life were all. They are living for a present advantage. They are concerned about a full measure of pleasure at any cost. They are ready to sacrifice any principle to indulge themselves in any practice.

There is a great and compelling moral persuasion in the resurrection. Let Christians awake! Let them be spiritually conscious! Let them be mentally informed! Let them be morally strong! Let them hold fast the hope of the resurrection and they will stand fast in the life of this present world.

Modern infidelity is making a desperate attempt to reconstruct human thinking and opinion so as to give us a universe without a God and a grave without a resurrection. Against this negative philosophy the Christian apologist must exert the fullest measure of his energy. The best we have must be put into the fight to save us from becoming a pagan civilization, if indeed we are not already in that state.

III. The Prospect of the Resurrection of the Christian. Verses 35-58.

The resurrection is now presented in terms of personal anticipation. It is not merely something past but something future. It is not merely a mystical thing which happened to Christ, but something practical for our own individual hope. Yes, it is something to which we look forward.

We are instructed in the nature and method of this coming resurrection as it pertains to our bodies.

1. The Character of the Resurrection Body. Verses 35-49.

We should be immediately impressed with the perfect order of argument with which we are now led to contemplate the great hope of the resurrection. It was built first on the certification of the gospel. It was next placed on the certainty of Christ's resurrection as the guarantee of our resurrection. With these things established, it proceeds to the next item of manner and method which is led off with the natural question, "How are the dead raised up? And with what body do they come?" How is this accomplished and what kind of a body does the resurrection provide?

We shall find out in three particulars:

(1) *The process and the product.* Verses 35-41.

"But some man will say, How are the dead raised up? and with what body do they come? Thou fool, that which thou sowest is not quickened, except it die: And that which thou sowest, thou sowest not that body that shall be, but bare grain, it may chance of wheat, or of some other grain: But God giveth it a body as it hath pleased him, and to every seed his own body. All flesh is not the same flesh: but there is one kind of flesh of men, another flesh of beasts, another of fishes, and another of birds. There are also celestial bodies, and bodies terrestrial: but the glory of the celestial is one, and the glory of the terrestrial is another. There is one glory of the sun, and another glory of the moon, and another glory of the stars: for one star differeth from another star in glory."

The process is explained in verse thirty-six—"that which thou sowest is not quickened except it die." Death is always the prelude to life. Nothing lives in nature except it dies. Jesus used this analogy to demonstrate the power and fruitfulness of the spiritual life in John 12:24, "Verily, verily, I say unto you, Except a corn of wheat fall into the ground and die, it abideth alone: but if it die, it bringeth forth much fruit." In man's spiritual life it is a spiritual process of dying to self. In man's physical life it is a chemical process of dying in natural life. Out of that death will come a new life.

What is now true of the universality of death was not always so. Man was created a deathless being. Death was introduced as a penalty for sin. Christ reverses the consequences of death and makes them serve our good by bringing life out of death.

The destiny of man was vastly different than what is witnessed in death. Enoch is a type of what that destiny was. Enoch lived without dying and passed through a remarkable metamorphosis which resulted in his change and ascension.

The product of this resurrection process is a new kind of body. In verse thirty-seven it says, "And that which thou sowest, thou sowest not that body that shall be." It is a body which is sown in death and a body which is reaped in life. One does not sow a body and reap a spirit. It is a new kind of body fitted for the new kind of life.

The person who asks this question is addressed as a "fool," not an imbecilic person but a foolish person. It is an unobserving skepticism, for had this man but looked at life around him he would have seen the answer to his questions in nature.

Out of surrounding nature Paul produces three illustrations to demonstrate the reasonableness of the change that takes place in the resurrection.

a. Plants.

The farmer scatters his seed in the certain expectation of a harvest—resurrection. The seed body which is sown is not the plant body which is reaped. It is the same in nature but not in manifestation. When that seed rots in death, it will spring forth into life; not as a bare seed but as a beautiful plant bearing a head of golden grain.

Each seed has its own body and within that body the characteristics of its resurrection. Plant three kinds of seeds in the same kind of soil and irrigate them with the same kind of water and they will bring a harvest of three different kinds of fruit. A watermelon seed, a squash seed and a pumpkin seed appear very much alike and yet they are very different. To each of these God has given its own body. The nature of the hidden life does not reveal itself until it passes through death and resurrection.

In the same manner all men appear to have the same bodies. They look alike. How then can one tell about the resurrection? There is only one way to tell. It is by the hidden nature of the individual. Just as various vegetables and fruit are different, depending on the nature of the seed, so in the resurrection the body will reveal the nature of the individual. Those who have natural life will be raised with bodies comparable to such a nature. Those who had spiritual life will be raised with bodies comparable to such a nature. All bodies will be raised just as all seeds will produce plants. The plant into which the seed passes will be determined by the nature which the seed possesses. So is also the resurrection of the dead.

b. Flesh.

There is first the principle that "all flesh is not the same flesh." There is human flesh, animal flesh, fish flesh, and bird flesh. Between these there is a biological difference. The reason for this difference is in the hidden nature of each. Man produces man. Animal produces animal. Fish produces fish. Bird produces bird. The resurrection is based similarly. It is according to nature. It will not be the same for all. The spiritual nature and the physical nature will produce diverse resurrections, but both will be raised on that great resurrection day.

In the hand of God matter becomes, in one case, the flesh of man; in another the flesh of beasts; in another the flesh of fish; in yet another the flesh of birds. Each flesh has it sphere. The man is adapted to an intelligent earth life. The beast is adapted to another kind of earth life. The fish is adapted to water life, while the bird is adapted to the air. In the resurrection, man's earthly body becomes the heavenly body adapted to its future expansive environment.

c. Stars.

The matter which composes the stars and suns of the heavens is identical. It is not only identical to the stars but to the earth. "The substances which form our air, our water, our stones, our blood and bones, are diffused throughout the universe and are everywhere the same." Yet there is a difference in what the scripture here calls their "glory." Each star or sun has its own splendor. We call it magnitude. There are stars of the first, second, third and twelfth magnitudes. They are not different in themselves but in their appearance to us.

The conclusion is—"so also is the resurrection of the dead." It will be a differing resurrection. All will not be raised in the forms of spiritual manikins to look exactly like the other. It was previously said, "and to every seed his own body." While there is going to be a certain similarity, there will also be a personal difference. No two natural bodies are alike and yet they are similar. The resurrection bodies will have variety and difference as "one star differeth from another star in glory."

As to every seed there is its own body, so to every spirit there will be its own body. It will be individualistic. It will reflect the degree of spiritual development in our present lives and characters. It will possess a perfection and beauty peculiar to itself. This being true, then, how important is our present attention to spiritual matters!

Time, energy and money spent on the present body end in the grave. All that is spent on the spirit finds its way into the body our spirits will wear throughout eternity.

The unique place of the resurrection in the Scriptures and in the Christian faith cannot be too frequently nor strongly emphasized.

The death of Christ is referred to in the Scriptures subsequent to the Gospels more often than the life of Christ. The resurrection of Christ is likewise referred to more often than His death. This is so because His resurrection establishes the efficient and vicarious character of His death; while His death establishes the purpose of His life.

If infidelity can persuade men that they die like beasts, they will then be persuaded to live like beasts. We need the ennobling and elevating teaching of the resurrection to permeate every feature of life in order that it may be lived on the high level to which it was lifted by Jesus.

We are discussing the character of the resurrection body.

(2) *The natural and the spiritual.* Verses 42-44.

> "So also is the resurrection of the dead. It is sown in corruption; it is raised in incorruption: It is sown in dishonour; it is raised in glory: it is sown in weakness; it is raised in power: It is sown a natural body; it is raised a spiritual body. There is a natural body, and there is a spiritual body."

The natural body has the characteristics of corruption, dishonor and weakness. The spiritual body has the characteristics of incorruption, glory and power. The natural body is sown a natural body and is raised a spiritual body.

This spiritual body is not a spirit. It is a body. It will have bodily characteristics and members. It will be able to engage in bodily activities. "Man in his higher state on the new earth will not only be master of the elements and forces: he will be himself a center of energy, shining like the sun, flying hither and thither at will, rising superior to weight" (Bettex).

This spiritual body is not a body made of spirit. It is a material organism perfectly constructed and adapted to meet the conditions of the new world, and is to be the vehicle of the purified and regenerated spirit of man.

The sum of this scripture is this: An old body is buried and a new body is raised. The question persists that was previously asked, "With what body do they come?" This resurrection body will be both identical to and different from the natural body. It is not going to possess the same particles of the old body but it will have the same identity. As it was in the case of the resurrection of Christ, the same body which was laid in the tomb was raised out of the tomb but it was possessed of new powers and life. It looked like the old body, but performed like a new body. It was identified by Mary in terms of physical likeness, but is was capable of previously impossible feats such as entering a room without opening its door.

On the Mount of Transfiguration, Jesus passed through the metamorphosis of the coming resurrection. He was recognized in His changed state, but His changed body was different in its parts from His ordinary body. The similarity and difference can be illustrated in connection with our present bodies. Our present physical bodies pass through a complete physiological change once in three and a half years. The body I have is not the same body I had. If you have not seen me for three and a half years, you have not seen me before. Yet you have, because the unity of appearance and personality is preserved throughout this change. My body, despite its changes, preserves its identity. Its molecules change. Life is preserved only by the constant process of throwing off dead matter and introducing living matter. The molecules of my last body three and a half years ago may be living in vegetable matter or animal matter. They may be painting the blush on a rose or enrobing the earth in the emerald glory of the grass. My body continues to be the same though it has new molecules. I have still the same organized body I started with when a boy. I still have the scar on my forehead that I received when I fell on a sharp stone. The blood that fell from my wound was replaced by other blood. All is different, yet all is the same.

This tells me that the resurrection of this body is no more an incomprehensible mystery than the fact that the change that takes place in my present body leaves me with my same body. The God who first formed it out of the molecules of matter, called dust, can set it up again. When it is so set up it will be the same body minus its liabilities of corruption, dishonor and weakness.

The spiritual body does not necessarily possess the exact particles of the mortal body. It will not be reconstructed necessarily out of the body put into the grave. It will not be produced by some indestructible germ lying dormant in the grave body. It will not result from natural forces which belong to our present body-life. It is not reviving the old life in a new form. It is not an ethereal body which inhabited our earth body as the nut meat inhabits a shell. It will not be a flesh and blood body for blood is the vitalizing principle of our earth body.

If it were necessary to collect the scattered molecules of our mortal body in order to form our new body, I do not doubt its possibility. This view is not necessary and is highly improbable. Science tells us that an adult does not have a particle of the same flesh he had as a child: yet he is the very same person by a continuous and progressive change, because what he now is is what has grown out of what he then was.

Our present body is called a "natural body." This is another way of saying soulish body. It is a body suited to the expression of our souls, and the soul is the seat of all our natural instincts and desires. Some day this soulish body will be slipped off and discarded as an old garment and we shall inhabit a "spiritual body." This spiritual body is exactly what the name indicates. It will be a body of the spirit. It will be suited to and fit for the spirit.

Dr. A. J. Gordon has said, "Now the body bears the spirit, a slow chariot whose wheels are often disabled and whose swiftest motion is but labored and tardy. Then the spirit will bear the body, carrying it on wings of thought whithersoever it will."

The natural body is the animal form of life while the spiritual body is that coming wonder of organized reality which is animated by the divine life. These two bodies are suited to two separate and diverse conditions of existence.

What is definitely and precisely indicated here in this distinction between the natural and spiritual bodies is the fact that while the body that is raised is like the one which has died, it will, nevertheless, be different, for it will have lost its weakness and corruption. It will thus be freed from all the liabilities and limitations of our present form of existence. It will be possessed of a new form of motion and expression. It will have powers and abilities of incredible proportions.

All of this change will be set according to a pattern. This pattern will be the present resurrection body of Christ which is called a "glorious body" or a body of glory. We are to have a body "like unto His glorious body." It will be like it in nature but distinct from it according to our own personality.

This is a solemn thought. What we are now we shall be. The cast of character will become the kind of eternal person we shall be. Yes, it is true that "we shall be like Him for we shall see Him as He is." Nevertheless, that likeness will take on the complexion and contour of our own individuality, for as "there is one glory of the sun and another glory of the moon, and another glory of the stars: for one star differeth from another star in glory. So also is the resurrection of the dead."

We must keep constantly before us the fact that all which pertains to the Christian life is a question of biology. It is a matter of life. The future life is entirely a biological question. There is nothing mystical about it. Jesus came into the world to introduce a new kind of life. He said, "I am come that ye might have life and that ye might have it more abundantly." How did Jesus propose to produce this life? Was it to be rubbed on like a medicinal liniment? Was it to be put on like a garment? Was it to be acted out like a play? Was it to be copied like an academic lesson? No! It was to be born in us and grow through us. It was to begin as any life would begin, through birth.

 The resurrection follows as the eternal phase of this new life. Jesus called it eternal life. The eternal part of it would not commence after death. It was to commence at the new birth. We have eternal life now as much as we will ever have it. No Christian will ever be any more eternal than he is now. Only it "doth not yet appear what we shall be." The resurrection will complete the physical part of redemption.

   (3) *The first man and the second man.* Verses 45-49.

> "And so it is written, The first man Adam was made a living soul; the last Adam was made a quickening spirit. Howbeit that was not first which is spiritual, but that which is natural; and afterward that which is spiritual. The first man is of the earth, earthy: the second man is the Lord from heaven. As is the earthy, such are they also that are earthy: and as is the heavenly, such are they also that are heavenly. And as we have borne the image of the earthy, we shall also bear the image of the heavenly."

 The fact is set forth here that there are two representative men who stand at the head of two races of men. These refer to Adam as "the first man," and to Christ as "the second man." This points out to us that in reality there were but two men. Adam was a direct creation. Adam was brought into being by creation and Christ, by incarnation. From Adam all members of the human race spring. From Christ all members of the new world of Christian men spring. After creating Adam, the creative process ceased. From Adam the race springs by natural law. After Christ the incarnation ceased. From Him the new race springs by spiritual law. Adam was not the product of the soil or the brute kingdom about him. He was the product of a divine process. Christ was not the product of circumstances or the improvement of the race. Nor are Christians merely improved human beings. The Christian is the result of a birth which is according to the spiritual law of the new life.

Adam and Christ do not produce the same life. Adam produced physical life which has suffered the corrupting liabilities of sin. Christ produces spiritual life which redeems man from sin and regenerates him into a new kind of life. This process will be completed at the resurrection when his body will receive the effects of this new kind of spiritual life.

Adam and Christ are not the same kind of life in themselves. Adam is said to be a "living soul" and Christ is said to be "a quickening spirit." One *has* a living existence and the other *is* a life-giving spirit. One is *living* while the other is *life-giving*.

In the sequence of life there is an inviolate order. There is first the natural and, after that, the spiritual. This is not reversed. No man has yet been able to reverse the order and possess himself of a spiritual existence before his physical existence. Hence, we must bear Adam's image in both patience and confidence until the day when we shall pass through the transformation of the resurrection.

There is not only a difference in the source of our life but in the sphere of our life. So it is said that, "The first man is of the earth, earthy: the second man is the Lord from heaven." Adam's sphere is earthly. Christ's sphere is heavenly. From Adam we derived a body suited to this present world. From Christ we shall derive a body suited to the coming heavenly life. This coming heavenly life is not a ghostly existence in some astral sphere but it is as definite and as material as our present life.

There is also a difference in the character of our life. It says, "As is the earthy, such are they also that are earthy: and as is the heavenly, such are they also that are heavenly." It goes further to say that the image of the earthy is received by the earthy and the image of the heavenly is received by the heavenly. Way's translation of this is splendid, "The first man was of the earth, a vessel of clay; the second man is from heaven. As was the vessel of clay, so are the sons of clay; And as is the Heavenly One, so are the sons of heaven. And, as we have borne the image of the vessel of clay, we shall bear also the image of the Heavenly One."

Here is the truth of a pattern, a process and a product. The pattern is the second man. The process is the resurrection. The product is the heavenly. According to this pattern, the resurrection is going to produce a change in us that will result in a body adapted to a new heavenly environment.

Since the first man is of the earth, earthy, we might also very properly add that he is of the dust, dusty, and of the dirt, dirty. To be identified with Christ through the second birth is to have a destiny of glory.

Just what does it mean when it says that "as we have borne the image of the earthy, we shall also bear the image of the heavenly"? In one case we have come to look like Adam, but in the resurrection we shall come to look like Christ. In I John 3:2 it says, "Beloved, now are we the sons of God, and it doth not yet appear what we shall be: but we know that, when he shall appear, we shall be like him; for we shall see him as he is." We are to be "like Him." Christ is to be the personal pattern of the resurrection change which will take place in our bodies. Christ is now the pattern of spiritual life. He will be the pattern also of the bodily change in the resurrection.

Does this mean that we shall all look alike and not be able to recognize each other? Not at all! There will be as much variety within the new species as there has been within the old species. We are now bearing the image of the earthy yet we do not all look the same. There are some two billion people on earth, but you never find two who are exactly alike. There is an infinite variety in creation which points to the infinite variety that will be true of the new creation. This, it seems, will correspond to that difference which was expressed before, where it spoke of one star differing from another star in glory.

This holds out to us the hope of the intimacy of eternal life. We shall know each other. It will be life continued on the basis of earth's friendships and relationships. In heaven there will be likeness without sameness. There will also be found "peace without molestation—plenty without want—health without sickness—day without night—pleasure without pain—and life without the least dread of death.

This should awaken in all sensitive souls a great incentive for living. This will not be some insipid religious feeling that will stimulate us for a few holy moments only. It will be a great urge, a deep longing, and a lasting determination to live with all these things in mind. We ought to measure the present moment by the future prospect. We ought to live today in the light of tomorrow. We ought to say, "I will be Christ-like today because I shall be like Christ in the days to come."

The wanton and deliberate destruction of civilian life and urban property in London by enemy planes was one of the darkest chapters of earth's history. It is scarcely believable that men with any degree of civilization remaining could conceive a destruction so vast and senseless. Londoners, however, looked toward a better and bigger city through the smoke and debris of their famed city's historic ruins. They already determined to turn Hitler's destruction into an opportunity for civic improvement. While dynamite squads tore down ruins, planning commissions sat in session to devise plans and prepare for reconstruction. As London arose greater and more magnificant after its historic fire in 1666, so London will rise greater and more significant from its recent catastrophe.

Do we think man is greater than God? Have we more foresight than He? Will He allow death to despoil permanently these temples which are our bodies? Must they dissolve into dust and never see a better day? The answer is emphatically, no! Man's reconstruction of destroyed buildings is matched by God's resurrection of dead bodies. We like these magnificent words: "So also is the resurrection of the dead."

2. The Change that Produces the Resurrection Body. Verses 50-58.

Let us read this passage according to Way's idiomatic translation. "So this I do assert, my brothers—material flesh and blood cannot inherit the Kingdom of God, nor may perishability inherit imperishability. Lo, the Mystic Secret is this that I tell you—

> We shall all—
> Not, sleep in death, but—
> In an instant, in the flash of an eye,
> At the Last trumpet-call
> For the trumpet shall sound,
> And the dead shall be raised imperishable;
> And we, the living, shall be transformed.
> For this perishable frame must clothe itself with the imperishable;
> This mortal frame must clothe itself with immortality.
> And when this perishable frame hath clad itself with the imperishable,
> When this mortal frame hath clad itself with immortality,
> Then shall come to pass the word that stands written—
> 'Death hath been swallowed up in victory!'
> 'Where, O Death, is thy victory?'
> 'Where, O Death, is now thy sting?'
> His sting is given to death by sin;
> Its power to hurt is given to sin by the Law.
> But to God be thanks, who is ever giving us the victory
> Through our Lord, Jesus the Messiah!
> Therefore, my brothers, dear ones, prove yourselves steadfast, unflinching, overflowing with zeal in the Lord's work always, knowing as you do that your toil is not fruitless in the sight of the Lord."

(1) *The need of the resurrection.* Verse 50.

"Now this I say, brethren, that flesh and blood cannot inherit the kingdom of God; neither doth corruption inherit incorruption."

The need of the resurrection lies in the present character and construction of our bodies. As a body of "flesh and blood," it is adapted to an earth-life but not to a heaven-life. The flesh part of our body is its earth substance. The blood part is its life principle. What is suited for one existence would be illsuited for a diametrically different existence.

The need for the resurrection is stated in these words, "flesh and blood cannot inherit the kingdom of God; neither doth corruption inherit incorruption." The word inherit means to obtain, and in this sense the flesh and blood body cannot obtain a spiritual existence, neither can a body of corruption obtain a sphere of incorruptibility. There must be a profound and radical change. Such a change will come. It will be a change on a new and eternal scale.

As Christ is the gracious pattern of all our present graces, so is He the greater pattern of our coming glory. He who now is the pattern of our souls will also be the pattern of our body. We shall have a body "like unto His glorious body." When He was raised from the dead, He said to His disciples, "Behold my hands and my feet, that it is I myself: handle me and see; for a spirit hath not flesh and bones, as ye see me have." His resurrection body is the pattern of our resurrection body. It was a body which was vitalized by a principle other than blood, for He said, "a spirit hath not flesh and bones." He had in that resurrected state a body of flesh and bone. He was not a spirit, but His body was spiritual; that is, it was vitalized and animated by a spirit-life. It was God the Creator's Spirit inbreathed into man which made him a living soul. It will be God the re-Creator's Spirit inbreathed into man which will give him an immortal body.

It is exceedingly important to realize that all of this ties into the redemptive and regenerative work of Christ. In His redemption He atoned for sin and conquered death. In His regeneration He passes on the benefits of that redemption to His disciples. The new birth is the beginning of eternity. We cannot live like animals and die to become saints. Death is not in itself a change for the better but rather for the worse. It cannot ever be seen as a blessing.

Much of the cheap poetic sentimentality about death is fit to be despised. Let us honestly face the facts. The facts are that death is a penalty and a process. It is a penalty for sin and a process that prevents the perpetuation of a race of godless human beings. To cancel the penalty and reverse the process we must partake of the regeneration of Jesus Christ. Thus, the resurrection of the body begins in the regeneration of the life.

(2) *The mystery of the resurrection.* Verse 51.

> "Behold, I shew you a mystery; We shall not all sleep, but we shall all be changed."

A mystery is only mysterious to the uninitiated. It is a "mystic secret." A secret is not something unintelligible. A secret is something not known to everybody. When you get into the inner circle and the secret is told you it is no longer a secret. It is something known to the people on the inside and when you get on the inside, you will find that the mystery is no longer mysterious and the secret is no longer secretive.

To us, the process by which the resurrection will change our bodies from corruption to incorruption is a secret. It is, for the time being, something we do not know. It is concealed from us because we are not in a position to know the laws by which this change will be produced. The prospect is that what is concealed will be revealed and what is a mystery will be made manifest.

This mystery which will be made manifest is the mystery of the change. It will not be the same change for all. It is true that "all will be changed." The change will result in the same thing, but it will not occur in the same way.

It says that "we shall not all sleep," referring to a generation which will be living at the time of Christ's coming. For those who sleep the change will be resurrection. For those who live the change will be translation.

Sleep is used as an emblem of death and since the resurrection can only be of the body, this sleep is only the sleep of the body. The spirit of the believer which leaves the body at death departs to be with Christ while the body is in a state of slumber in the grave. The resurrection is the change which will bring it forth to life. This change takes place, not at the time of death, but at the time of Christ's return. It will produce the transformation of resurrection in those who sleep and the transformation of translation in those who live. Resurrection is the change from physical death to eternal life for the body. Translation is the change from physical life to eternal life for the body.

Several important facts must be kept in mind in order to keep our perspective clear. We must not become confused as to the time of the change and the subject of this change. The time of the resurrection will be at the second advent of Christ. Furthermore, it will be the resurrection of believers and not a general resurrection of all beings. It does not concern those patterned after the first man, Adam, but those patterned after the second Man, Christ.

Another thing to be kept in mind is that this is definitely the resurrection of the believer's body. It is the body which sleeps. During the interval between death and the Lord's return the spirit of man has been in conscious existence with Christ.

> "This body is my house—it is not I;
> Herein I sojourn till, in some far sky,
> I lease a fairer dwelling, built to last
> Till all the carpentry of time is past.
> When from my high place viewing this lone star,
> What shall I care where these poor timbers are?
> What, though the crumbling walls turn dust and loam—
> I shall have left them for a larger home.

What, though the rafters break, the stanchions rot,
When earth has dwindled to a glimmering spot!
When Thou, clay cottage, fallest, I'll immerse
My long-crampt spirit in the universe.
Through uncomputed silences of space
I shall yearn upward to the leaning Face.
The ancient heavens will roll aside for me,
As Moses monarch'd the dividing sea.
This body is my house—it is not I.
Triumphant in this faith I live and die."

The Christian conception of death is not only advanced by the solid affirmation of Scripture; it is supported as well by analogy from nature. Here we stand upon the shore of the sea. We watch a great ship slip from its moorings. Its cables loosed from their earthly anchorings are drawn aboard, and under the impulse of its hidden power the majestic vessel moves out. On the blue of the ocean she is an object of symmetry and beauty. As we stand and gaze she diminishes in size and shape until at last she is but a speck against the sky. Then before our very eyes she disappears beyond the horizon. We say, "There she goes." Where has she gone? Not out of existence, only out of sight. She is the same ship she was before. She has not changed a bit in size or shape, but she is gone. Yet to others who stand on another shore in another land she will soon appear. They will soon be saying of our ship, "Here she comes." That is what dying is for a Christian. We watched the fleeting breath as he slips farther out toward the other land. Farther and farther he goes and when the last breath comes, we say, "There he goes." Where has he gone? Not out of existence. He is no less existent and conscious now than he was then. He has only gone beyond our sight and our sense. On another shore other watchers looking this way will say, "Here he comes." Yes, that is dying for a Christian— a going out and a coming in. Here the shout, "There he goes." There the shout, "Here he comes." He has exchanged earth for heaven, time for eternity, us for Christ.

(3) *The manner of the resurrection.* Verse 52.

"In a moment, in the twinkling of an eye, at the last trump: for the trumpet shall sound, and the dead shall be raised incorruptible, and we shall be changed."

The resurrection is not a process of evolution. It is not a gradual transformation. It will occur in the suddenness of "a moment." It will happen as noiselessly as "the twinkling of an eye." This will be in the flash of an eye. Twinkling means a scintillation. It refers to an eye wink which occurs almost imperceptibly and entirely without noise. The hinges of the upper eyelid are so precisely hung and so instantly responsive to nerves and muscles that they move with a stealth and quickness that is scarcely noticeable. We can then imagine the beautiful timing and remarkable swiftness of the change that will take place at the resurrection.

This change in our bodies will not only be "in" the flash of an eye but it will be "at" a certain time. The time elapsed will be an eye-flash. The time this eye-flash occurs will be "at the last trump." Just what does it mean by this statement? In Thessalonians it says, "For the Lord himself shall descend from heaven, with a shout, with the voice of the archangel and with the trump of God: and the dead in Christ shall rise first." Thus, the rising of the dead will be at the sounding of a trumpet. This trumpet is described as God's trumpet. Will it be a literal trumpet heard by all the world in a spectacular moment of time? We think not. The character of the trumpet will be such as will produce an announcing sound heralding the most thrilling spectacle of all time. As radio hurls a voice through the air which is picked up only by those tuned to the same wave length, so the trumpet sound will be heard only by those concerned. We conceive of this sound not directed so much to the sleeping bodies, because the spirits are not in the grave, as it is a great heralding notice of a new day.

This trumpet has no connection with the seven trumpets of the book of Revelation where, in the eleventh chapter, it speaks of the seventh angel sounding the last of seven trumpets. Those are trumpets of judgment and are blown by angels. This is a trumpet of blessing and is blown by God.

This trumpet may have its meaning in a military custom of the ancient Romans of Paul's time. If an army was about to break camp for a march, trumpets were used. The first trumpet blast meant to strike tents and assemble arms and equipment for the march. The second trumpet blast meant to fall into line in companies. The third and last trumpet blast meant to march. If this was Paul's idea of the resurrection trumpet, it speaks to us once more of the military precision of this great event. A previous statement was, "every man in his own order." This referred to the order of military movement as it now refers to the assembling of the units of this movement for the final march.

We believe there is a deeper meaning than this behind the blowing of this "last trump." Trumpets were significant in the earthly life of Israel. There was a redemptive pilgrimage which in both symbol and sacrifice set forth the meaning of redemption. There was a sacred feast of trumpets which called the people together for worship. The trumpets used were the silver ones described in Numbers 10:1-10 which were made of the silver atonement money required of the people. The sounding of the first one assembled the leaders. The sounding of the second and last one was a general call for all the people. It was the order to march.

Keeping this in mind, we notice that the trumpet is used variously. Israel will be gathered from all the earth by the trumpet. The heavenly hosts are marshalled to Armageddon by the trumpet. The trumpet will proclaim the world's final and complete conquest by Christ. It will be the signal for the resurrection. Since the trumpet was made of one piece from the redemption money of the people, how significant are its uses! Redemption is to be completed in the regathering of Israel, the victory of Armageddon, the conquest of the nations, and the resurrection of the dead. This, indeed, is the vast scope of the redemption of Christ. In that redemption is the principle of every great consequence yet to come for man's good. Peace, prosperity, health, and resurrection are all wrapped up in Christ's redemption. When this last trumpet sounds, it will not be the last trumpet in point of time. Other trumpets will sound in the world after the notes of this one have echoed past the open grave of resurrected saints. This will be the last trumpet as far as the Christian is concerned. It will be his summons to the glad company of the redeemed. It will be his summons to those climatic events which will usher in the new era.

The sounding of the last trump will be heard and answered by a transforming change in two classes of people. The trumpet shall sound and the dead shall be raised first; and second, the living shall be changed. Notice how accurate the language is. It does not say "all" will be changed or that "all" will be raised. It says that certain ones will be changed—the living. One is resurrection and the other is translation. Here is a soul-thrilling prospect to look forward to, and while we are looking we are sustained by the presence of One who said, "I will never leave thee nor forsake thee."

Time has been called "the chrysalis of eternity." There is only a measure of truth in this statement. Time is, in reality, an interval between two eternities. Time is but a convenient measurement of existence for human beings. Beyond us there is no oblivion any more than there was an oblivion behind us.

The Christian looks forward into eternity through the open portal of a resurrection tomb.

(4) *The imperative of the resurrection.* Verse 53.

"For this corruptible must put on incorruption, and this mortal must put on immortality."

It says "this corruptible *must*" and "this mortal *must*." This is the resurrection's imperative. A certain condition in man makes the resurrection imperatively necessary. It is the con-

dition of mortality in those who are living. This is spoken of
the Christian. When dead he has a corrupting body. While
living he has a mortal body. This condition refers strictly to
the body, for spirits are neither corrupting nor mortal. It is
the body which puts on incorruptibility and immortality that
it might be the fitting garment and vehicle for the spirit which
possesses eternal life.

When the Bible speaks of immortality it speaks of it as
"deathlessness" and "incorruption." This can only mean the
body, because the spirit or soul of man is capable neither of
death nor of corruption. It is a body condition. Jesus is spoken
of as having "abolished death and hath brought life and immortality to light through the gospel." This He did by His
resurrection and we shall share in that at our resurrection.

Man has always had the quality of everlasting existence,
but the Bible carefully distinguishes between everlasting
existence and eternal life. The believer has eternal life. The
non-believer has everlasting existence. The believer has, in an
accomodated sense, an immortal spirit and a mortal body.
Some day what is true of his spirit will be true of his body.
The body will put on incorruptibility and immortality. The
things which cause corruption will be absent in the new order
after the resurrection. Bacteria and disease germs will no
longer be present. However, incorruptibility is not just a negative thing consisting of the absence of bacteria and germs.
It is a new quality of life. It is a new structure of body. In
fact, it is a new physical creation of immortality to match
our present new spiritual creation of character.

"Immortality comes from the word "athanasia" and appears
much like a modern word called "euthenasia." There is a
science of euthenics that correlates to the science of eugenics.
Euthenics is "the mode or act of inducing death to secure
more efficient human beings." Man may induce death but he
cannot produce deathlessness. This is something beyond the
reach of the scientist's brain or hand. No formula he can
arrange can produce a single atom of immortality.

(5) *The triumph of the resurrection.* Verses 54-57.

"So when this corruptible shall have put on incorruption, and this mortal shall have put on immortality, then shall be brought to pass the saying that is written, Death is swallowed up in victory. O death, where is thy sting? O grave, where is thy victory? The sting of death is sin; and the strength of sin is the law. But thanks be to God, which giveth us the victory through our Lord Jesus Christ."

The resurrection will be a long-anticipated victory. It will be the climaxing part of redemption so far as the believer is concerned. This victory was written in Isaiah 25:8, "He will swallow up death in victory; and the Lord God will wipe away tears from off all faces." Death has caused more tears than any other human happening. When death is gone, the most potent source of tears will be gone.

At present, both the process of death and the place of the grave are experiences that confront all men. While the experiences are the same, the effects of these experiences are not the same. All must experience death and the grave in the normal expectancy of life. Yet, for the Christian, death has no sting and the grave has no victory. It is true that it appears so because the Christian and the non-Christian suffer the same consequences of death and the grave. The Christian dies and the Christian is buried, but this is only relatively true, for there is a fact to be borne in mind. That fact is the resurrection. It will nullify death's present sting and make empty the grave's present victory.

The question is asked, "O death, where is thy sting?" The word "sting" refers to an organic weapon belonging to such insects as bees. It is the same word used in Revelation 9:10 where it speaks of an awesome brood of locusts which have "stings in their tails." In the bee the sting is a sharp organ of offense and defense connected with a poison gland and used in wounding and innoculating its enemy with a poisonous secretion. When the honey bee strikes an enemy with its stinger, that organ is left in its victim. It has lost its future effectiveness because its sting is gone. When death struck Christ on the cross it lost its sting and, hence, its future effectiveness. Whenever it strikes a believer, it is with a stingless process. Death has lost its sting and the grave has been robbed of its victory. The final and complete victory will come when death is swallowed up and abolished. Now death's sting is gone. Then death's existence will be gone.

To some, however, death has a sting. It is only to those who are yet in sin and out of Christ. In Christ, death is stingless. Out of Christ, death is still a penalty. In Christ, only the process of death continues while the penalty ceases. No Christian dies in penalty for sin. Christ did that for him. All Christians must suffer the process of death.

If behind death we find sin, then behind sin we find the law. The law is "the strength of sin." The law gives sin its penalty and its teeth. The law still exacts its sentence. You will be careful to notice that the law is not the strength of salvation. The law does not bring salvation. It is that which gives to sin its power to hurt. As long as sin is here, there will be death's penalty. As long as there are those living under the law, there will be subjects for that penalty. In grace there is a stingless death and a defeated grave.

The source of this victory is carefully identified. "But thanks be to God, which giveth us the victory through our Lord Jesus Christ." Christ is our victor because He has fulfilled the law and vanquished death.

(6) *The incentive of the resurrection.* Verse 58.

"Therefore, my beloved brethren, be ye stedfast, unmoveable, always abounding in the work of the Lord, forasmuch as ye know that your labour is not in vain in the Lord."

The resurrection gives a new meaning to life. It is no longer the frustration of life by death. What is the use of life if its efforts and endeavors are nullified by death and absorbed by the grave? The answer is, no use. The Christian life has both a plan and a progress. Life is laid out on an eternal scale. Time merges into eternity. Thoughts, plans and deeds do not end with a grave but continue into another world. Life is not an exile's existence in an isolated world. Death transfers life to a higher and better plane. Death continues what life commences. Labor here becomes labor over there. Fellowship now is fellowship forever. Hence, we are to be "steadfast, unmoveable, always abounding in the work of the Lord" because such labor "is not in vain in the Lord."

The world tries to pre-empt the Christian philosophy of death. It dare not because it cannot. This philosophy is the exclusive property of the Christian. Have Christ and you will have a life laid out on the scale of eternity. Go out then, to live, to love, and to labor. To live without love is to miss the greatest virtue. To live without labor is to miss the highest purpose.

> "If I have strength, I owe the service of the strong;
> If melody I have, I owe the world a song.
> If I can stand when all around my post are falling,
> If I can run with speed when needy hearts are calling,
> And if my torch can light the dark of any night,
> Then, I must pay the debt I owe with living light.
> If Heaven's grace has dowered me with some rare gift;
> If I can lift some load no other's strength can lift;
> If I can heal some wound no other hand can heal;
> If some great truth the speaking skies to me reveal—
> Then, I must go, a broken and a wounded thing,
> If to a wounded world my gifts no healing bring.
> For any gift God gives to me I cannot pay;
> Gifts are most mine when I give them all away;
> God's gifts are like His flowers, which show their right to stay
> By giving all their bloom and fragrance away;
> Riches are not in gold or land, estates or marts;
> The only wealth worth having is found in human hearts."

CHAPTER XVI

THE CHRISTIAN AND SERVICE

I *Corinthians* 16

THE FINAL chapter of this great book with its story of a maturing life does not leave us suspended in some fantastic religious experience that is without point or purpose. It leaves us where all matured and adult Christian life should be, in the activity of service. It harnesses life, intellect, emotion and will, and energizes them with a practical spirituality. This, indeed, is the fitting climax of a life that is matured.

This book of life began with the problem of a perverted Christian liberty. Christians released from the bondage of legalism were going to the extreme of an unrestrained liberty. They failed to understand the true meaning of liberty. Liberty is not a question of doing as we like but doing as we ought. Liberty is life devoted to the best interests of all. It is in this large place of liberty's wide interest that the final phases of this chapter place us.

Amidst the ravages and activities of war the bishops of the church of England gathered to discuss their church's future. It is reported that "with great coats wrapped around them, they gathered day after day in the paralyzing cold of unheated Malvern College to hear speaker after speaker denounce present-day failure to identify Christianity with any great cause except 'nosing out fornication.'" Ours is the failure to see the great causes identified with Christianity. The New Testament everywhere identifies it with the great cause of world evangelization and Christian humanitarianism. It is identified further with the great cause of faithfulness in little things. Causes are not great because of size. World dimensions do not make a cause great. Jesus was dedicated to the cause of the individual. He was dedicated to the cause of the heart, the head, and the hand. He saw in humility the first step to greatness. We have misjudged greatness because we measure by human standards.

Let us look into this final chapter and see life identified by a greatness of service that is calculated to challenge the least and the greatest.

I. STEWARDSHIP. Verses 1-4.

   1. The Principles. Verses 1, 2.

> "Now concerning the collection for the saints, as I have given order to the churches of Galatia, even so do ye. Upon the first day of the week let everyone of you lay by him in store, as God hath prospered him, that there be no gatherings when I come."

The occasion for this bit of stewardship instruction came as a result of the distress of Christians in Jerusalem. That city had first felt the sharp edge of persecution's sword. They had suffered the despoiling of their goods. Their faith had cost many their life. To relieve this distress, Paul is gathering an offering to be taken to them.

Immediately after saying in the previous chapter, "Therefore, my beloved brethren, be ye steadfast, unmoveable, always abounding in the work of the Lord, forasmuch as ye know that your labour is not in vain in the Lord," Paul says, "Now concerning the collection." The practical application of the incentives of the resurrection is immediately linked to the taking of a collection.

What relation does labor have to money? It said in the previous chapter, "your labor is not in vain." Your money is your labor in the form of capital. He who gives his money is giving his labor. Even when days of labor have ceased, money continues to be our labor. Some give their labor in time. Some give their labor in talents. Others give their labor in money.

You perhaps have heard ministers say rather flippantly, "we do not take collections; we receive offerings." That sounds good but it is not a distinction with a difference. It is speaking here of a "collection" which means the gathering of money. It is only by such means as this "collection" that Christians have of assembling their resources for the administration of the affairs of the church. In this case it was the social aspect of the gospel. There is a social aspect and we do well to remember it. The spiritual aspect is first and the social, next.

You are careful to notice that the collection was not taken for the sake of the collection. It was taken "for the saints." Every collection should have a purpose. Here it was very beautifully stated "for the saints." It does not say for the poor, or the indigent, or the less fortunate. They were not asked to give to a condition or a calamity, but to kindred souls.

This collection was not received for the benefit of their own selves and their local assembly. It was to go to fellow-Christians they had never seen. It was to go to a place they had never been. Here is Christianity identified with a great cause. The cause was not only great but the manner in which they went about it was equally great. Many times we dishonor a great cause by the little way in which we do things. That is true of many of the financial affairs of the church. The great cause of world evangelism is belittled by our commercialized and secularized money raising. Imagine Paul attempting to gather a sum of money for the relief of the saints in Jerusalem by conducting a sale or serving a supper. We have belittled the greatness of Christianity's cause by the littleness of our financial methods.

In all the Greek manuscripts there is not even a period or a comma between the fifteenth and sixteenth chapters. We step from the scenes and incentives of resurrection into the scenes and necessities of a collection. Doing this, we must carry over the greatness of the resurrection into the necessities of the collection. If we are faithful and observe this spirit of greatness, we shall never become involved in the

personal pettiness of a lot of people nor the shameful com-
mercialism of a lot of churches. We shall measure life by
the broad sweep of eternity. We shall consider substance,
not as a thing to hoard and hang on to, but something to
exchange for immortal things.

If every Christian were to venture his life in such a plan
as this, it would transform the whole character of Christian
work. The confining restrictions in which we now find ourselves would be gone. The meager flow of means would become a mighty stream.

If we were careful to divide our profits, we would find God
dividing to us the lasting and abiding profits of a great life.
We do not believe that generous giving is in itself a guarantee
of temporal blessing. Other things must be equal, but if
they are equal, it is still true that "godliness is profitable to
all things."

"In the latter part of the last century a girl in England
became a kitchen maid in a farmhouse. She had many styles
of work and much hard work. Time rolled on, and she married the son of a weaver of Halifax. They were industrious;
they saved enough after a while to build themselves a home.
On the morning of the day when they were to enter that home,
the young wife arose at four o'clock, entered the front dooryard, knelt down, consecrated the place to God, and there
made this solemn vow: 'O Lord, if thou wilt bless me in this
place, the poor shall have a share of it.' Time rolled on and
a fortune rolled in. Children grew up around them, and they
all became affluent. One, a member of parliament, in a public
place declared that his success came from that prayer of his
mother in the dooryard. All of them were affluent. Four
thousand hands in the factories. They built dwelling houses
for laborers at cheap rents, and where they were invalid
and could not pay, they had the houses for nothing. One
of these sons came to this country, admired our parks, went
back, bought land, opened a great public park, and made it
a present to the city of Halifax, England. They endowed an

orphanage; they endowed two almshouses. All England has heard of the generosity and the good works of the Crossleys."

The ethics of the Christian church in the matter of finance is one of the greatest tests of its purity and sincerity, but on this very basis it has a shameful record. Everywhere one sees and hears of unethical and unscriptural financial practices.

One could wish that the church would be as careful to keep beyond reproach as was true of the last American Olympic Committee. The Committee was financially harassed up to the time of the team's departure for Europe. They received an offer of $100,000 from a breakfast food concern in return for the inclusion of the product on the athletes' menu and permission to advertise the fact. Their chairman said, "Though tempted to accept this means of solving most of the money worries, the committee finally rejected the offer on the ground that it would be unethical and set a precedent injurious to sport." Are we as zealous for the cause of Christ? Do we guard its interests so as not to set a precedent injurious to Christ?

The high ethics of church finance is revealed in the manner which Paul laid down for the gathering of the benevolent offering to be taken for the Judean saints.

(1) *Periodically.* Verse 2.

". . . upon the first day of the week . . ."

The recognition is made here of "the first day of the week." This day was recognized as the Lord's day and was the day when the Christians met for worship. It was distinguished from the seventh day which was identified with the law of the old, and now obsolete, dispensation. The first day was identified with grace and the resurrection of the new dispensation. You will find repeated references to the disciples gathering for Christian worship on the first day.

This first day began with the resurrection. No law changed it. No council decided it. No committee arranged it. It was as spontaneous as Pentecost.

This first day was a beginning day. It was the memorial of the beginning of redemption as the seventh day was the memorial of the beginning of creation.

This first day was a Christian day. It was to be a memorial to Christ as the seventh day had been a memorial to God. Hence, when the disciples gathered on this first day they observed the Lord's Supper.

This first day was a day of spiritual preparation as the seventh day had been a day of physical rest.

On this day they stood on resurrection ground with a new and significant emphasis upon Christian service and activity. It is fitting that our money should have a place as well as our manhood.

This taught the principle of systematic Christian giving. In the Old Testament the tithe was an annual tax. Here it was to be a systematic contribution. It would be a remedy for occasional spasms of charity. It would not be dependent upon stirring emotional appeals. It was to be a deep-seated, systematic habit of giving.

The observation is obviously needed, yet it should be made for the sake of emphasis that this sort of systematic, periodic Christian giving would solve the financial problems of the whole Christian enterprise.

(2) *Personally.* Verse 2.

" . . . let everyone of you lay by him in store . . . "

It is very specific, "let everyone of you." This would obviously apply to all members of the Christian community of believers. It applies to old and young, rich and poor. The churches of Macedonia gave out of what Scripture says was "deep poverty." The Lord accepted the mites of the widow. While their proportion was more than the gold of the rich, their portion was not only accepted but required.

The principle of the gift lies in the giver as the proportion of offering lies in the offerer. Giving is something personal. Dollars are not just dollars. Money is not just money. Money is life and labor. It is time and thought. Giving depends upon the giver. Paul says in II Corinthians 8:5, "And this they did, not as we hoped, but first gave their own selves to the Lord." When one has given himself his money will follow.

The thought conveyed in the phrase "lay by him in store" is quite suggestive. In Way's translation it says "forming a little hoard." This is the proper kind of hoarding. Behind it is the idea that the existence of the hoard and the size of the hoard is our own personal business. It is not something to be levied on us by ecclesiastical treasurers. It is to be a personal proportion of our own choosing and knowledge.

(3) *Proportionately.* Verse 2.

". . . as God hath prospered him."

The amount of the individual's contribution to the collection was to be a proportion determined by that individual's prosperity. There is no legalism here. There is no specific measurement anywhere in the New Testament of the amount we are to give. The Christian is under a new covenant. His life is actuated by grace and not regulated by law. It is a matter of liberty and not constraint. He is God's son and not a slave. Having passed through the refining and ennobling effects of love, the matured Christian is prompted in his benevolence by the spontaneous generosity of his heart.

Paul says in II Corinthians 8:12, "For if there be first a willing mind, it is accepted according to that a man hath, and not according to that he hath not." The basis of expectancy is personal ability. This automatically makes the proportion of our contribution flexible.

While the New Testament does not make the tithe legally binding, any more than the Sabbath, we cannot recklessly assume that there are no principles inherent in the New Testament which govern both the use of money and time. The New Testament attitude to time is no less strict than the Old Testament. In the New Testament every day is sacred and, likewise, all means is the capital which Christian stewards are to manage.

The early Christians set a noble example that far outstripped any Old Testament regulation. They forsook all, sold all, sacrificed all, and gave all. It was necessary in that day to mobilize every resource for a total, all-out war against paganism. The intensive defense of the faith and the extensive offense of the gospel required a Christ-minded discipleship that would give all.

The Christian principle of proportionate giving on the basis of personal prosperity would certainly consider the tithe as a minimum standard. This would not be a legal matter at all. His giving is something subject to the control of the Holy Spirit. If He is to the guide and director in all other departments of life, He should be in stewardship, also.

Fritz Kreisler, the noted violinist, is reported saying, "I have a right to use for myself only that which will make me more efficient and more fit for the purpose of the kingdom of God." That is ideal for Christian giving.

The reason for laying down this kind of periodic, personal, and proportionate giving is expressed in the final phrase of the second verse, ". . . that there be no gatherings when I come." This means that Christian giving should not be dependent upon emotional appeals or financial crises. The present manner of giving in the church is the very thing Paul sought to prevent. We give, not in keeping with a proper plan, but in response to emotions and emergencies. The reason for the emotional appeals and the emergencies is the depleted treasury of the Lord's work. If we give scripturally, the treasury would be sufficiently full to meet any need and, hence, no emergencies would exist and no emotional appeals would have to be made. Appeals for money are not right but they are made wrongfully necessary because the Christian church is not right in its giving. The correction of the financial problems of Christianity is not in stopping appeals but in starting scriptural giving.

There is money on hand for the exploitation of every kind of material enterprise on earth, yet the greatest work in the world languishes. It does its work on a pitiful religious dole when it might be supported by a bursting treasury. It is not overstating the case to say that the enterprise of world evangelization depends as much on our *paying* as our *praying*.

We find ourselves still lingering about the opening verses of this final chapter. They deal with the Christian's money matters. They are as important as his spiritual life; in fact, they are his spiritual life. Spirituality and liberality belong together.

There may be a deeper reason for the paucity of gifts to the Christian enterprise than we ordinarily suspect. If the ministers can charge the members of the church with failure in giving, the members can charge the ministers with falsity in asking and laxity in handling gifts. Appeals are made so often from unworthy motives and for purely personal gain. Improper administration is another reason for lack of giving. It was these very things which Paul had in mind in the next verses.

2. The Application. Verses 3, 4.

> "And when I come, whomsoever ye shall approve by your letters, them will I send to bring your liberality unto Jerusalem. And if it be meet that I go also, they shall go with me."

Paul saw to it that the appeal had the very highest motive. It was not a fictitious need. It was not an invented emergency. It was not a personal financial racket. The occasion for this collection was an actual necessity of fellow Christians. To relieve that necessity was as much "the work of the Lord" which Paul spoke of in the final verse of the previous chapter as the evangelization of Africa.

The spontaneity of their response in this collection was to be from the great fact of the resurrection in which they were reminded that their "labor is not in vain in the Lord." All of this would combine to lend a legitimate and proper reason for their giving, and these things should be true of every bit of financial activity in the modern church.

There was another thing in this incident that we do not dare overlook. It was the careful provision for the wise handling and administration of the money. Paul said, "And when I come, whomsoever ye shall approve by your letters, them will I send to bring your liberality unto Jerusalem." He is here pointing to the safeguard in handling Christian finances. It was the fact that he avoided going out to solicit funds without reputable methods for handling those funds.

He took the precaution of instructing this church to take this particular offering in his absence so it could not be charged against him that he was a financial promoter. Then he provided that they appoint accredited and reputable delegates who would handle the money. Paul refused to take the responsibility of handling the funds personally. No doubt he would have been impeccably honest, but the provision he made was wise. More Christian workers have sinned in the mishandling and misuse of money than ever went wrong in doctrine or morals.

Just one more observation before we pass on. Paul speaks of their "liberality unto Jerusalem." It is something he has anticipated for, at the present writing, the collection had not been received. Paul evidently was sure of his ground.

An offering is not small because of its size. A small offering may be liberal and a large offering may be contemptible. An offering is small when it is *less than it might be.*

What is liberality and generosity? It is something which is relative. A person may be generous when he gives away a dime. Another man may be stingy when he gives away $100,000. Liberality is not to be judged by the amount of money we give. On the contrary, it is to be judged by the amount we have left after we give.

II. BROTHERLINESS Verses 5-12.

Three contemplated visits are referred to:

1. The Visit of Paul. Verses 5-9.

"Now I will come unto you, when I shall pass through Macedonia: for I do pass through Macedonia. And it may be that I will abide, yea, and winter with you, that ye may bring me on my journey withersoever I go. For I will not see you now by the way; but I trust to tarry awhile with you, if the Lord permit. But I will tarry at Ephesus until Pentecost. For a great door and effectual is opened unto me, and there are many adversaries."

It is interesting to notice that Paul took thoughtful care of, and gave wise planning to his work. He did not follow his whims. He combined, what all of us should observe, the intelligent use of his own faculties with the faithful acknowledgment of divine leadership. He spoke of prolonging his visit to Corinth "if the Lord permit." He was under orders from God, yet he was planning his work and not living a haphazard life.

The delay at Ephesus was a great and urgent opportunity for service. It probably would have been more pleasant to go immediately to Corinth. He could enjoy the hospitality of many friends. But Paul was not consulting his pleasure. He sacrificed his pleasure to enter an open door of opportunity.

He called it "great" because it was wide and challenging. He called it "effectual" because it promised many opportunities for work. Paul called it a "door" because it was an opening of providential, divine arrangement. We dare say he would have been none the less interested if it had been only a small door instead of a great door. "How often do we sigh for opportunities for doing good, whilst we neglect the openings of Providence in little things, which would frequently lead to the accomplishment of most important usefulness! Good is done by degrees. However small in proportion the benefit which follows individual attempts to do good, a great deal may thus be accomplished by perseverance, even in the midst of discouragements and disappointments."

The open doors of opportunity surround all of us. If you are on a bed, there is a door for you. If you are on crutches, there is another door for you. Each of us has his Ephesus. All of us have our great doors and effectual. Are they unentered and unoccupied? Enter while the door is open. The next time you pass it may be closed. Speak while the ear is listening. Act while the strength is sufficient. Work while it is yet day; the night cometh when no man can work.

> "The bread that giveth strength I want to give;
> The waters pure that bid the thirsty live;
> I want to help the fainting day by day —
> I'm sure I shall not pass again this way!

> "I want to give the oil of joy for tears
> The faith to conquer cruel doubts and fears.
> Beauty for ashes may I give alway —
> I'm sure I shall not pass again this way.

> "I want to give good measure running o'er,
> And into hungry hearts I want to pour
> The answer soft that turneth wrath away!
> I'm sure I shall not pass again this way.

> "I want to give to others hope and faith;
> I want to do all that the Master saith;
> I want to live aright from day to day —
> I'm sure I shall not pass again this way."

Paul recognized another thing. The advantage of the open door had the disadvantage of "many adversaries." There is never an opportunity without an adversary. Success always generates opposition. This, in turn, must generate perseverance and perseverance, in turn, builds greater and greater heights of the soul. Success breeds jealousies, envyings, murmurings, backbitings, and various kinds of oppositions. Their presence will never be a hindrance if we only keep our eyes on the opportunities and off the adversaries. It is when we look at the adversaries that we lose the vision created by the opportunities. Peter failed in his venture of faith when he

looked at the water and not at the Lord. We shall fail as
ignominiously if we follow his course.

Paul accepted the opportunities, ignored the adversaries
and succeeded by following this strategy. Success, however,
does not come just by blinking one's eyes to his difficulties.
We must acknowledge, even if we do not accept them. The
text reads that a "great door and effectual is opened unto
me, and there are many adversaries." The words "there are"
are italicized. The Scripture actually said, "a great door and
effectual is opened unto me and many adversaries." The adversaries were as real as the opportunities. Let us be practical
enough to acknowledge them but wise enough not to accept
them as hindrances and obstacles to our success. Paul's strategy in dealing with the open door of Ephesus was to
acknowledge his adversaries but *not accept* them. What we
emphasize in our respective life situations has a lot to do
with our attitude to life.

There is a poem, read but now forgotten, which speaks
about two girls who played one day in a strange garden. Each
reported to her mother what their adventures revealed. One
said, "It was such an ugly place." "But why was it ugly?"
was the mother's query. "Because every rose bush had the
sharpest thorns." The other said, "It was such a lovely place."
"And why?" Because every thorn bush had the loveliest
roses." One saw a rose bush with thorns and the other, a thorn
bush with roses. It makes a difference where we put the emphasis. With some, the thorns are the big things. With others,
the roses are the big things. With Paul, the oportunities were
more significant than the adversaries.

Paul next turns from his own proposed visit to Corinth to
Timothy's.

2. The Visit of Timothy. Verses 10,11.

"Now if Timotheus come, see that he may be with you without
fear: for he worketh the work of the Lord, as I also do. Let no
man therefore despise him: but conduct him forth in peace, that
he may come unto me: for I look for him with the brethren."

We call this young man "timid Timothy." He was not only young in contrast to Paul's maturity, but he was shy and self-conscious and probably suffered from what we moderns call an inferiority complex. Paul begs for a charitable and generous brotherliness. See how nobly and self-effacingly he does it. He says, "See that he may be with you without fear: for he worketh the work of the Lord, as I also do." Here is a complete absence of jealousy. Paul is saying in effect, "treat him as you would me." He says, we are both in the Lord's service. He is just as good a worker as I am. Think of that and then let shame cause our faces to blush when we consider the jealousy that exists among Christian workers. A new pastor comes to a church; he cannot stand to see his people treat the former pastor with love and affection. Not Paul! He urges them to treat Timothy as he would be treated. Give him a cordial reception. Help him to overcome his sensitiveness. Do not let him feel conscious of receiving anything he does not deserve. He deserves all you can do for him because he is one of God's choice workers.

There is much to learn in these little niceties of Christian conduct. Christianity consists as much of the way we act as in what we say. If one says that he is impressed with the heresies of modernists, then we say that we are impressed with the hypocrisies of fundamentalists. It is about time we began to inspect the *conduct* of our creed as much as we insist on the *correctness* of our creed.

3. The Visit of Apollos. Verse 12.

"As touching our brother Apollos, I greatly desired him to come unto you with the brethren: but his will was not at all to come at this time; but he will come when he shall have convenient time."

We cite this brilliant preacher's deferred visit to point out the difference between his delay and Paul's delay in visiting Corinth. Paul deferred because of the opportunities of

Ephesus. Apollos deferred for a different reason. It was not opportunity, but opinion. Paul thought he ought to go immediately to Corinth, but Apollos thought differently, for "his will was not at all to come at this time; but he will come when he shall have convenient time."

Apollos' "convenient time" was not the matter of selfish convenience. It was a difference of leading. You see, Paul was not an archbishop who presided over the regional church, who sent one here and another there. All of that came later. Here they were leaders subservient to the leadership of the Spirit. It was the Spirit who detoured Paul's visit to Corinth by way of Ephesus. It was the same Spirit who deferred Apollos' visit to Corinth until a more convenient time. It might not have been convenient because of the factions at Corinth in which Apollos was involved. Hence, the deference. The judge of the convenience of the time was left to Apollos to decide in his own conscience and by the light of divine guidance.

How much we have lost by the cumbersome machinery of ecclesiasticism in which personal initiative almost completely obscures the guidance of the Holy Spirit can only be imagined. It must be a tremendous loss. What we lose collectively we may retrieve personally. Let us each determine to seek and follow the kind of guidance that detoured Paul, deferred Apollos and opened the way for Timothy.

III. MANLINESS. Verses 13, 14.

> "Watch ye, stand fast in the faith, quit you like men, be strong.
> Let all your things be done with charity."

The church was instructed to act with Christian brotherliness. The Christian is now being instructed to act in the spirit of manliness. Manliness and womanliness befit the individual Christian as brotherliness befits the collective church. They were to be wakeful sentinels at the outposts of duty who stand fast and firm in their faith. Duty and faith go together. No one can be faithful in his duty who is not true in his faith.

Duty and faith require qualities of honor. The word "quit" is the opposite from a quitter. In the French it comes from the same root. In Greek it means, "to act like a man." They were to acquit themselves of any accusation of weakness. Spirituality to some is synonymous with weakness and femininity. Actually it means strength.

The Corinthians were now to be men in contrast to their previous condition of childish carnality. They were to stand at their posts of duty in the midst of a mad paganism as matured men of faith and action.

At the beginning of this letter Paul spoke to them "as unto carnal, even as unto babes in Christ." Now he speaks to them as matured Christians who are to act in all the strength, dignity and privileges of Christian manhood and womanhood. Their disputes were to be a thing of the past. Energy was now to be directed to the great task of evangelizing the world's paganism, rather than in the internal controversies of carnality. Their gifts were to be directed by love. Their means were to be dispensed by an intelligent and practical plan of Christian giving.

Everything was to be done in the crowning virtue of Christian character—LOVE. "Let all your things be done with charity." Thus, love was not incompatible with manhood, strength or maturity. It is that which keeps manhood loveable, strength pliable, and maturity gentle.

IV. SERVICE. Verses 15-18.

"I beseech you, brethren, (ye know the house of Stephanas, that it is the firstfruits of Achaia, and that they have addicted themselves to the ministry of the saints,) That ye submit yourselves unto such, and to every one that helpeth with us and laboureth. I am glad of the coming of Stephanas and Fortunatus and Achaicus: for that which was lacking on your part they have supplied. For they have refreshed my spirit and yours: therefore acknowledge ye them that are such."

We are attracted to the expression, "they have addicted themselves to the ministry of the saints." Here is a blessed kind of addiction. We have all heard of dope addicts and liquor addicts and nicotine addicts, but who has heard of addicts of kindness? To be an addict means one who is devoted. It literally means "ordained." They were ordained devotees to the cult of Christian kindess. They had so arranged and set the ideals and activities of their lives as to be instantly ready to help the saint in need.

In keeping with their high service, Paul gives high honor. He says, "submit yourselves unto such." Here was true honor. Here was a recognition of real worth. We honor men for their place. They should be honored for their service. Their service should, in turn, be such as Paul describes in the house of Stephanas—addicts of kindness.

The conclusion of First Corinthians parallels Romans to a large degree. It is a record of intimate courtesies extended to those whose conspicuous service has been a valuable aid to Paul. Here he carefully singles out such friends as Stephanas, Fortunatus, and Achaicus. They are part of a roster of remembrance. The Corinthians are forthwith charged to accord a full and fitting recognition to such as he has mentioned and to all others who have rendered a similar service.

An effort was made to find the ten men who were members of Sergeant Alvin York's squad which performed the most acclaimed feat of heroism in World War I. In wiping out a nest of machine guns in the Argonne, they killed 25 and captured 132 enemy soldiers. A movie version of this feat was to be made and the production company sent a scout to find the ten men in order that the use of their names might be authorized. After an arduous search, they found these ten men, to each of whom they gave $250. Where do you think they found them? Two were found farming, in fairly comfortable circumstances. One was driving a truck for a Massachusetts city. One was working in a mill; another was a mill watchman; another was a porter in a barber shop. Still another was in a veteran's camp. That accounted for seven. But the other three? One was a hopeless drunkard, a saloon bum. Another was living beside a Philadelphia city dump, ekeing out a living of what he could salvage from the smoking debris, and keeping a few goats. The third was living in a one-room shack in a Texas town, and refused so much as to show his face. When they returned to this country these men rode up Broadway with Sergeant York in a storm of cheers and ticker tape. A grateful nation, they were told, meant to show that nothing was too good for them. But that was years ago.

There is a place in the roster of remembrance for those whose faithfulness has aided the cause of righteousness. This remembrance is not to the high and mighty but to those who have blessed little places with large lives; who have done small things in a big way.

V. Salutations. Verses 19-24.

The concluding words contain two salutations:

1. The Salutation of the Churches. Verses 19, 20.

"The churches of Asia salute you. Aquila and Priscilla salute you much in the Lord, with the church that is in their house. All the brethren greet you. Greet ye one another with an holy kiss."

A tender bond of Christian affection evidently existed between the various Christian churches. These churches, you must understand, were not great bodies of ecclesiastical dignity which met in magnificent edifices. They were, instead, communities of humble disciples which met as conveniently as they could. Some of these groups met in houses like the one which gathered in the house of the distinguished Aquila and Priscilla. It was called "the church that is in their house."

This church in the house was as genuine and as proper as the church in any cathedral in the world. In fact, we have an idea that it might be a great deal more sincere and spiritual in the absence of the accumulated pomp and ceremony. The church needs the good offices of persecution to purge it from these accretions. In England where the dire consequences of war are winnowing the souls of men, the bishops are preparing for a less liturgical and more practical worship. We need the purge in our souls and in our churches.

The Corinthian church was filled with an overflowing measure of hypocritical fellowship. Its members were pretending a genuine Christian affection for each other but were so factionally divided as to make a sincere fellowship impossible. Paul invokes an ancient custom upon them that they might demonstrate the sincerity of their love. He says to them, "Greet ye one another with an holy kiss." We notice the adjective "holy." The memory of Judas with his kiss of betrayal was current among them. It was a sacred thing for them to kiss. It was a pledge of honor. In fact, it literally means "the kiss of consecration." When they kissed, it meant a consecration of friendship and faithfulness. And so Paul invokes this custom with all its solemn sacredness as a means of purging hypocrisy and strengthening their fellowship.

We feel sure that this custom is not binding upon us. After all, it was a custom and not a law. We respect the custom for them but do not require it for ourselves. If there be those who are legalistically inclined who insist that the veil-wearing custom is essential to modern Christian worship, then this custom of the greeting-kiss is equally binding. We have no right to omit one and insist on the other. If one prefers either or both as a personal practice, that is his right, but it is not his right to require it of all.

One thing, however, we ought to observe in this custom is the sincerity of our salutation. One has said, "as a man's salutation, so is the total of his character; in nothing do we lay ourselves so open as in our manner of meeting and salutation." There is much unholiness in our greetings. They are often filled with hypocrisy and insincerity. There are those who are effusive in their greetings to one's face and abusive in their attitude to one's back. This is shameful hypocrisy. Let our greetings measure the grace of our honest hearts.

Let hand possess the earnestness of inner warmth. Let us live in good fellowship that is as transparent as the air. Let face answer face as one that looks into the crystal pool and sees there the reflection of himself.

2. The Salutation of the Apostle. Verses 21-24.

"The salutation of me Paul with mine own hand. If any man love not the Lord Jesus Christ, let him be Anathema Maranatha. The grace of our Lord Christ be with you. My love be with you all in Christ Jesus. Amen."

Paul adds his personal saluation in his own handwriting. This sacred document is autographed by its author to establish its authenticity and insure its authority.

This personal salutation is threefold:

(1) *A warning.* Verse 22.

"If any man love not the Lord Jesus Christ, let him be Anathema Maranatha."

Here was a solemn warning to specious Christians. It was not giveth to pagans. It was intended for inside consumption. Corinth's colony of Christians had its Judases. It had its false professors. It had its shallow camp followers. These are solemnly warned.

"Anathema" means accursed. It was the epithet hurled upon Jesus by pagans. It is now used to reveal the awful tragedy of mistaken identity—the mistaken identity of false Christianity. Men and women who professed and did not possess.

"Maranatha" was a Syriac formula in Greek characters meaning "the Lord cometh." His sure coming will reveal the false professor. In view of that certainty, Paul warns all such against further pretense. He strips hypocrisy from them and makes them stand in the light of Christian reality.

(2) *A benediction.* Verse 23.

"The grace of our Lord Christ be with you."

His letter is a hand of literature laid upon their heads to impart a blessing of grace. He invokes the all-sufficient, ever-sustaining grace of Christ upon them.

(3) *An affection.* Verse 24.

"My love be with you all in Christ Jesus."

Whatever the criticism, whatever the warning, it was tempered with love. This tempering made the message none the less serious and important. It did reveal its genuineness, and, we feel sure, made its obedience more attractive.

The writing is ended. The truth goes on. It is not only ours to read and reason, but to heed and follow. We shall find life maturing into the attractive and fruitful thing it was with Paul!